C000029057

CHARGING AGAINST NAPOLEON

CHARGING
AGAINST
NAPOLEON

Diaries and Letters
of Three Hussars
1808–1815

Eric Hunt

LEO COOPER

First published in Great Britain 2001 by
LEO COOPER
an imprint of Pen & Sword Books Ltd
47 Church Street, Barnsley, S. Yorkshire S70 2AS

Copyright © Eric Hunt 2001

ISBN 0 85052 827 5

A catalogue record for this book is
available from the British Library

Typeset in 11/13 Sabon by
Phoenix Typesetting, Ilkley, West Yorkshire

Printed and Bound in England by
CPI UK Ltd

For Rebecca, Anabel and Madeleine

CONTENTS

MAPS

PREFACE

Writers, taking their lead from the Great Duke, have often criticized the British cavalry in the Peninsula. Wellington was particularly scathing about the behaviour of the 18th Hussars after the Battle of Vitoria, threatening to dismount them and send them home if he heard any further complaint. Not surprisingly, Regimental histories tend to brush criticism under the carpet and, in *Memoirs of the Eighteenth Hussars*, Harold Malet referred to the unhappy episode only briefly, but it had been picked up at the time by the press in England and influenced attitudes for some time afterwards. As tends to happen, the distinguished performance of the 18th on other occasions between 1808 and 1815 is often overlooked.

But these are not just accounts of battles and rows with Wellington. The diaries and letters of officers of the 18th provide a fascinating insight to the manners and mores of cavalry officers of the period, as well as delightful descriptions of the countries through which they travelled and of their inhabitants.

Place names

Many of the places referred to by the various writers are difficult to identify on modern maps, but I hope my guesses are correct. For better or worse, I have used the spelling of the country rather than the anglicised version. That still leaves problems in Spain and Belgium, where place names may be in Spanish or Basque, Flemish or Walloon.

Spelling

Endearing as much of it is, it would have been wearing for the reader to be faced with the spelling of the originals and I have therefore 'corrected' it.

E.E.H.

ACKNOWLEDGEMENTS

Over the past few years I seem to have bothered any number of people for information and advice and I am afraid some may now be overlooked. If so please forgive me.

When I joined the 13th/18th Royal Hussars in 1949 I first encountered Ralph Dodds, with whom I have been friends ever since. We were both in A Squadron – known as 'the Eighteenth Squadron' since amalgamation of the 13th and 18th in 1922. From an early stage he has helped me with both research and comment on this book, but particularly in undertaking the French translation of some of George Woodberry's diaries back into English. Another friend from A Squadron is Peter Waddy, whose kindly expertise in matters photographic has, I fear, not been put to as good use as it deserves.

Gary Locker at Home Headquarters of The Light Dragoons first drew my attention to the Kennedy letters and has assisted me in all sorts of ways, particularly in finding illustrations. Anthony Weldon helped greatly, not least in pointing me towards Henry Wilson of Pen & Sword, as well as in providing photographs of his Kennedy memorabilia. I am indebted to the Assistant Archivist at Bangor, Elen Wyn Hughes, for all her help with the Hughes diaries. David Murphy, of the *Dictionary of Irish Biography*, provided with alacrity a wealth of material on Irish families.

My wife Gill has not only endured the whole process with remarkable equanimity, but has also helped me with checking transcription of the lengthy original manuscripts – Woodberry in particular was verbose to a fault – as well as drafts and proofs of this book.

I am also grateful for permission from:

The National Army Museum to quote from the first volume of Woodberry's original diary, as well as from Loftus Otway's brief diary.

Sir Anthony Weldon to draw extensively on Arthur Kennedy's letters, which have remained in his family since one of Kennedy's daughters married the fifth baronet.

The Trustees of the Kinmel Estate, to make use of the Hughes diaries (now lodged with the Department of Manuscripts of the University of Wales, Bangor) and a copy of the portrait of James Hughes.

John Mollo to use the photographs of Robert Bolton's and John Dolbell's portraits from his book *The Prince's Dolls*.

The Queen's Own Hussars Regimental Museum to quote both from the diary of Edward Hodge and the correspondence of William Verner of the 7th Hussars (which is being painstakingly transcribed by Peter Hard).

The Trustees of the 13th/18th Royal Hussars Regimental Museum to use photographs of items from their collection.

E.E.H.
Mappowder   *July 2001*

INTRODUCTION

A Welshman, an Irishman and an Englishman

The story follows the fortunes of the 18th Hussars, from 1808 to 1815, through the diaries and letters of Welsh James Hughes, Irish Arthur Kennedy and English George Woodberry, as well as other contemporaries including Loftus Otway of the 18th and officers from other regiments.

James Hughes (JH) was born in 1778, third son of Edward and Mary Hughes of Kinmel Park, Denbigh. He was commissioned in 1800 and served as a cornet in the 16th Light Dragoons until 1802. After obtaining a captaincy in Hompesch's Mounted Rifles he transferred to the 18th Light Dragoons in 1803.

Arthur Kennedy (AK) was fourth son of John and Elizabeth Kennedy of Cultra, County Down. His father died in1802 and Arthur was commissioned in 1803 into the 24th Foot, transferring to the 18th Light Dragoons in 1804.

Loftus Otway (LO) was the fourth son of Cooke Otway of Castle Otway, County Tipperary. He entered the 5th Dragoon Guards in 1796, remaining with them until 1803. After two years in the 8th Dragoons he served on the staff in Canada and transferred to the 18th Hussars in 1807.

The background of George Woodberry (GW) remains a mystery, beyond saying that he was born in 1792 and came from Worcestershire. He briefly served as an ensign in the 10th Foot, before obtaining a cornetcy in 1812 in the 18th Hussars.

Their Regiment

Charles Moore, Earl of Drogheda, had raised the 19th Light Dragoons in 1759 during the Seven Years War.[1] The new regiment was re-numbered 18th during cutbacks at the end of the Seven Years War, but as often as not were known as 'Drogheda's Horse'. The war with Revolutionary France had been waged for three years before they first left Ireland in 1796, for the West Indies. There they had few battle casualties, but horrific losses from cholera and on return to England in 1798 the Regiment had almost to be re-raised. That task was tackled with great vigour by their new commanding officer, Charles Stewart, in time for the Allied expedition to Holland in 1799. (Arthur Kennedy was related to Stewart through his great-grandmother, Martha Stewart.)

During the brief peace after the Treaty of Amiens, regimental strengths were speedily reduced, but war and enlargement of regiments returned in 1803, when the 18th were stationed in northern England. Later in the year they moved to Ipswich, where Captain James Hughes joined. In 1804 the Regiment returned to Ireland and amongst a number of new officers was Cornet Kennedy. Four of the light dragoon regiments, the 7th, 10th, 15th and 18th, were converted to Hussars during 1805 and 1806, and dressed in uniforms copied from Hungarian light cavalry.[2] For the 18th that was:

> a dolman, or jacket, trimmed in front with bars of lace, having three rows of buttons. The pelisse was trimmed all round the edges and at the cuff with a light grey fur. The head-dress, a fur cap, having a bag of a blue colour with a plume of white springing out of a smaller red one, confined by a ring between the two colours.[3] The cuffs and collars were white, as also were the small clothes. The sash was of yellow, with blue barrels in front. Horse equipment, with white sheepskins and blue shabracue trimmed with a vandyked edging of lace. In this attire the Regiment delighted the gay eyes of the Dublin citizens.

In 1804 Napoleon Bonaparte had been crowned Emperor of an empire which stretched south from the Elbe across Italy and from the Pyrenees to Dalmatia. The crushing defeat at Trafalgar in October 1805 put paid to his plans for the invasion of England. Instead, with the Berlin Decrees of 1806, he tried to isolate Britain by banning France's client nations from trading with her.

2

The First Peninsular Campaign

Nearly half Portugal's trade was with England and the Portuguese ignored the Decrees. This could not be tolerated and in October 1807 the French occupied Portugal, in collaboration with Portugal's old enemy, Spain. Napoleon then made a fundamental error. Several of his relatives already ruled over dependent countries and he thought Spain ripe for similar treatment. In May 1808 he placed his brother Joseph on the Spanish throne – and opened his 'Spanish Ulcer'.

The armies of Spain and Portugal were no match for the forces of France and her allies and both countries appealed to Britain for help. A British expeditionary force was sent in response, initially under command of Arthur Wellesley, youthful victor of Assaye. His instructions from Lord Castlereagh were to support Portugal and Spain in 'throwing off the yoke of France, and the final and absolute evacuation of the Peninsula by the troops of France'. Meanwhile the Spanish, against all the odds, had inflicted a series of major setbacks on the apparently invincible French. The situation was so serious that the newly installed King Joseph thought it prudent to withdraw himself and the bulk of French troops from Madrid and retreat to the north.

Until then, resistance in Portugal had been minimal. Now, encouraged by Spanish example, there was a rising in Oporto and disturbances elsewhere. Both Spanish and Portuguese civilians reacted fiercely against the cruelty and greed of the invaders. Junot had to concentrate in and around Lisbon and, at the beginning of August, Wellesley's force of some 13,000 men reached Mondego Bay, north of the Portuguese capital, where about 2,000 Portuguese joined them. The only cavalry with Wellesley were the 20th Light Dragoons. However, two more regiments had embarked at Northfleet on 17 July: the 18th Hussars and the 3rd Hussars of the King's German Legion (KGL). (The 18th had been back in England since 1807, in Lord Paget's brigade at Ipswich.)

After defeating the force Junot sent against him at Roliça, Wellesley won a major victory over Junot himself at Vimiero on 21 August – as the ships with the 18th Hussars and 3rd Hussars arrived off Mondego Bay. Another 10,000 men, pulled back from an abortive foray into the Baltic, were soon to arrive under Sir John Moore, but before that, two more senior generals, Dalrymple and Burrard, superseded Wellesley. The French sued for peace and the Convention of Cintra allowed Junot to evacuate his force in British ships with weapons, artillery and baggage – including their Portuguese plunder. In England there was public indignation and the signatories to the Convention were court-martialled; Wellesley, who had opposed the agreement, was acquitted.

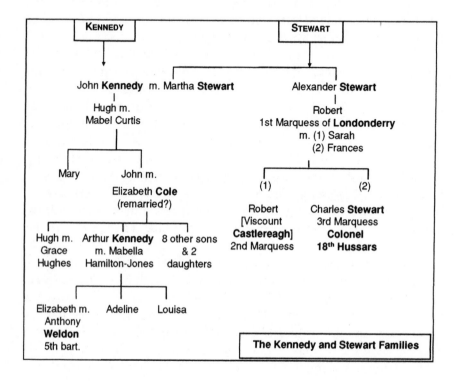

The Kennedy and Stewart Families

PART I

WITH MOORE TO CORUÑA

CHAPTER 1

THE MARCH UP COUNTRY

October to November 1808

Lisbon to Vila Viçosa

Otway, Hughes and Kennedy were among the 745 officers and men of the 18th Hussars, who had embarked at Northfleet. 'Followers' included families and officers' servants, but ninety-one wives had had to be left behind.[1] In Mondego Bay they stewed in their transports until the Convention of Cintra was signed when the convoy moved up into the Tagus and began landing at Cascais.

The success at Vimiero encouraged the British Government to order Moore to take the expeditionary force into Spain, together with re-inforcements under Sir David Baird. The army was still concentrated round Lisbon and it took until mid-October before Moore could get them on the march.[2]

Napoleon determined that he must take a personal hand in the Peninsula. Substantial reinforcements were needed, but before they could be freed from the Rhine and Danube, he had to guard against renewed opposition from the Austrians. In September he hurried to Erfurt to confer with his new ally, Tsar Alexander, but secured no more than vague assurances of Russian support in keeping Austria quiescent. He was back in Paris on 29 October and on the road again for Spain at 4 a.m. next day. Meanwhile 100,000 of his veterans were on the march for Bayonne.

Eventually, leaving the heavy baggage in Lisbon, but not, alas, the women and children, Moore's troops were also on their way. Three columns left by different routes over the mountains; the fourth, with

7

most of Moore's artillery, took a longer road through Extremadura. He had been advised that his artillery could not negotiate the more direct routes of the other columns.

Most of Baird's ships had arrived off Coruña, but the local Junta made difficulties about their landing and disembarkation could not begin until 26 October. His cavalry, who should have been ready to lead the advance, did not leave England until 2 November.[3]

Charles Stewart commanded Moore's cavalry, the 18th and the 3rd Hussars KGL, and was succeeded in the 18th by Oliver Jones. Otway took Jones's place as 'second lieutenant colonel'. With four battalions of infantry, all under Sir John Hope, they formed the escort for five of Moore's six batteries on their roundabout route across Spain. The 18th were ferried across the Tagus en route for Villa Viçosa, near the frontier with Spain, and the rendezvous for the cavalry brigade.

17 October

[JH] March'd for the second time to Lisbon to embark, part of my troop having embarked with Allen. Lost my valise, rode Law's horse to Aldengaliga, overtook Captain Jones with a detach't of my Troop and his own. Guide lost his way & stray'd ab't the woods the whole of the night.

It was 2 a.m. before he arrived at Setúbal and next day, after a 'long & tedious' march, they found only one house at Pinheiro – and no water or provisions. The 19th brought a 'better road & better march' and at Alcáçovas Hughes found a 'physician-minister who spoke French & attended my sick *pour l'amitié*'. Évora was 'imposing & handsome . . . but its riches & magnificence is entirely ecclesiastical – the remainder of the inhabitants live in poverty.' At a convent he had 'some conversation at a double gate with some nuns, not interesting'.

Kennedy wrote of a country in 'a state of miserable destitution, with fields unsown, hamlets ruined and deserted'. By Redondo 'our horses were knock'd up and one lay down incapable of moving', but the *Juge de Foi* gave Hughes billets, stables and forage; and 'a comp'y of Portuguese cav'y who march'd in as I arrived, moved for our accommodation'.

At Villa Viçosa he was billeted with a priest with whom 'bad Latin the only means of communication' and men and horses were put up in the 'the Palace of the Bragança'.[4] The French had left numerous traces behind them in the gates and walls of convents and private houses, 'this appears in most cases to have been purely wanton, as their balls have indiscriminately perforated nunneries, churches & houses'.

While Hope's force assembled there was time for sightseeing – and seeking female company.

25 October

[JH] Watering order a great many sore backs; our sick not numerous, rode to Borba, prettily situated, bought tea & wine.

28 October

[JH] Visited a nunnery Donna Enriqueta, Rosa & Lucretia Mendoza.

29 October

[JH] Went to 2 nunneries with Hay promised Enriqueta to go to mass tomorrow

30 October

[JH] Went with Hay to the Convent of — had a long conversation with the Abbess of nuns in the parlour. Sister Maria a fine woman and interesting.

Stewart arrived and 'commenced his artillery' including a request that Major Allen 'send a written statement of his unfortunate march'. But 'no news from England or anywhere else, Stewart brought no letters' – a complaint familiar to soldiers in every century. Orders arrived to march on the 6th, in two divisions.

Baird at last managed to disembark and his infantry were on their way on 26 October, the cavalry five days later.

Perhaps Hughes's evening activities at Vila Viçosa, including '*tropo de vino* with spice', led to his being late for an early morning punishment parade and receiving a reprimand from Jones 'in the field'. He clearly did not appreciate this and, from his shorthand scribbles, it was not the first time he had fallen foul of the new commanding officer. On those grounds or a separate row with Stewart, he composed an 'address', copies of which were signed by most of the captains. However, he had been persuaded to withdraw it by the time that the march was renewed.

31 October

[JH] Last accounts of the French, their left was at Pamplona in Navarre, their centre at Estella, with a corps advanced to Viana, on the right bank of the Ebro. I forget where their right was, but they form'd a semi-circle convexing to the front; it is said that the Spaniards beat them at Sanquissa. If so & the Spanish, united with the English who landed at Coruña, are pretty strong on their right, their position must be nearly turn'd; indeed it is reported today that they have passed the Pyrenees, that they attack'd a pass occupied by the Spanish & fail'd, but on renewing the attack they were successful after a bloody conflict, the Spanish however attack'd them in their turn & recover'd their positions.

Unknown to Hughes (and Moore), the French in Spain had already begun to receive the reinforcements that were to bring their forces to some 250,000.

In Portugal, 1 November was, 'by the number of people going to the churches I believe a Holy day'.[5] Hughes's landlord dined with him and provided the latest rumours, 'the Portuguese gazette contain'd an account of the French having abandon'd Spain on account of a yellow fever – & that the Turks & Austrians had joined against the French & had raised a numerous army.'

Hughes 'went a boar hunting, too late, shot at eagles', and on the 3rd, after arranging baggage on the horses for the march, went to see the castle, 'very ancient and appears to have been tolerably strong – covering a considerable extent of country but it is in a state of decay . . . Parade for inspection of arms, all good, a few trifling repairs.'

Vila Viçosa to Navalmoral de Mata

On the 6th, Hughes bade farewell to 'Enriqueta', 'made up the business' with Colonel Jones, and set off in heavy rain for Elvas and Spain. Kennedy:

> crossed the Guadiana at Badajoz, the capital of Extremadura, and so entered Spain. The Army was, out of compliment to the Spanish nation, ordered to wear the red cockade in addition to their own black one. These were ordered for the purpose for the N.C.O.s and men, but officers were requested to provide themselves and put them on when they passed the frontier.

There was 'already a remarkable difference in the appearance of the people particularly the women, who are charming'. In Badajoz, 'a good town', Hughes losing his way back to an 'execrable billet' was 'near sleeping in the streets; quarrelled with the Patrol & discovered it accidentally; a Spanish officer almost in the same room'.

They entered Mérida 'over a fine old bridge, the river fordable, but navigable I shd. think . . . town surrounded by ancient and ineffectual wall'. Hughes went forward to find quarters and forage at Medellin. There was a slight frost and a 'very fine morn'g' on the 11th and, when the troops arrived, 'carriages & a great crowd of people assembled at the bridge to meet them'. The 18th 'gave three cheers for Spain which was very well received'. Hughes dined at Otway's quarter, 'several courses & much attention, but Spanish cookery is oil, fire & molasses & is enough to kill one unaccustom'd'.

Following his advance party with an orderly they lost their way crossing a marshy plain before finding their destination, Miajadas, 'a dirty & uncomfortable town'. But he was 'tolerably well put up, mulled some wine & went to bed'.

After arranging billets and waiting for the troops to arrive, he set off for Trujillo, 'six very long leagues' over a hilly and rocky road and his horse 'quite knocked up'. Next day was 'rainy & tempestuous' and the troops did not arrive till after three o'clock, 'most wretchedly tired & wet'. The church bells rang 'to our honour which we return'd with three cheers. Stewart express'd himself pleased & so he ought.' Charles Jones took Hughes's place with the advance party, while Hughes presided at a court martial into a robbery by members of his troop. Byrne of Hay's troop had been 'stilettoed by a Spaniard'.

11

He dined with the 'Intendant General of the Post' where they 'danced *fandangos* &c', but was up at three o'clock to inspect led horses and then march to Jaraicejo, 'a miserable village, fill'd with thieves & having apparently no other occupation'. However, he had a 'tolerable good billet . . . at the house of a sacristan who sang & play'd on a sort of pianoforte'.

Crossing a high mountain on 16 November they:

[JH] continued to ascend thro' a rocky & woody country, until we came nearly to a rocky pinnacle crown'd by a turret & where there is a post-house, here we began to descend & saw before & far below us an immense extent of country, hill and dale & the whole terminated by mountains cover'd with snow, the clouds floating beneath us, on the whole a most magnificent scene.

Descending a zigzag road they came to the Tagus, crossing it by a high stone bridge into Almaraz.

17 November

[JH] March'd for Navalmoral . . . We were met here by two deputies of the Junta of —, who entertained us but as usual Spanish cookery did not agree with me . . . A court martial sat at my billet for the trial of Mason &c which adjourn'd till the

18 November

[JH] Stewart did not approve of the sentence & the court re-assembl'd but would not revoke the decision, referr'd to General Moore.

As Hope's column entered Spain, Napoleon arrived in the north from France and on 10 November Soult defeated Spanish troops at Gamonal. Moore reached Salamanca on the 13th where he heard that Blake, one of the Spanish generals with whom he was trying to link up, had also been defeated.[6] He wrote:

The positions of the Spanish armies, I have never been able to understand. They are separated, the one in Biscay, the other in Aragon, on the two flanks of the French, leaving the whole country of Spain exposed to their incursion, and leaving the British army to be exposed to be attacked before it is united.

He instructed Hope and Baird to join him as quickly as possible, although a junction would be 'very precarious'.

Navalmoral de Mata to Arévalo

The instructions to speed up reached Hope's cavalry when the officers were dining with the local *Junta*, at Navalmoral de Mata, ' we are order'd to make a forced march to Calera'. The night was cold and dark, several men were drunk and there were several falls. Marching through open, cultivated country they could see in the distance 'a high chain of mountains cover'd with snow that run from the Pyrenees to Portugal & divide New & Old Castile'.

Next morning they halted and fed at Oropesa then on to Calera y Chozas. At Talavera de la Reina, where they were 'greeted by the populace', there was bad news, 'communications with Sir John Moore supposed to be cut off, but I could not be persuaded that our case was deplorable'.

A steep climb took them to Santa Olalla where Hughes's servant James 'caught a Franciscan in a peculiar situation with my patroness'. At Santa Cruz del Retamar there was 'a Spanish wedding at the house of Captain Jones – a singular scene'. By 24 November they were at Navalcarnero, and Kennedy heard from his brother Hugh's wife:

My dear Grace, you cannot conceive how happy I was to hear you were all well, more especially as it is the first letter I have received from Ireland since I arrived . . . I have been sent forward to procure billets on the march for the Regiment in consequence of my having picked up the lingo of the country . . . We arrived at Almaraz on the Tagus about 18 days since . . . In the evening whilst the officers were partaking of a grand dinner which the Deputies of the Government had provided for them, an express came for the Cavalry Brigade and park of artillery to proceed by forced marches to Escorial to join the division of the Army under General Hope, intelligence having arrived of the column of the French having defeated General Blake the Spanish General and having arrived at Valladolid, intended to cut off our communication with Sir John Moore at Salamanca.

. . . Today we are within 5 leagues of Madrid but I am sorry to say we are not allowed to enter it; we leave it to the right and proceed to the Escorial, one of the finest palaces in the world . . .

We may expect daily to be engaged with the French who, 'tis said, are not far from Madrid at present . . . although so near where the French are supposed to be, we can get no good information of them. . . . Long before this reaches you the bloody battle will have been fought. God grant it may be glorious for England and old Ireland . . . The Flame of Liberty is completely lighted in this country, the Spaniards are flying to arms in all directions and from the Pyrenees to Gibraltar and the Mediterranean but one spirit seems to reign universal, detestation of the tyranny of Bonaparte and determination either to conquer or die. . . . I think it is the happiest time of my life to be a witness to the glorious scene. Everywhere we are received with the greatest joy by the natives who seem much indebted to England for her great exertion in their cause.

On the 22nd Baird reached Astorga. There he heard of the Spanish reverses and that both Soult and Lefebvre were within one hundred miles and probably closing on Leon, less than 50 miles away. He sent a message to Moore, telling him that he would be prepared to withdraw to Coruña.

Hearing rumours of Spanish successes, Kennedy was more sanguine:

Escorial, 25th. I stop the press to announce my arrival at one of the most romantic & beautiful places I ever saw. . . . The situation is the foot of the Somosierra Sierra Mountains, an immense range of hills or rather rocks 'mazingly high, the most romantic you can conceive. The front of the Palace commanding a view of about 40 miles including a view of Madrid distant 7 leagues or 27 miles. The Palace itself is so large you see it very plain at a distance of 26 miles. The view all round is really delightful and the fineness of the weather, which is as warm as your June, adds much to the scene.

. . . I believe we are the first British cavalry the natives here have seen for some time as all the people flock round me as if I had horns, enquiring when the rest of the English cavalry are to come in. All the young *señoras* are dressing themselves out awaiting with impatience the arrival of the Regiment, which will be in today.

. . . you cannot conceive anything so pretty as my ride here. The fine views along the road, the fineness of the day and the people in every village stopping my horse to make me drink wine and from every corner of a street and even from behind the hedges and ditches crying out with the greatest enthusiasm and joy strongly depicted on their countenances. '*Viva Gran Bretana, Viva Fernando VII*' . . . In short the nearer we approach the Grand Army the more the enthusiasm seems to increase.

News arrived yesterday of the Spaniards under Blake having destroyed about 15,000 French and of Bonaparte having arrived at Bayonne with a large army and in consequence of Blake's victory having retreated back to Paris. However nothing certain can be depended on but this, that we are within about 30 leagues of the main body of the French. Large parties of their cavalry are even in the mountains near this plundering and marauding and when pursued they run back to the main body.

Hughes also visited the Escorial:

27 November

built in the form of a gridiron by Philip 2nd in commemoration of the Battle of St Quintin gain'd on the anniversary of that saint who was fried on a gridiron, the situation of this place is high on the side of a rocky mountain, which frowns over it, & takes from it the appearance of its size, notwithstanding which it still looks enormous. I join'd the party of Ld. Wm. Bentinck, Stewart, &c & went over it & to the top of it . . . it is not very high in itself but from its situation it commands an immense tract of country, & the prospect, tho' not beautiful is certainly magnificent. The Mausoleum of their Kings is built of dark polish'd marble – & also the tombs & ornamented with brass. There is a large convent within the Palace & a large but gloomy church. There are also several good pictures – & plenty of bad ones; these & a closet containing a variety of costly trifles & highly precious religious toys form in my opinion the whole interest of the Escorial, which is large without being noble & fine without being handsome.

While the military tourists were at the Escorial, Sir John Moore was wrestling with two courses of action; he could play for safety and withdraw on Portugal or continue with concentrating his force and assist such Spanish forces as still remained intact. He decided the risks did not justify his abandoning the Spanish and on the 26th ordered Baird to stop his withdrawal. Nevertheless, he was bitterly disappointed at the Spanish failure to provide the support which he had been promised. He was also infuriated by urgent pleas to advance from the Supreme Junta in Madrid, supported by Frere, the British ambassador. He wrote to the latter:

15

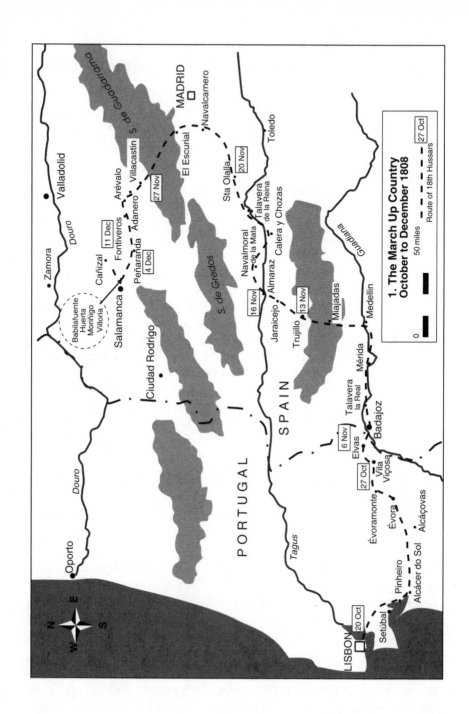

1. The March Up Country
October to December 1808

50 miles

— — — Route of 18th Hussars

PORTUGAL

SPAIN

MADRID

LISBON

20 Oct

Setúbal
Pinheiro
Alcácer do Sol
Alcáçovas
Évora
Vila Viçosa
Évoramonte
27 Oct
Elvas
6 Nov
Talavera la Real
Badajoz
Mérida
Medellin
Guadiana
Miajadas
13 Nov
Trujillo
Jaraicejo
16 Nov
Almaraz
Calera y Chozas
Navalmoral de la Mata
Talavera de la Reina
20 Nov
Sta Olalla
El Escurial
27 Nov
Navalcarnero
Toledo
Villacastín
Arévalo
Adanero
4 Dec
Peñaranda
Fontiveros
11 Dec
Cañizal
Salamanca
Babilafuente
Huerta
Moriñigo
Villoria
Ciudad Rodrigo
S. de Gredos
S. de Guadarrama
Zamora
Valladolid
Oporto
Douro
Douro
Tagus

N
E
S
W

16

Madrid is threatened; the French have destroyed one army, have passed the Ebro, and are advancing in superior numbers against another which from its composition promises no resistance, but must retire or be overwhelmed. No other armed force exists in this country: I perceive no enthusiasm or determined spirit among the people. This is a state of affairs quite different from that conceived by the British Government, when they determined to send troops to the assistance of Spain. It was not expected that these were to cope alone with the whole force of France: as auxiliaries they were to aid a people who were believed to be enthusiastic, determined, and prepared for resistance. It becomes therefore a question whether the British army should remain to be attacked in its turn, or should retire from a country where the contest, from whatever circumstances, is become unequal.[8]

On the evening of the 28th he heard that the Spanish had been defeated at Tudela. Before midnight, 'overwrought by irritation and despondency', he gave orders for retreat. The columns with him were to prepare to march back to Portugal, Hope was to move by Peñaranda on Ciudad Rodrigo and Almeida, Baird was to return to Coruña and go by sea to Lisbon.

The 18th marched for Villacastin on the 28th, crossing 'the great chain of mountains which divide Old & New Castile'. Hughes came up with General Hope, who appeared 'much alarm'd lest he should not effect his junction with Moore. The French advancing on our right & seem to avoid us, their flankers and advanced parties near Segovia, many reconnoitring parties sent out, much on the alert; quartered at a convent of Franciscans, cold & miserable.'

Next day, Hughes's squadron 'remain'd for the protection of the rt flank of the infantry'. The rest of the Regiment marched north and Kennedy wrote:

> though the Regiment had traversed a large portion of Spain and during the last few weeks had been almost constantly in the immediate presence of the enemy, yet, strange to say, they had never exchanged shots. That event occurred for the first time on the night of 29th November when the vedettes furnished by the picquets at Arrivola came in with a report of the French advancing in some force. We withdrew from Arrivola, but at daylight, finding the enemy had withdrawn, returned there. From the hour we quitted Lisbon, up to the day of joining the main body of the Army at Salamanca, this was the only event that befell us.[9]

17

CHAPTER 2

DISPLAYING 'ADDRESS AND SPIRIT'

30 November to 24 December 1808

Hope took 'a flank movement to the left by Avila & keep the heights to avoid the enemy's cavalry' while the 18th and the 3rd Hussars KGL 'march'd over the plains' to protect him. At one village they dismounted to feed and, 'while we were doing so Q.M. Grady gallop'd up to inform us that Colonel Stewart was engaged with the enemy in a wood about half a league off, in consequence of which we bridled up, & mounting all the horses we could we proceeded with rapidity towards there, but it proved a false alarm & Messrs Burke, Grady, & Stewart saw with quixotic eyes.'

Hope's infantry and guns hurried past Fontiveros and on the night of 30 November the infantry slept in square without piling arms. During the next thirty-six hours they marched 47 miles before being allowed to rest at Peñaranda.

At Fontiveros on 1 December Hughes was 'alarm'd in the middle of the day by the drunkenness & misconduct of a vedette, & turn'd out, told off the squadron & advanced, again a false report'. On 3 December the infantry and guns at last joined Moore at Salamanca. Hughes marched to Peñaranda; still across 'a plain & corn country':

4 December

[JH] Right Squadron for Moriñigo and a village adjoining it, march'd westerly a little S. the remainder of the Regiment more to the right. General Alten & a corps of riflemen here in consequence of which diminish'd the guard, tired & very cold.

19

Moore was under great pressure to stay and fight, from British diplomats and from the Spanish themselves. He seems most to have been influenced by the appeals from Madrid, where the residents had risen against the occupiers. His force was too small to relieve the capital; the best he could do was to attempt to draw off Napoleon's army. Late on 5 December he countermanded the withdrawal instructions:

> I was aware that I was risking infinitely too much, but something must be risked for the honour of the Service, and to make it apparent that we stuck to the Spaniards long after they gave up their cause for lost.[1] I mean to proceed bridle in hand for if the bubble bursts and Madrid falls, we shall have to make a run for it.[2]

Madrid survived only two days of siege and the French occupied the city on 4 December, but it was a week before the news reached Moore. Meanwhile, he ordered an advance towards Valladolid preceded by a cavalry screen. On the south bank of the Douro, the 18th and 3rd Hussars KGL pushed towards Alejos and Tordesillas, while north of the river Baird's cavalry made a forced march from Astorga to Toro.

Stewart's brigade heard of the fall of Madrid five days before General Moore – and the rumour-mongers made the worst of it, only to change their tune when the orders to advance were received:

5 December

[JH] march'd to Aldealengua, here the Regiment muster'd. Stewart arrived, bad news, it is said that we are to embark immediately *re infecta* & that the French at Madrid carry it all; this national disgrace thoroughly mortified and afflicted me, arrived at Murisco where the right squadron halts, 2 companies of the 95th here, reconnoitred the place & made arrangements for its security, at 7 o'clock a party order'd to be station'd at Petigua a village 2 leagues and half in our front on the road to Valladolid, and I was ordered to proceed & post their vedettes &c. Very hard frost & at first foggy, took a hasty dinner & proceeded having sent the picquet before. Overtook & passed them, taking a sergeant with me. Went the wrong road & was attack'd by my own party, found a Quartermaster General in the town, advanced for intelligence & settled everything with him & returned home, told the good news.

6 December

[JH] Better news today. The French have suffer'd much at Madrid and retreated to the Escorial, rode Don Juan and reconnoitred – sketched – & wrote this.

Hughes's diary for this campaign now ended with a note to 'send James to Salamanca for letters maps butter & cheese &c' and 'no fight till 12th'.

Fortunately, on 10 December, when the 18th were covering the north eastern approaches to Salamanca, Loftus Otway opened a small notebook and wrote on the first page 'Journal of the operations of the 18th Hussars in Spain':

11 December

Marched from Villares, outpost from Salamanca, to Canizal 5 leagues. This is a small village commanded on all sides. Country open and well suited for cavalry. A Hanoverian deserter came in and reports that he left 4 squadrons of Dutch and Hanoverian *chasseurs à cheval* near Valladolid on the 10th inst.

Rueda

Captain Dashwood, one of Stewart's ADCs, followed up that report. Disguised as a peasant, he found a French patrol in the village of Rueda – eighty men from the 22nd Chasseurs and some infantry.

12 December

[LO] March from Canazel to Naval del Rey 6 leagues, an open corn country like most parts of Spain that I have seen. Several commanding positions, arrived at Naval at 4 o'clock pm heard that a detachment of French cavalry and infantry were at Rueda. Colonel Jones after feeding his horses marched with 100 men to the neighbourhood, to attack it, at 10 o'clock.

The 18th dismounted a number of men to act as infantry for the action.[3]

13th December

[LO] I left Naval del Rey, with Major Hay and Lieutenants Conolly & Johnson and joined Colonel Jones ½ a mile from Rueda about one o'clock am, accompanied by Brigadier General Stewart, who immediately arranged a plan for the attack on a hill close to the town. A picquet of forty infantry and a few dragoons were posted; in the centre of the town the remainder of the infantry, about 30, were stationed; the cavalry about 20 were distributed thro' the town – the plan of attack was as follows.

Forty of our hussars were dismounted and ordered to attack the infantry in the town who were advantageously posted, being surrounded by houses in a small space, the entrance so blocked with bags of cotton that 2 men could with difficulty enter together, but nothing could long stop our brave fellows, the French retired to their guard house, the door was forced, the enemy fled by the back door. This attack was ably led by Colonel Jones. The attack on the picquet on the hill was entrusted to me and this was made with so much celerity that we were in on the picquet before they had time to form and we succeeded in capturing, dispersing and destroying it only sustaining a loss of two hussars wounded and two horses killed. The enemy lost on this occasion six killed and 26 taken and 12 horses. Colonel Jones in the attack conducted by him had one hussar killed and two wounded.

Thus the first blood was drawn in Spain and our success obtained us 500 bags of cotton value £3,000.

Captain Hodge of the 7th Hussars, with General Baird's column, added a nought to the estimated total:

Gen Stewart of the 18th came up. From him we learnt of the good fortune of his regiment, two detachments having fallen in with two of the French and not only made a Lieutenant Colonel of Dragoons prisoner, but have taken an escort of money and cotton valued in £30,000 which will be shared by the regiment. Such prize money rarely falls to the lot of the Army.[4]

Despite the news of the fall of Madrid, Moore decided he could still help the Spanish by threatening French communications in the north. From questioning the prisoners taken by the 18th it was apparent that the French still thought that the British were retreating to Portugal. This was confirmed when Moore received an intercepted dispatch from Berthier telling Soult to overrun the kingdom of León, and seize the towns of León, Zamora and Benavente; he would find no opposition, as the English were in full retreat on Lisbon.[5]

When Captain Gordon of the 15th Hussars reached Tordesillas on 14 December, the reported value of the cotton captured by the 18th had again increased:

> the 18th Hussars and 3rd Hussars of the German Legion, who had marched from Portugal with Sir John Hope's column, arrived soon after us; a party of the former regiment having on the preceding day surprised a detachment of the enemy's cavalry at Rueda when several wagons laden with cotton, said to be worth £80,000 fell into the hands of the victors. The loss of the Eighteenth was inconsiderable, and several of them appeared on parade next day equipped with the broad buff belts and gauntlet gloves of the French dragoons, which caused some repining amongst our men at the superior luck of the Eighteenth. Orders were given out this evening for the cavalry to proceed to Simancas . . . but in the morning there was a change of plan at headquarters – in consequence of the information contained in an intercepted letter from Berthier to Soult. The brigade divided on the march. General Slade halted with the Fifteenth at La Mota, four leagues from Tordesillas; the other regiments occupied St. Cyprien, Valmoase, Pedrosa del Rey, and Villa Don Diego.[6]

Oman wrote:

> on December 15th, the whole army suddenly changed its direction from eastward to northward. The left-hand column of the infantry crossed the Douro at Zamora, the right-hand column at Toro. The cavalry, screening the march of both, went northward from Tordesillas to the banks of the Sequilla, pushing its advanced parties right up to Valladolid, and driving back the dragoons of Franceschi, several of whose detachments they cut off, capturing a colonel and more than a hundred men. They intercepted the communications between Burgos and Madrid to such effect that Bonaparte believed that the whole British army was moving on Valladolid, and drew up his first plan of operation under that hypothesis.[7]

Valladolid

Oman added a footnote:

23

Franceschi actually evacuated Valladolid and retired northwards. Napoleon at first believed that Moore had occupied the place: but . . . mentions that no more happened than that 100 hussars swooped down on it on Dec.19, and carried off the Intendant of the province and 300,000 reals (£3,000) from the treasury. This exploit is omitted by nearly every English writer. Only Vivian mentions it in his diary, and says that the lucky captors belonged to the 18th Hussars.

However, Loftus Otway had recorded it:

19 December

we arrived within 2 miles of Valladolid at 12 of night when I sent my interpreter and a Spaniard forward to the town for intelligence. They soon returned with information that the French had retired with precipitation a few hours before, leaving some men and horses and their sick behind. At 2 o'clock I entered the town and an officer and 22 privates surrendered. Early in the morning I arrested the French Intendant General (Dr Zavier D'Urbina) and left Valladolid at 9 o'clock being then 40 miles in advance of the outposts. On my return I heard the [inhabitants of Rueda] cry 'Ay Jesus, corre, aqui vengan los franceses', 'Oh Jesus, run, here come the French', with screams and — they all turned about and were soon in their houses. I thought it a false alarm and I ordered an officer to reconnoitre, however, he had not advanced many yards before I was satisfied that I had fallen in with a detachment of the enemy cavalry. I instantly resolved to attack supposing it was a party sent out to cut me off – drew swords formed line to the front (so as to fill the road) Gallop March. The enemy who had halted when first they saw us now got into motion and after a short advance halted to wheel about. We charged and after a few discharges of their pistols and carbines which did us no harm, they fled and then it was 'sauve qui peut' we soon gained upon them and when the affair was over I found we had taken one Lieutenant Colonel (Antignac) two —s two L—s and 22 rank and file all of the 22nd Chasseurs à Cheval.

We likewise captured two ladies one the mistress of the Lieutenant Colonel the other wife of the 2nd M—. My party consisted of one lieutenant, one corporal and 26 hussars, that of the enemy 35 men and 100 infantry, the latter from the impatience of the colonel to arrive early at Valladolid were too far behind to be of any assistance to him. The lieutenant was with the infantry that morning so that he escaped; four were killed and the rest got off. I lost no time in collecting my men and prisoners and marched that day and part of the night to Castronuño distant forty-four miles being the quarters of the 18th and the outposts of the British Army.

Having joined up at last with Baird, and changed direction from east to northward, Moore formed four divisions, in which units recently arrived from Coruña were mixed with those who had marched from Lisbon. The commander of the cavalry, Lord Paget, was supposed to leave the cavalry in their original brigades: the 7th, 10th and 15th Hussars under Slade, the 18th Hussars and the 3rd Hussars KGL under Stewart. Knowing Slade to be incompetent he nevertheless transferred the 7th to Stewart's command.[8]

The 18th moved on through Villalôn de Campos, reaching Villada on 20 December. On 21 December Lord Paget led Slade's brigade, with a troop of horse artillery, to clear some 700 of Franceschi's cavalry from Sahagún. With the 15th he inflicted some forty casualties in a brilliant attack and took over 160 prisoners, including a number of officers.

Moore followed Paget into Sahagún on the 22nd and began making plans to attack Soult before reinforcements could reach him. Orders for the advance to continue were given and he issued a General Order to the Cavalry:

> The different attacks made by the Cavalry upon those of the enemy during the march have given them the opportunity to display their address and spirit, and to assume a superiority which does them credit, and which the Commander of the Forces trusts will be supported upon more important occasions. The attack conducted by Brig-Gen the Hon Charles Stewart and the 18th Light Dragoons, when upon the Douro, and that by the Lt-Gen Lord Paget upon the enemy's cavalry at this place, are honourable to the British cavalry. The Commander of the Forces begs that the Lt-Gen and Brig-Gen will accept his thanks for their services; and that they will convey them to Brig-Gen Slade and the offrs, NCOs, and men of the cavalry under their command, for their conduct in the different affairs which have taken place.[9]

On the 23rd Moore advanced towards Soult's position, between Saldana and Carrion in three columns, covered by the 10th and 15th Hussars on the left, the centre by the 7th and on the right the 18th and 3rd German Hussars.

Just as the advance began, reports coming in confirmed that a much larger force would soon confront Moore. The whole of the French army was on the move from Madrid, commanded by Napoleon. Moore decided reluctantly that, after all, he must retreat. He wrote to the Spanish general Romana: 'It would only be losing the army to Spain and to England to persevere with my march on Soult. Single-handed I cannot pretend to contend with the superior numbers the French can now bring against me.' He asked Romana to take his men back across the river Esla by the most northerly route, leaving the road to Astorga and on into Galicia clear for the British. The retreat began on Christmas Eve.

CHAPTER 3

RETREAT

24 December 1808 to 16 January 1809

From exultation at prospects of both fighting and booty, the mood of the army was reversed. The weather was deteriorating and worse was to come as they climbed into the mountains. There was little food or shelter and their sick had to be abandoned. Morale sank and discipline, already tenuous in an army with a large number of criminals, almost disappeared in some units. From being heroes to the local inhabitants they became as dreaded as the French. Yet, 'When the sound of the French trumpets was borne on the wind, the pallid British scarecrows would instinctively face about'[1] and when they did reach Coruña, they did so to such effect that they were able to repulse Soult's army and claim a victory of sorts.

Before that could happen, some of them won themselves a place in the history books, as the Rearguard kept the French at bay throughout those three terrible weeks.

Snow fell during the approach to Sahagún and after a brief thaw and heavy rain, returning frost created roads covered with sheets of ice. Some men 'got frostbitten, and one poor woman, a trumpeter's wife, died from the cold'.[2]

The 18th spent 24 and 25 December in skirmishing at Sahagún and on Christmas Day the baggage was sent on to Mayorga. But the enemy occupied the town, and the baggage was captured. The 10th Hussars recovered most of it, but there is a note with the 1808 muster rolls of the 18th:

the Adjutant's Rolls in which the same were inserted having been taken by the Enemy on the 28th December together with the baggage of the Regiment; the Men and Horses Present & Absent at the Musters taken for 28 October and the Horses Present and Absent at the Muster taken for 24 November could not be inserted.[3]

Villaramiel

Elsewhere, thirty of the 18th attacked and routed a hundred French cavalry:

[LO] At Villaramiel was very near being made prisoner, having entered that village about 8 o'clock the evening of the 26th not knowing it was in possession of the French, having only two hussars with me and Captain Wates, General Stewart's ADC. I passed through this village a few hours before with one captain and lieutenant and 40 hussars and could learn no intelligence of the enemy ... 5 miles further on the road to Placentia I ordered the horses to be fed, whilst Captain Wates and myself reconnoitred the country in front.

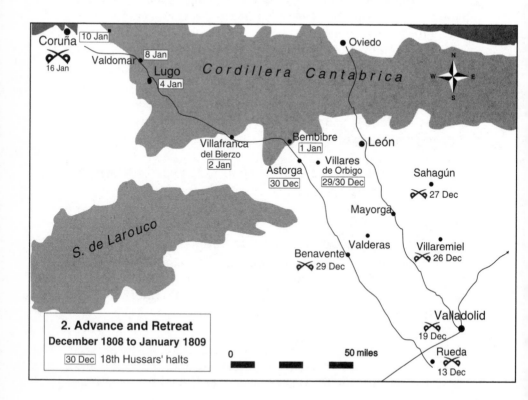

2. Advance and Retreat
December 1808 to January 1809
30 Dec 18th Hussars' halts

Meanwhile Charles Jones heard that a French patrol was in a village about 5 miles away and, without waiting for orders, set off to attack them. A messenger sent to Otway was 'so slow that the affair was over' before he heard that the French were in the neighbourhood. He returned 'as fast as our horses could carry us' and found:

one of our men concealed in a house who told me his horse had been killed, in an unsuccessful attack Captain Jones had made about an hour before in a field not far off. That the French so outnumbered them, that they were surrounded and he feared many of our people must have suffered. He was pursued into that village, and escaped by running into the house where I found him. I made him mount behind one of the men and the *Alcalde* advised us to retire as quickly as possible as the French had a strong picquet posted in the village; the night was dark, to which we owe our safety. I saw their dismounted men cross me in the main street and on leaving the village we were pursued for half a mile, and obliged to quit the road and after wandering about for 6 hours having no guide but the stars we reached a village.... On arriving there I found Captain Jones and 16 or 17 of the party had arrived and that the affair was not at all disastrous. On the contrary he took a lieutenant and 3 prisoners in the charge and their horses. Not able to dislodge the French he crippled them so much that they did not molest him in his retreat. In the course of the day and in the event the remainder of the party of my men came in, bringing 2 more prisoners.

The infantry could march to Benavente without being attacked and all, including the rearguard, were across the Esla by the 27th:

Paget's cavalry, however, had a much more exciting time on the last two days. Finding that he was not attacked, Soult began to bestir himself on the 26th: he sent Lorges's dragoons after the British Army, in the direction of Mayorga, while with Franceschi's cavalry and the whole of his infantry he marched by the direct road on Astorga, via the bridge of Mansilla.

Lorges's four regiments were joined, first by Colbert's brigade and then the cavalry of the Guard, followed a little later by Lahoussaye's dragoons.

It is a splendid testimonial to the way in which the British horsemen were handled, that they held their own for three days against nearly triple forces on a front of nearly thirty miles. No better certificate could be given them than the fact that the Emperor estimated them, when the fighting was over, at 4,000 or 5,000 sabres, their real force being only 2,400. Moore was not exaggerating when he wrote on the twenty-eighth that 'they have obtained by their spirit and enterprise an ascendancy over the French which nothing but great superiority of numbers on their part can get the better of'.

The 18th Light Dragoons turned back to clear their rear six times on December 27, and on each occasion drove in the leading squadrons of their pursuers with such effect that they secured themselves an un-molested retreat for the next few miles. At one charge, near Valencia de Don Juan, a troop of 38 sabres of this regiment charged a French squadron of 105 men, and broke through them, killing twelve and capturing twenty.[4]

Kennedy described that action for his mother:

I was so fortunate as to be the first personally engaged with the Imperial Guards the day before the action at Benavente in which Lefebvre was taken. I had command of an advanced picquet near Villapanda within 2 leagues of Bonaparte's quarters[5] . . . In the morning at 7 o'clock I observed a picquet of his cavalry advancing towards my post. Instantly turned out and gave them chase which they did not relish but on the contrary took to flight, we pursuing them into the town where their main body was, where fifteen squadrons of them turned out and gave us chase in turn, their advanced party which was about 500 yards in front of the main body was nearing us fast when to their no small surprise (I believe) I halted and faced about and charged them, killing wounding and making prisoners of almost all the party before the main body came up. Finding that we must inevitably be taken had we delayed a moment longer I made off thinking myself lucky indeed to carry away two mounted dragoons of theirs and to have only eight of our men and an officer wounded and one horse killed.

Every one of Paget's five regiments had its full share of fighting on the 26th and 27th, yet they closed in on to Benavente in perfect order, with insignificant losses, and exulting in a complete consciousness of their superiority to the enemy's horse. Since the start from Salamanca they had in 12 days taken no less than 500 prisoners, besides inflicting considerable losses in killed and wounded on the French. They had still one more success before them, ere they found themselves condemned to comparative uselessness among the mountains of Galicia.[6]

With the partial thaw and the amount of traffic the roads were now extremely heavy, and 'the artillery horses were scarcely able to drag the guns through the sloughs'. Several villages showed 'mournful proof of the shameful devastation committed by the infantry which had preceded us. . . . The inhabitants shouted, "*Vivan los Franceses*", and we overtook some stragglers who had been stripped and maltreated by the Spaniards.'[7]

Action at Benavente

They crossed the Esla on the 27th, leaving picquets on the right bank under Otway:

> The Cavalry retired to Benavente, I was named Field Officer for the Outlying Picquet. Remained all night at a small village with 50 of the 18th Hussars. Got on my horse at daybreak – saw the whole of the French cavalry on the other side of the river near a bridge which was rendered impassable by us during the night. I observed their motions, saw them return up the hill and presently discerned [them] opposite a place, where in dry weather there is a ford. They attempted the [crossing] in two places, at length they proceeded swimming the centre of the stream; sent an officer off to give notice.
>
> Instantly I called in a small party of an officer & 20 men posted about 1/4 mile off, to another party of the same strength at the bridge, sent my orderly dragoon to the village to desire the 10th to join us as quick as possible, as likewise to an officer & 20 men of the Germans posted a little below the bridge; retired with the first two picquets towards Benavente (distant 2 miles) skirmishing with the enemy. Within ½ mile of the town joined by the small picquet of the Germans. Had then 60 men, took a position on the road, flank protected by old mud garden wall. Country quite open. Some old mud walls which served to cover my flanks, strengthened the skirmishers, told off the picquets by files & by threes, observed the enemy advance & a large force in rear to support their advance, the whole not less than 600 or 700 men, the enemy continued to advance, tho' slowly, I held my ground. At this moment I was joined by Sergeant Major Jeffs & 25 men of the 18th & the Inlying Picquet under Col.— [Quentin] 60 men of the 10th Hussars, they came up on my left, wheeled the outlying picquet by threes to the left & thus uniting ordered the whole to advance at a walk.
>
> The enemy halted at this time, one squadron was somewhat in advance of the others, thought it a favourable time to charge – gave the word – the men gave a loud shout & rushed upon the enemy. Their squadron was broken in an instant, tho' composed of Bonaparte's best

cavalry, his Imperial Guards. After the charge gave the word to halt but in vain our men continued to pursue & whilst dispersed the 2nd squadron of the enemy advanced on our left & took us in flank & rear. This brought our people to their recollections & in 2 minutes the French & we were completely intermingled. When this moment had the French general advanced upon us (with his reserve) we should have been cut to pieces & he might have entered Benavente before the cavalry could get to their alarm posts.

However we had better fortune for General Stewart with a squadron of the Germans was approaching from the town. We rallied upon them & the enemy took the same moment to collect their scattered people and did not attempt to advance, we lost a good many men but not so many as the enemy, the officer who commanded the advance was killed & I got his sword. When General Stewart had got us all in our places he determined to attack the enemy who by this time had brought their force more together, tho' not in line. The General placed himself at the head of the Germans. I continued with the picquet & was about 50 yards to his right & rather outflanked the French. In his advancing to the charge I gave similar orders to the Picquet & from my position, I kept the left squadron of the enemy in check whilst he broke the squadron opposed to him & my bringing the right shoulder forward, I came in contact with the right squadron of the enemy which had wheeled to their left & had taken the general in the rear. Thus were we a 2nd time completely intermingled with the French & both parties withdrew to collect, a little fatigued with the use of the sabre. In this attack I think I may safely say the enemy fared the worst, as we took their general prisoner (Lefebvre) & they certainly did not stand so firm as before. The distance between us was not more than 130 or 150 yards & a constant fire was kept up on both sides whilst the men were regaining their places.

In a few minutes we were joined by more of the Germans & the picquets were strengthened by the 50 men I had sent for to the village. Lord Paget also came out to us & took the command. He soon put us in proper order for another attack, but would not allow us to charge till the 10th Hussars & 18th Hussars on the march from the town were near enough to act as a reserve. On seeing those advancing to our support, the French determined to retire, by alternate squadrons, but we were too close to them to allow them to manoeuvre & Lord Paget led us on to the charge in gallant style, for a little while they kept together, but we at length broke them, took about a 100 prisoners & drove the rest head foremost into the river & whilst they were swimming the river killed & wounded at least 100 of them with our pistols & carbines. When they crossed the river they formed & began to fire at us but they were soon routed by two of Captain D—'s [Downman's] guns who destroyed several of them with shrapnel shells & who just arrived as they formed on the other side.

It may be right here to observe that the French did not in course of this morning advance to the charge. They always waited our attack & I think to advantage except in the final instance when I attacked them on hard ground, but all the other charges we made were in deep ground, wheatland, the horses above fetlock deep, & in consequence the horses always came up blown & feeble.

My conduct this day earned me the thanks of Lord Paget in front of my Regiment.

Napoleon was said to have watched the action from a bluff on the southern bank of the river. He found it difficult to accept that Imperial Cavalry had met their match and later that day wrote to the Empress Josephine that the British were 'flying in panic'. Soon after, hearing rumours of plotting against him in Paris and warlike preparations by

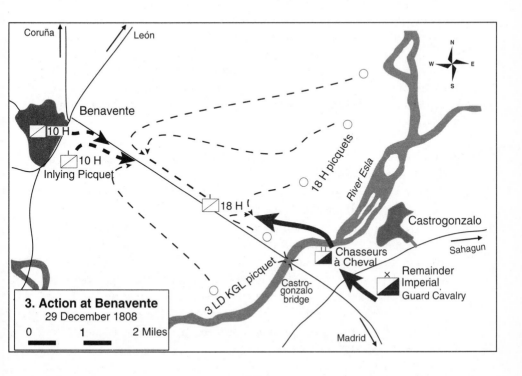

3. Action at Benavente
29 December 1808

0   1   2 Miles

Austria, he set off for France. Soult was left to complete the destruction of the British Army.

There was now little scope for mounted action and the British cavalry concentrated in and near Astorga. The Spanish were retreating over the same route and the houses of Astorga were filled by Spanish troops, amongst whom typhus was raging. Roads were covered with men who had fallen out, foundered horses and broken carts. Almost all the baggage mules of the 18th were knocked up. 'We resembled rather a crowd of insubordinate rebels in full flight before the victorious soldiers of their Sovereign than a corps of British troops, executing a series of military movements in the presence of their enemy.'[8]

Marching by night the 18th halted for a day at Villares de Ôrbigo and then on to Astorga and Bembibre. Early on 1 January, the 15th overtook a number of wagons 'loaded with the cotton which was taken at Rueda by the Eighteenth; we also passed several cars filled with the sick and wounded belonging to our army. Owing to the deep snow and the dreadful state of the roads, these carriages made little progress, and were all taken up by the enemy before night.'[9]

From Villafranca del Bierzo the country was far more bare and desolate. Horses were losing their shoes on the rough and stony road and, as soon as a horse was unable to keep up with the Regiment, he was shot by his rider to prevent him from falling into the hands of the French. 'Many witnesses of the retreat state that the incessant cracking of the hussars' pistols, as the unfortunate chargers were shot, was the thing that lingered longest in their memories of all the sounds of these unhappy days.'[10]

Moore made a stand at Lugo where, on the 7th, the French 'made a vigorous attack on our position, but were repulsed with considerable loss'. Gordon thought, 'Nothing could be more gratifying than to remark the total change' in the conduct of the infantry. 'It appeared that, with the prospect of being led against the foe, they had at once recovered all those qualities for which British soldiers are peculiarly estimable; every order was obeyed with alacrity, and not a trace remained of the discontent and insubordination which had been so general for the past few days.' But they were to be disappointed; the French 'did not think fit to accept the battle we offered'.

Moore had no alternative but to continue the retreat; the supplies at Lugo were nearly exhausted.

Watch-fires were left burning on the ground, which were kept up during the night by the picquets, who remained to observe the enemy's motions. The different columns retired with the utmost regularity, and in such perfect silence that the French did not discover our evasion until after daylight. The night was extremely dark, which favoured this manoeuvre. Our route to the town lay over broken ground and through intricate lanes; the country was also much intersected by dry stone walls, enclosing the fields and vineyards, which made it difficult to keep the squadrons together, as no man could see his own horse's head, much less his file leader.[11]

On 10 January they were near Betanzos and Kennedy wrote:[12]

in the various actions and skirmishes in which we have been engaged, the enemy must be convinced that in the proportion of two, and in some instances three, to one their cavalry are unable to contend with ours or even resist our attack whilst the men who have returned have learned more of real warfare in this campaign than they could have acquired in many years of ordinary service, but on the other hand our loss must necessarily be many for independent of the killed many wounded men returned that are rendered incapable of further service. . . . I feel that I have given you but an imperfect sketch of our operations in general but particularly of the various sufferings and privations which the troops underwent.

On the 12th they reached the outskirts of Coruña and were posted round the village of Elvina, commanding the Betanzos road. Two days later a despairing Otway wrote, 'We are now at Coruña and what is to be our fate I know not. The transports are not yet arrived & perhaps it may be our fate to join the 5,000 men now prisoners we took in the retreat.'

Death of Sir John Moore

A stand by the rearguard at El Burgo meant that it was 15 January before Soult was able to close on Coruña. By then, the exhausted main body had had time to recover and to be re-equipped from the Coruña depots. Moore sited two-thirds of his force well back, covering the western approaches to the town and shielding the embarkation.

Cavalry patrols reported on the French advance and screened the final preparations for defence and embarkation. Picquets (one under James Hughes) stayed out until the morning of the 16th and battle was not joined until that afternoon when Soult made a preliminary attack on the centre. After heavy fighting he thought the way clear for him to make his main assault to the west. There, however, two divisions confronted him and his attack was not only halted, but driven back into the hills. The French were also falling back on the other flank and Moore had a victory in sight when he was fatally wounded. By the time Hope could take over command the momentum of the pursuit had been lost. By dusk the fighting was over.

Evacuation

Embarkation continued that night and all next day. Many of the horses that had survived now had to be slaughtered:

> The horse artillery and wagon-train shipped all their horses which were worth bringing away. The officers of the cavalry were allowed to take all their horses, but the number of troop horses was limited. . . . Many hundred fine animals were shot to prevent the French from benefiting from their services; and in executing the order for the destruction of these irrational companions of their toils, the hearts of the soldiers were more affected with feelings of pity and grief than by all the calamities and misery they had witnessed during the retreat . . . the town exhibited the appearance of a vast slaughterhouse. Wounded horses, mad with pain, were to be seen running through the streets, and the ground was covered with mangled carcasses of these noble animals; for, in consequence of their uncertain aim with the pistol, the men were latterly directed to cut the throats of the horses instead of attempting to shoot them.[13]

All that the French could do was bring down artillery fire at long range onto the harbour – to the discomfort of Kennedy, as he wrote after landing at Portsmouth, on 23 January:

> With no small degree of satisfaction do I sit down to inform my dearest mother of my safe arrival here yesterday evening after a passage of seven days from Coruña. . . . I am happy to say that the numerous prayers you mentioned to have put up for my safety have been heard

and that you are in favour aloft for such a retreat or rather escape as I in common with the rest of the army have had I believe is not to be paralleled in history, and on the whole the entire business has been disastrous indeed to the British nation . . . although our army (the best perhaps that ever left England), performed prodigies of valour and were uniformly victorious in every action with two, three and even four to one in some instances, yet the result has been melancholy indeed. Our hussars in particular have immortalised themselves and the French will long have reason to remember us.

In short nothing could equal the bravery of our men but what can you suppose 30,000 are to do against the whole population of the Continent, which you may say were brought against us. All the force that could be mustered on the Continent, to the amount of 300,000 at least, were in motion to attack us and at one time were nearly surrounded by 4 columns of 25,000 each, one of which was commanded by Bonaparte in person . . . suffice it now to say that from the circumstances of our being in the rear of the army covering the Retreat I have witnessed scenes I could not possibly have believed had I not actually seen them.

[From the 29th] . . . until we arrived at Coruña we had almost daily encounters with them. The Light Infantry at the latter part of the business bore the brunt of the business among the hills when we could not act; to our great joy we reached Coruña after a most harassing and fatiguing march indeed on the 11th Jan. but judge our situation when we were informed there were no transports to receive us and likely to be a scarcity of provisions. With the sea roaring at one side of us and the enemy on the other daily receiving great reinforcements. In this happy situation our army took up a position about ½ a league from the town and the enemy another close by us. The sentinels of the 2 armies close to each other. They of course lost no time in erecting field works and batteries to attack us. In this posture they remained from Wednesday 11th until Monday 16th. During which time, as the transports arrived on Saturday from Vigo, we were embarking our troops by degrees while the enemy on the contrary were daily receiving large reinforcements. At length on Monday about 2 o'clock our Regiment was marched down to the quay and had just commenced their embarkation when the attack commenced on our lines. Never was there known so sanguinary or so obstinate contested a business; our gallant fellows, the 42nd and 50th in particular charging them up to their guns with the bayonet. The result was we drove them back to their trenches with prodigious slaughter and when night put an end to the battle our troops continued embarking as quick as they could and by daylight we had almost all on board except 300 that got into the town and defended themselves until evening, when I hope they all got off.

At daylight the enemy, finding we had retreated to the town and ships, advanced as usual, and on their arrival at the first gate were received with a discharge of grape shot which made them glad to escape. They however took possession of a hill near the town, which completely commanded the shipping in the harbour. Here they brought their cannon and were employed for a few hours erecting a Battery to attack us. It is impossible for me to give you an adequate idea of our situation at this critical time. Our ships close under their guns, in a little harbour surrounded with rocks a strong contrary wind blowing so as to prevent the possibility of the ships in the inner harbour from getting out. 300 sail of ships all close to each other, the men-of-war, thirteen sail of the line, so far off as to be of no manner of use in covering us. The ship I unfortunately was on board was one of the nearest of any to the Battery. In this state, I may conceive about 12 o'clock, a tremendous fire of shot and shells opened on us. You may easily now form an idea of our pleasant situation. The Captains of the inner vessels all deserted their ships and among the rest was your humble servant, who with the assistance of a boat rowed down the harbour and got on board the first ship I met out of range of the guns, every moment expecting a shell to terminate my career. Such a scene of distress I never before witnessed and hope I never shall again. Many transports full of troops ashore on the rocks. The Bay covered with boats picking up the poor fellows. But I am sure many must have perished as the wind blew so fresh. We got on board a very good ship twenty-two officers and about 250 soldiers in all, of different regiments. The officers all without anything but what they had on their backs, without sea stores. We thought ourselves lucky to pack on the cabin floor in blankets and to eat salt provisions.

You may therefore suppose our joy at seeing the Isle of Wight yesterday morning after encountering a severe gale the night before. We ran a single ship without convoy. . . . I find we are likely to go to Southampton as our two troops are there now, however I shall know tomorrow morning. There are only five officers of ours come as yet one of them is Hoey, the rest of our crew were — as we are at present having shot all our horses at Coruña. I am happy in telling you I never was better in my life thank God.

I have so many letters to write on business as I command the party here at present that I will thank you when you decipher this to send it to Cultra for their information.

PART II

INTERLUDE
1809 TO 1812

CHAPTER 4

REGIMENTAL DUTIES IN ENGLAND

The ships from Coruña reached England between 23 January and 8 February. Storms went on for several days, several ships were wrecked and nearly 300 evacuees were drowned, including fifty-six officers and men of the 7th Hussars.

> the ignorance of the ship-masters in general was so gross that it is surprising so few of the vessels were lost, especially when it is considered that they were ill-manned, their sails and rigging in the worst state, and many of them scarcely sea-worthy.

and the state of their returning soldiers appalled the public:

> The haggard appearance of the men, their ragged clothing, and dirty accoutrements – things common enough in war – struck a people only used to the daintyness of parade with surprise. A deadly fever filled the hospitals at every port with officers and men, and the miserable state of Sir John Moore's army became the topic of every letter and the theme of every country newspaper along the coast.[1]

After disembarking, the 18th marched to Deal. Like everybody else they were in sorry condition, very different from when they left for the Peninsula. As Gordon wrote of the 15th:

> Then, well mounted, completely equipped, and filled with anticipations of future glory, we moved in all the 'pride, pomp and circumstance of war'. Now . . . reduced in numbers, weakened by sickness, baffled in our hopes of fame, ragged, and on foot, we bore no resemblance to our former state.

41

Remounted and re-equipped, the 18th were employed for the next two years helping the Revenue on the south coast against the thriving smuggling trade. The task was not without its compensations as the Collector of Customs paid a reward for seized goods – eventually.[2]

Officers often had other pursuits and, as the Commanding Officer had authority only to grant up to two days leave to officers, 'the chronic overstaying of their leave came to such a pass that an example had to be made in the case of one, Lieutenant Sir Godfrey Webster, when his supersession seems to have stopped the irregularity.'[3]

In June 1811 the 18th took part in a review on Hounslow Heath by the recently created Prince Regent[4] of three of the regiments of Hussars, the 10th, 15th and 18th, with two troops of Horse Artillery. Charles Paget wrote to his brother Arthur:

> It was truly fine and Paget was quite in his element after it. The Prince and all the Brothers,[5] with all the Staff and Officers of the Brigade, repaired to the Castle at Richmond, where a most sumptuous déjeuner, or rather a d—d good dinner, was prepared by Paget's order. It was of the most luxurious style, I suppose about 200 sat down to it, and as Turtle, Fish, Venison of the best quality and quantity was provided; as Champagne, Hock, Burgundy, and Claret, Vin de France and Hermitage was drunk in copious libations; as Peaches, Nectarines, Grapes, Pines, Melons and everything most rare in the dessert way was provided in abundance, it was a feast worthy of the magnificent piece of Plate, which had been (unknown to the moment) in readiness to present to Paget by the Prince, the Dukes, and the officers of the Hussar Brigade.[6]

Loftus Otway was seconded to the Portuguese Army and in August 1811 the Hon. Henry Murray took his place,[7] assuming command of the 18th the following January. The Regiment was now stationed at Hounslow, with detachments at Kensington Gate, Twickenham, Hampton Court, Chertsey and Richmond. On 11 January the Prime Minister, Spencer Perceval was assassinated and the 18th were ordered to London because of fears of public unrest. However, the likelihood of disorder diminished when it emerged that the assassin was a bankrupt, who blamed the Government for his troubles.[8]

There was also 'Royal Duty', such as providing escorts to members of the Royal Family. Arthur Kennedy, promoted to captain in July 1811, was at Windsor a month after the Perceval alarm and frequently saw the King and Queen. He wrote to his mother from Windsor in June 1812:

Yesterday we were received by Stewart at Hounslow; he was dressed as a general of hussars and most uncommon splendid drapery as you ever saw and was most highly pleased with the appearance and performance of the old 18th. We gave him a grand déjeuner or rather dinner afterwards as the principal ingredients were turbot, turtle, venison, champagne, hock etc. . . . The General looked remarkably well and was received in a most flattering manner by the officers. Health drank with great applause and fine speeches in return. In short it must have been very gratifying to him. Lady Caroline, Matilda etc. were there as high as you please. He goes to Ireland immediately and I hear does not return to Portugal, this however is not certain.[9]

I went to the Opera a few nights ago and afterwards to Lady Castlereagh's. His Lordship was civil, looks rather thin since his return to office.[10] We had a grand assemblage of nobility there at supper. I don't think somehow that London will be a good market for the Stewarts. Matilda does not seem to improve, but I think Octavia a very nice girl much the best of the two at present there – Charlotte and I are still on the same footing that great people ought to be.

I have the happiness of a Royal nod and smile every day. They are as regular as clockwork in their morning and evening excursions to the Park and Frogmore etc. I fear I shall not be able to accomplish a visit to you sooner than October when the leave comes out. We have so few officers with the Regiment at present. Tell M her old flame poor Captain Underwood who was at the Hotwells has departed this life, he came up to London from Bristol and died soon after his arrival about a fortnight ago, his death gives me another step in the Regiment.[11] Called on your friend Lady Templetown, the old lady has been near making her exit. She had a sudden fit of either apoplexy or some such thing and was near dying she is however better. I hear Lord Templetown and his Lady came here on an excursion yesterday; they have lately lost one of their children and she is in very low spirits. I never saw anyone so much altered for the worse as she is. . . . He as usual glad to see me. I believe they were a little surprised after dinner by the familiar manner in which Charlotte saluted me. We were standing on the balcony of the inn when she passed by with Lady de Clifford to take her evening drive in the Park, Lord T. took off his hat and bowed, which she returned favourably, and instantly nodded laughed and kissed her hand to the blue jacket. His Lordship looked rather astonished as you may suppose. Old Snuffy and the Old Prince are gone off today to dine with the Princess of Wales at Kensington under an escort and don't return till the day after tomorrow. It is rather a novelty their patronizing the Princess of Wales as they are [not?] supposed to be great friends. Little Charlotte dines there tomorrow.

July 1st. I did not write to you about the letter to Castlereagh because I concluded you did not send it as the administration was not changed, consequently there was no occasion for any hurry in troubling his Lordship. Therefore I hope you did not send it, although I think it was very properly worded. I think we had better wait till Alick comes over himself which I think he will very soon.[12] I am sorry to hear of your W. India produce having been seized. I shall expect to hear often from you now that you have got a member of Parliament near you.[13] . . . Mrs Siddons has made her exit from the stage; such a crowd never was seen at Covent Garden as on Monday.[14]

We have just heard that the 10th have got a route from Brighton in march the day after tomorrow. If so we may expect to go on Monday from here.

The 18th marched to Brighton in August 1812, shortly after Cornet George Woodberry joined. Five months later the Regiment, with the 10th and 15th Hussars, were under orders once more for the Peninsula.

CHAPTER 5

WHILST IN THE PENINSULA

England had been appalled at the state of her army returning from
Coruña and what seemed ignominious defeat. With news of further
Spanish defeats, pessimism reigned. Politicians argued that a British
army should never again set foot on the Continent. However, by the
spring of 1809, that had been succeeded by indignant belligerence:
France and Bonaparte had to be brought to book. Austria joined
Britain in yet another Coalition, the Fifth, and began campaigning on
the Danube and in Italy.

In the Peninsula the outlook remained bleak. The 16,000 British
troops remaining in Portugal could only defend Lisbon, not take any
offensive action. Oporto was reoccupied by Soult in late March. Some
135,000 Spanish troops remained under arms, but they were defeated
in several battles in the first three months of the year and the garrison
of Zaragoza had at last to surrender after a siege of eight months.
Nevertheless the Spanish, both soldiers and guerrillas, fought on
across the country. With such an example, it was as well that the
British Government showed equal resolution and accepted promptly
Sir Arthur Wellesley's contention that Portugal could and should be
held.[1]

Three months after Coruña, Wellesley landed in Lisbon. Two
weeks later he moved north to tackle the French under Soult before
the other two French armies in the Peninsula could concentrate and
outnumber his force. In a brilliant operation, the river Douro was
crossed in mid-May and Soult driven out of Oporto – and Portugal.
Wellesley now had to tackle what was to be a persistent problem:
cooperation with Spanish generals. A second French army under

45

Victor was beaten at Talavera in July 1809 despite, rather than with, the help of Cuesta's Spanish forces. The success was welcomed with great enthusiasm in England and the victor was created Baron Douro of Wellesley and Viscount Wellington of Talavera.

In the same month, however, Britain's ally Austria had been defeated at Wagram, had to seek an armistice and in October signed the Treaty of Vienna.

Despite his success, Wellington's position in Spain was precarious. To avoid being cut off from his Lisbon base he had to withdraw to Badajoz on the border with Portugal. This brought recrimination from the Spanish, but, 'till the evils of which I think I have reason to complain are remedied I cannot enter into any system of cooperation with the Army'. A Spanish force under del Parque defeated the French in October at Tamames, only to suffer two more defeats themselves in November, at Ocaña and Alba de Tormes. This increased the French threat to Portugal and Wellington withdrew across the frontier into winter quarters. By then he had reconnoitred with his chief engineer the 50 miles of fortifications that were to be the Lines of Torres Vedras.

In the spring of 1810 Napoleon sent another 100,000 men to the Peninsula, making a total of some 325,000; another French invasion of Portugal seemed probable. The new peer was forced to remain on the defensive; his army was sufficient only to secure Portugal and the Portuguese troops had yet to be tried in battle. However, they were showing promise under the training of General Beresford (created a Portuguese Marshal to give him the necessary status) and other British officers like Loftus Otway.

The Spanish were much less cooperative than the Portuguese and Wellington was reluctant to be involved with their soldiers unless they were put under his command. He concentrated on preparing men and defences for the likely French invasion of Portugal and persuaded the Portuguese to accept a 'scorched earth' policy. He also built up an intelligence system which would keep him better informed over the next four years than his enemies, often knowing more about their plans and dispositions than did their own generals.

The Spanish frontier fortress of Ciudad Rodrigo held out against a French siege from May until July 1810. Almeida, in Portugal, was also expected to hold out, but by bad luck, its magazine was hit by French artillery fire. Many of the garrison were killed and it had to

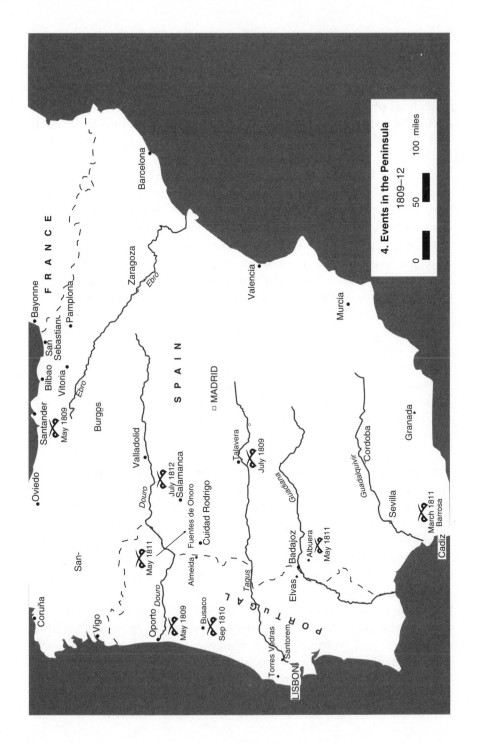

4. Events in the Peninsula 1809–12

be surrendered in late August. Massena was free to advance into Portugal, but was soundly defeated at Buçaco. Then came the carefully planned withdrawal into the Lines of Torres Vedras, north of Lisbon, the existence of which remained secret until the leading French troops came up against them. The Allied force was able to spend the winter of 1810 securely behind the Lines whilst the French suffered badly in inhospitable terrain and at the end of a tenuous supply line.

The year 1811 began with Wellington's army secure behind the Lines and Massena's army struggling to survive at Santarém. Soult was besieging the other main Spanish border fortress of Badajoz. In early March came a British victory at Barrosa against the French besieging Cadiz, but a few days later Soult bluffed his way into Badajoz. This meant that, although Massena had withdrawn to Spain, Portugal was still vulnerable to attack on two routes – via Ciudad Rodrigo and Badajoz. Wellington sent Beresford to attack Soult and recapture Badajoz whilst at Fuentes de Oñoro he blocked Massena. Beresford had to abandon his siege of Badajoz in order to counter Soult's drive north at the bloody battle of Albuera.

Ciudad Rodrigo was recaptured in January 1812, after an eleven-day siege and the following month Wellington was not only advanced in the United Kingdom peerage as an Earl, but was also created Duke of Ciudad Rodrigo and a Grandee of Spain. In April the Allied army stormed Badajoz.

Napoleon's plans were now well advanced for the invasion of his recent ally, Russia. In June the Grand Army crossed the River Niemen en route for Moscow. In the same month hostilities broke out between Britain and the United States, partly over Britain's insistence on her right to stop and search neutral vessels suspected of carrying contraband, partly over American ambitions to acquire parts of Canada. American privateers were soon a serious threat to the Peninsular Army's maritime supply line.

Wellington defeated Marmont in July 1812 at Salamanca and entered Madrid a month later. Further honours were poured on him. He was created Marquess of Wellington and, as Generalissimo of Spanish armies, could now exercise direct authority over Spanish troops. In October, however, he had to withdraw from a siege of Burgos, first to Salamanca and then once more into Portugal. Napoleon's Grande Armée had been forced at the same time into an infinitely more serious retreat – from Moscow.

At the end of the year, Wellington was in a much more favourable position than when the year's campaigning began. The French had been cleared from Andalucia, Estremadura and Asturias and their overall strength had been reduced by some 30,000. They had also lost considerable amounts of equipment including some 3,000 guns.

PART III

EJECTING THE FRENCH FROM SPAIN

CHAPTER 6

EN ROUTE FOR PORTUGAL

January 1813

The war with France must have seemed unending, but 1813 was to be the beginning of the end, with 'The Spanish Ulcer' playing no little part in the final defeat of Napoleon.

Wellington needed both cavalry and infantry to reinforce his army and make up the casualties of the 1812 campaign. He was reluctant to accept green units and would much rather have had the depleted veterans brought up to strength. He told the Commander-in-Chief, the Duke of York, that 'he would like to have the horses of the four hussar regiments which were being sent to him from England to give to his old Peninsula troopers, rather than the regiments themselves'. Fortunately for their *amour propre*, when the Hussar Brigade was ordered to Portugal they were not aware of that correspondence with Horse Guards.

Major James Hughes, now second-in-command to Henry Murray, returned to his diary at the end of March 1813. He briefly noted the events of the preceding months, before resuming it on a daily basis, some of it in French and some in his own shorthand.

> I think that it was towards the end of December that I received news that the Regiment had been ordered for embarkation. . . . Apparently we had no more than two or three days to make preparations and to confirm that I went to Portsmouth where I learned at the agent for the transports, that none had arrived that they knew of; they had received the instruction, but when they arrived it would not be possible to fit them out for the reception of cavalry in less than fifteen days. It was

53

what I expected . . . Indeed I suspected that we would not embark in less than five months! It happened, however, at one and the same time that I went by horse to Portsmouth when I was told that all was ready and that we would embark in two days; I returned home at full gallop, made what arrangements I could and next day left before daybreak for London. I returned quickly having made my farewells to my brother etc.

Young George Woodberry began the New Year as he intended to go on, opening a new leather-bound book (inscribed with the arms of the Blount family) and heading the first page: 'The Idle Companion of a Young Hussar during the year 1813'.

He made an entry almost every day, often filling several pages with his record, not just of daily happenings, but of the places and people he encountered. A green subaltern, imbued with romantic ideas of himself as an officer in a smart cavalry regiment, he was also a romantic in his literary tastes. (The 'Idle Companion' all too often included examples of his own verse.) At Brighton his love was Amelia Perkins, herself still a schoolgirl, but he would still be attracted by a variety of *beaux yeux* over the next two years, in Portugal, Spain and France.

At the end of 1812 he was at Portchester Castle, between Portsmouth and Fareham.

1 January 1813

The Eighteenth Regiment of Hussars marched this day from Brighton, on their route to Portsmouth to embark for Portugal. I was commanding a detachment of twenty men here when I heard the orders for embarkation had arrived, Lieutenant Morris was immediately dispatched to relieve me and I posted off to Brighton to take leave of my friends Mrs Perkins and Amelia.

2 January

Slept at the Castle and left Brighton about 4 o'clock Sunday morning, meet the Regiment at Havant orders having arrived for them to remain there until the transports are ready to take us on board. Smith and his wife, with Miss Moseley, were at Emsworth, dined with them, when Miss M. gave me a small parcel, containing a note and a seal from Amelia, and a gold pencil case and pen from Mrs Perkins; how kind they have always been to me, what return can I make equal to it.

His agent Van Voorst came to Portsmouth to see him off and Woodberry rode back to Brighton to snatch a few more days of seeing 'Miss Amelia'.

13 January

I returned to Havant and found the order for embarkation had arrived and the first division of the Regiment marched into Portsmouth to embark. I found Mr Van Voorst waiting impatiently for my return. We went together to Portsmouth, got there just as my horses were put on board the *London* No 287 – my bay horse, pony, grey horse 'Crafty' – God send they may go safe.

He stayed ashore a few more days, going to the theatre several times and seeing 'Mr Betty perform several of his most favourite pieces'. His personal provisions for the voyage were:

12 live fowls	24 lemons & oranges
2 hams	2 cases portable soup
3 dried tongues	3 quarts of grits & rice
6 half-quarten loaves	3 doz red herrings
3 lb butter	3 doz porter
1 lb coffee	3 bottles brandy
9 lb sugar	2 bushel potatoes
3 lb wax candles	2 lb cheese

After going aboard the *London* with Charles Hesse, his first experience of life at sea was much to his liking:

18 January

The Commodore's ship, the *Aboukir* 74 guns lays near us; he hoisted the blue ensign this evening for all officers and men to repair on board their respective ships. The wind this evening remained fair. This being Her Majesty's Birthday all the men-of-war in Portsmouth Harbour and Spithead fired a royal salute. It had a beautiful effect and gave me some idea of a naval engagement. Slept in an hammock or cot last night for the first time; like the berth very well; may I never lay on a worse place or sleep less comfortable than I did in it.

Hughes remembered the voyage as being without incident, noting no more than his embarkation on the *Bellona* and: 'without any adventures and a reasonable voyage we were in the Tagus'.

But Woodberry had much to record:

19 January

About ½ past 9 o'clock this morning we set sail from Spithead; the whole convoy got under weigh and had a very pleasing effect, about ninety-eight sail, most part transports having our Regiment, the 15th Hussars; and detachments of several others. Strong breeze blowing all day; we lost sight of land this afternoon.

20 January

This morning found the fleet off Plymouth had a beautiful view of Eddystone lighthouse and the convoy for miles round. This afternoon we lay'd to for the fleet in Falmouth to join the convoy. The sea very rough all night. Hesse and most of the people on board was seasick this night.

21 January

The sea very rough, the blowing very hard yet we were obliged to lay before this wind waiting for ships out of Falmouth Harbour. Soon after 3 p.m. the Commodore and the Falmouth fleet appeared in sight, about 12 sail; we now set sail again – with a south east wind – went all night about 7 knots. Hesse very ill, likewise my servant.

22 January

Wind remains still fair, if it continues we shall be there [Lisbon] about Sunday night next. Lost all sight of land. Entered the Bay of Biscay about 12 this day, rather disappointed the sea not more blustery than in the Channel.

Since America had declared war their privateers had had a number of successes against British ships and aided the French considerably by harassing convoys to and from the Peninsula.

23 January

saw the Lisbon packet sail through the fleet. . . . Two women on board very ill, one brought on deck in a fainting state, gave her some brandy &c. This night an American privateer chased us, but we sailed too fast for her. We saw large shoals of porpoises jumping out of the sea round the vessel . . . the fleet much dispersed. Hope to God none of our transports are taken by the French or Yankees, several suspicious vessels have been seen this evening.

24 January

The fleet this morning off Cape Finisterre, out of the Bay of Biscay, God be thanked. About 10 a.m. we hove to waiting for the Commodore & the fleet to windward to come up; the convoy much dispersed this morning, some of the ships appeared twenty miles off us. Set sail again about 12, the wind much abated and getting more to the south; the weather now more like June or July than January. It had a surprising effect on all on board. The women I found walking on deck for the first time; Hesse much better, so was my servant Ipper. About 3 p.m. was completely becalmed, the sea as serene and smooth as the Thames . . . the convoy carrying all the canvas they were able had a beautiful effect, but it was all of no avail, we could not proceed. . . . We made about one knot all night.

25 January

Calm continued all night and much the same all day. All on board recovered of their sickness, very surprising. I have not been seasick myself, never having been to sea before in my life. . . . About 8 p.m. a light breeze sprang up; we sailed about 4 knots. This day I dined with Hesse on board the *Thomas*, Captain Williams, bound for the coast of Africa. The Captain made us pretty well tipsy. Hesse very ill after this frolic.

26 January

Calm again, we saw land for a short time, supposed to be Vigo. Two strange sail among the fleet but owing to the calm the Commodore could not make sail after them; they looked very like American privateers. Hope none of our convoy are captured. Only sixty-two in sight this morning, out of near one hundred and twenty. This evening a breeze sprang up and from the south, was therefore oblig'd to haul to against the wind

Domestic strife amongst the 'lower orders' offended Woodberry:

27 January

The wind very much against us; kept tacking about in hopes of getting on. The Commodore made signals to the fleet, which our Captain did not perceive; he fired a shot at our vessel which had nearly gone into the cabin. Hesse & self were sitting at dinner when we heard the shot whiz.

The hold in an uproar this morning owing to a man (ie a brute), breaking a bottle in his wife's head. We had the fellow confined in the forecastle and stopp'd his grog & upon our making inquiry respecting the woman & quarrel, found the fault on her side, allowing the black cook to kiss her, therefore her grog was stopped likewise. The more I see of the world, the more I am disgusted with Man and Woman of the lower order. Fancy a brute such as the one mentioned above striking a woman on the head with a wine bottle, and then the woman so far degrades herself as to allow the black cook (the ugliest man I ever saw) take liberties with her person and that in the eyes of her husband. I cannot form an idea which of the two deserves most blame.

The Rock of Lisbon was sighted on the 29th but strong easterlies kept them from the Tagus until 2 February. Most of the carefully chosen provisions were gone and Woodberry had only three fowls left. He gave one to Mrs Sweeney, a Troop Sergeant Major's wife, 'poor woman, she is still very ill' and was himself 'rather unwell, have a bad cold, begin to get low spirited being kept here so long'.

1 February

This morning the Captain called me up soon after six o'clock to see the eclipse of the sun, which appeared as the sun arose about 7 a.m., and remained partially eclipsed till ten minutes to 8 o'clock. It was a most beautiful sight. . . Still beating about, the wind remaining in the same quarter. A thief on board — two of the men lost things, one a cloak the other a pr boots. I made complaint to the Captain and he ordered his sailors on deck during which time my sergeant and the Mate went into the forecastle and search it over when at last they discover both articles hid under some sails &c; it was afterwards ascertained that a sailor named Scott had stole them. The Captain wished to have the fellow punished by running the gauntlet, but I persuaded him not. The wind changed two points this afternoon & we were able to make more sail and got very near the Tagus during the night.

2 February

Was much pleased this morning on finding we lay so near the mouth of the Tagus, Lisbon Rock on our left and Cape Espichel on our right. We got into the Tagus about 2 o'clock p.m. when a complete calm came on. The scenery here appear'd very grand. Fort St Julian and the distant view of Belém and Lisbon one of the most pleasing sights that can be conceived. The Rock had a romantic & grand appearance when contemplated from a distance of a few leagues. Thank God we got past the bar before 9 o'clock this evening and cast anchor. I then went to bed more happy than I had been for many days past.

CHAPTER 7

LISBON

February to March 1813

Most of the 18th Hussars landed at Belém by 3 February, but an American privateer had captured one ship – with half a troop on board. The new arrivals found plenty of social life in Lisbon, Wellington's principal base. Supplies and reinforcements were coming in from England while in the opposite direction went a stream of casualties and sick. Hughes was soon pursuing the favours of the ladies:

> After disembarking Murray and I went to the house of the Town Major, where we wrote our names; after that I paid my respects to General Leith who asked me to come with my companions to the Ball given by the British Ambassador, Charles Stuart. I met Lord Worcester[1] . . . the recognition, which pleased me most, was by a pretty lady of the house of La Cerde who recalled when I was in Portugal four years before. I did not remember her, but naturally I pretended that I did, whereupon I was introduced to the whole family and in particular, I paid court to Donna Maria de Carmi; I sensed that this was not at all to the liking of the lady who first remembered me.
>
> In a short while we marched to Benfica &c, a pleasant place near Lisbon where I was quartered at the home of Da. Michiella Van Hogward, an acquaintance which I shall never forget.

Thus the old campaigner; for young Woodberry, all was new and exciting:

2 February

Thank God! Landed safe at last . . . I had every eye on me as I came on shore at Black Horse Square. I then kept walking on not knowing

61

where to go. At last I met Hesse; we took a turn through all the principal streets and afterwards went to an hotel kept by a Mrs Benson, an Irish woman, got a good dinner, afterwards went to the Opera. Considering that the actors repeat verbally what the prompter reads and that often louder than the actor, they get thro their parts with much spirit. The music is pleasing and they dance a sort of pas-de-deux, with castanets, called a *bolera*, and a *fandango* with much exertion but with little grace.

A Lieutenant Wallis, 82nd Regiment, refused after dinner to drink Lord Wellington's health. I find he is much disliked by all the officers who have come from the army. . . One of our transports is reported to be captured by the Americans; has forty-five men and sixty horses on board belonging to Captain Turing's troop. . . Got the men landed on Friday from the *London*, all well with them. Marched them to Belém Barrack. Called and delivered my letters of introduction.

Lisbon was 'not so fine a city as you are led to expect on viewing it from the Tagus. The streets are narrow but there are some very good streets.' When the Regiment marched to Luz and Benfica he thought the country fine, the views beautiful, the roads very bad. Luz was 'surrounded by gardens all most enchanting and romantic, planted with orange, olives & vines.' The poorer class of Portuguese appeared to think of 'nothing but religion and whiskey, which is cry'd about all day, like sprats or mutton pies in London'. Like many of his countrymen Woodberry had a considerable prejudice against Roman Catholic practices and institutions.

7 February

Last night in the bustle some rascally Portuguese stole my cloak – the very thing I shall most want up the country to wear on night picquet.

On the 10th the missing transport arrived; the Americans had released her after the Captain signed a bond for £3,000 ransom. They also disarmed the soldiers and 'took a part of their appointments'. After an inspection of the Hussar Brigade by Generals Leith and Peacock,[2] who 'expressed themselves pleased with our appearance', the 18th were played back to their quarters by the Regimental band.

14 February

Last night the house, wherein Kennedy, Smith & Dolbell sleep at Benfica was attempted to be broken open by a banditti of 9 fellows. Dolbell fired a pistol at one, and Smith discharged the contents of a — at another; they then made off.

Enos Smith was put under arrest by Colonel Murray for 'wilful neglect of duty and coming out to Portugal in a different ship to what he was appointed, by which means many of the men's necessaries were lost &c. The Colonel intends making him pay for every thing they lost on board.' Smith was later released from arrest after a severe lecture from Murray, but was 'very indignant at Kennedy & the Colonel'.

18 February

General Stewart's horses are arrived, likewise an excellent pack of fox hounds. . .[3] It is reported General Earl Uxbridge is coming out to command the whole of the cavalry here. I wish it may prove true.[4] . . . The Portuguese live very frugally. The name of an Englishman is much respected and the women look upon us with compassion: 'What a pity that such brave men should be such heretics!'

One day Ipper, was 'much scalded, bringing the soup to table at our mess his foot slipped and he fell soup and all'. But he was fit enough to go out of bounds the following evening, whilst his master was at the Theatre St. Carlos:

21 February

saw an Italian opera & a ballet, with plenty of dancing. Several songs rapturously applauded, so was several dancers, particularly Madam Norah. I never wish to see a better dancer in one point of view, and a more indecent one in another; she quite shocked my modesty. On my return to Luz found my servant Ipper lock'd up in the guard house, went there & relieved him . . . the Patrol found him in the village after 9 o'clk.

At another review, on the 23rd, General Peacock 'with his staff and about fifty officers mounted, some on horses, others on mules &

asses, enter'd the ground and was received by the Brigade with a general salute. . . .The 10th Regiment was dressed in complete marching order. The 15th in complete review order, shell bridles, &c. I think we look'd as well as either.'

Orders for Review February 1813

Luz 22nd February 1813

The Regiment will assemble at Leon, in Review order, to morrow morning at ½ past 8. Neither officers or men are wear their cloaks which are to be left at home.

As the Officers have not their Horse Review Furniture, only the plain blue Shabracque & Regiment. Sheep skin to be worn, & leather horse Collars, and plain Hussar Bridles.

The Officers will wear White Leather Pantaloons, White Leather sword & pouch belts. Regimental Fur Caps, Cap lines & feather. Regimental Jacket, Hussar Sash, with three rows of Gold knots in front according to order. The Regimental sabretache. The Officers as well as the Men must wear their Pelisses slung. The orders on the subject of Officers dress being thus fully detailed, no excuse will be taken from any officer appearing dress'd in any other manner. The Lieut. Colonel trusts that both officers & men will turn out in a Manner creditable to the Regiment. If the Men turn out ill they have no excuse whatever for they have every thing requisite for their appearance in Review Order. Though the Officers have not their Review Furniture still if they make their servants turn out their plain bridles & furniture well cleaned, they will have quite as soldierlike Appearance as the more splendid review furniture of the two other Regiments of Hussars.

Afterwards Woodberry went to Cintra for a few days' and on the first morning encountered Marshal Beresford:

walking in the garden of the New Palace with General Hamilton who I was some years ago introduced to; immediately recognized me & introduced me to the Marshal who invited me to dine with him. Sixteen sat down to a most elegant dinner. . . . We dined in the room where the famous (or infamous) Convention of Cintra was signed. The Marshal was most superbly dressed for dinner in a marshal's uniform in the Portuguese service with a rich star on his breast. General Hamilton was particular attentive to me the whole evening; asked me if I would come on his staff; intend asking Colonel Murray, as I should like it of all things.[5]

Back in Luz, he thought his friends in England might be 'enjoying themselves round a roaring fire, while I am here sitting in the shade writing this sweltering to death with the heat of the sun.' Smith heard his wife was pregnant: 'Alas poor Enos, surely you are mad; poor fellow he has already too great a plague, what would she be if surrounded with a family; I sincerely pity him.' Woodberry's own daydreams were romantic:

Love is the most delightful of all passions; love makes my homely meal comfortable . . . In health and cheerfulness I arise from the mean repast & retire to a bed, which many would think hard, but on which I sleep as soundly as ever prince slept in a Palace. It is love for my — and an honest heart that causes all my happiness.

But he was happy to spend an hour or two 'learning the language off the beautiful Hannah, my Portuguese neighbour'.

Woodberry seems to have been a devout man and noted disapprovingly one Sunday that, although a church parade had been ordered, 'no parson came'. However on 9 March, 'Divine Service was performed by the Brigade clergyman to the Regiment', when 'the scorching heat was very annoying'.

Colquoun Grant inspected the 18th on 12 March, 'We had the whole of the Regimental as well as private baggage of the Regiment with us.' A few days later 'being a particular day among the Portuguese, the Host was paraded in very grand style round Lisbon. Colonel Grant of the 15th Hussars whom every one knows to be a great "blood", on riding past, in saluting it, unfortunately his wig came off with his hat, which caused great laughter, even to the monks, friars &c.'

16 March

[GW] Lieutenant Dunkin wrote to Colonel Murray from Brighton that he felt himself much hurt when he heard I was come out with the Regiment over his head, that his greatest wish was to go on service with the Regiment . . . All very fine talking; he knew I was coming out near a fortnight before we sail'd, yet never troubled himself till near two months after: so much for Dunkin & the white feather.

Murray ordered Dunkin to join the Regiment which Woodberry thought 'will astonish him a little'.

An optimistic Regimental Order was issued:

Saint Patrick Day

The Retrait will not sound to night till 10 o'clk at which every Man must return quietly home. Ireland looks to the 18th as Pecularly her own, to uphold her name by their good conduct abroad, and she has had reasons to be proud that they did belong to her. But on the long list of Crimes, discreditable and mean, which of late have prevailed in the Regiment, their Country can look with no feelings, but those of Humiliation & Regret. It is hoped however that the recurance of the Festival of their Patron Saint will recall to the recollection of every Irish Soldier that a high sense of honour above every mean or dishonest action is equally characteristic, with undaunted courage & nature of a True born Irishman.

17 March

[GW] About 3 o'clock this morning was serenaded by our Band with the tune of 'St. Patrick's Day in the morning' under my bedroom window. Finding that the custom in the Regiment on this day is, that the English officers should treat, I asked Bolton, Brook, Dean, Chambers, Rowlls & Pulsford; I made them pretty groggy & they departed in peace about 12 o'clk. The Portuguese keep this day as strict as the Irish. Many broken heads in the Regiment this evening: one man carried in the hospital more dead than alive.

On return from Cintra, Woodberry found Dolbell at odds with Kennedy. An apology averted a duel, but the quarrelsome cornet continued to annoy his fellow-officers. When Woodberry dined at Benfica: 'Smith, Foster & Dolbell began a conversation on riding, which ended in very high & abusive language from each to the other. Kennedy interfered and told Dolbell, who was certainly much in the wrong, the impropriety of his conduct. At one time I expected nothing less than a duel would be the consequence between Smith & Dolbell.'

On 19 March it was 'All hurry & bustle, expecting to receive our rout immediately', but Woodberry then heard the 'great scarcity of forage up the country' meant that they would remain a few weeks longer. 'By this delay our horses will get in excellent condition. The Regiment have not lost more than eight horses since we left England and . . . not more than seven men sick, none of those dangerous.'

A frigate came in, 'By her we are informed of the glorious success

of the Russians over the French, & the surrender of Danzig.'[6]
Rumours of peace began when news came of the large drafts having
to be sent from Spain to help with the creation of Napoleon's new
Grande Armée.

News of the appalling defeat in Russia did not reach King Joseph in
Madrid until February. He had to send some 15,000 men of all arms
to the Army of Germany. That still left him with a substantial force,
but a sizeable proportion was tied down by the activity both of
Spanish guerrillas and of a small Anglo-Sicilian expeditionary force
at Alicante.

Woodberry was put out by 'talk of Peace and of the Brigade going
home in three months. I would rather stay here a year or two & see
a little service.' He thought such reports reassured:

> the married men with Mr Dolbell & a few others . . . I think I am as
> much beloved by my brother officers as any one out. On the contrary
> there's Mr Dolbell the whole have cut and shall not be surprised to hear
> of his leaving the Regiment. The unmanly manner in which he boasts
> of his amour with Lady Charlotte Howard at Brighton will bring down
> on him the disgust of every man of honour, and if General Howard by
> chance hear of his boasting, its likely a horsewhipping may be his
> reward.

News came of the loss of the frigate *Java*. 'This is the third frigate
the Americans have took. Fault must attach somewhere. Oh, that the
ever to be lamented hero, Nelson, was now alive; he would soon be
revenged for this national disgrace.'

Woodberry ordered 'four prs of Lisbon shoes for Amelia' and on
the 26th he 'Found a most beautiful dog, cream colour, if I am lucky
enough to preserve him during the campaign, & take him home with
me, what a handsome present he will be to Amelia.'

Meanwhile he solaced himself with Portuguese girls, who he
thought 'lively creatures'. 'I tease Hannah & Louisa (my pretty neighbours) to death about their religion and many other things equally
disagreeable to me. I observe to them that their sex must be dirty devils
to be eternally l— themselves, when Louisa coolly observed, then how
much more dirty you who never l— yourself at all.'

Smith thought he would have to call Dolbell out 'before he can bring the fellow to a true sense of honour & good behaviour, living in the same house with Dolbell, Smith is compelled to put up with a great deal of insolence, and it's more than Kennedy & Smith can do to keep him at all in bounds.'

Entertainment and Sport

At the 'English Envoy's Ball at Buenos Aires' Woodberry 'saw some charming women' and was introduced to 'several nice girls, but I declined dancing. Lord Worcester danced the whole evening (country dances) but about an hour before the ball broke up, waltzing commenced. Hesse attempted. Worcester and an officer of the Portuguese waltzed very well.'

He was an enthusiastic theatregoer and was much taken by a dancer:

> at the Saliteres Theatre. . .The dance (what I went to see) went off with great elation particular a *bolera* by a Spaniard and a little woman with thick legs. I shall never forget her, the more she shew'd her shapes, the more applaud it, till at last she ———. The scenery & transformations at this theatre are the best I ever saw. If they had a few of those at Covent Garden Theatre in a pantomime it would be a serious rival to Mother Goose.

When Lent approached Lisbon was en fête: 'the people all mad, throwing water, oranges, flowers, nuts and every kind of nuisance at each other. We got a pail of water over us & was struck several times with oranges; many I saw sporting masks & curious drapes.' And immediately after the Minister's ball, 'several of the ladies threw a white powder over many of the gentlemen which they had brought with them for that purpose. It created great mirth, for some of the gentlemen felt rather displeased and was therefore laugh'd at.' On Shrovetide, 'Lots of fun this morning with my sweet neighbours, throwing water, flowers, & oranges at each other.'

At a race meeting, 'Close had a marquee on the ground with plenty of refreshment which proved a desirable accommodation from the heat of the weather.' Another day 'General Stewart's pack of hounds came over to Luz . . . I took them round the neighbourhood, but had no sport.'

Heavy drinking was not confined to the men. Woodberry confessed: 'Very much annoyed all day with a confounded headache, fancy I must have been a little groggy last night. Smith & Cotton were dam'd drunk, so was Rowlls. Cotton, in going home, fell off his mule, & it stray'd away; was oblig'd to walk near three miles.'

But he was a great sightseer and one day:

rode with Smith and saw the Palace. The apartments are very beautiful, particular those painted & decorated under the directions of Junot when here in 1808. The gardens are laid out with more taste than any I have seen in this country & the fountains are superior to any I ever saw in my life. Like all the palaces & beautiful buildings I have seen in this country this charming place is going fast to decay, every part of it neglected.

He also took lessons 'to learn the German flute of Mr Kennie, master of the Band. The waltz composed by Mr Kennie, call'd by him after my name, has become a great favourite here. It was called for first by one of the officers at the Minister's Ball and have ever after been a great favourite, particular with the Portuguese.'

Crime and Punishment

There were early indications of disciplinary shortcomings in the Regiment:

8 February

Sat on a court martial this morning for the first time, on two men for unsoldierlike behaviour to their officers; they were both punished this afternoon before the Regiment. No one can detest corporal punishment more than I but subordination must be kept up or we shall all go to the dogs. I am much afraid some of our men will get themselves into serious trouble when we join Lord Wellington's army for if they go on with any of their drunken tricks there Lord W. may perhaps shoot some of them which I should be extremely sorry for. I look forward with pleasure for the Regiment to go into action. Am confident they will not disgrace themselves and return home, whenever we may, it will be with laurels.

69

Murray wrote to Hughes (at Benfica):

The man who refused to carry the corn must be marched for three hours with two carbines clubbed . . . He must, however, take this exercise in the shade, as it is not one which is easy to be practised in this climate. The horses will not eat half their corn, and though there can be no question that the surplus ought to go into the general store and not to be turned to the men's profit, yet I am convinced no severity will stop the practice, and I know no means that can so effectually put a check to it as the diligence of the officers in visiting their stables. Example is the only legitimate end of punishment, and, on service, the commission of crimes is so frequent that, if each offence met with severity, it would be take from punishment the only benefit that can be derived from it. . . . For my own part I am convinced of the impolicy of frequently resorting to the utmost extent of powers in our hands, and therefore do not intend to flog these men. I should, however, be particularly obliged to you if you would suggest anything that occurs to you short of that, for I do not by no means, intend them to escape without punishment.

Drunkenness and insubordination were not the only crimes; theft from local inhabitants was such that a nightly patrol round the cantonments was ordered:

Last night some of our men broke open a house and robbed it of many valuable pictures and candlesticks: very bad beginning indeed. . . . There are, doubtless, vagabonds who disgrace the name of soldier, but is judgment to be passed on a whole profession because individuals are dishonest? Every profession, every trade, have their delinquents; and the soldier occasionally transgresses the rules of order; what class of civilians have not also rioters among them?

But when, 'most of our men discovered to have sold their horses' corn', he thought 'some example must immediately be made'. He sat on more courts martial:

Sat on a court martial most of this day, trying four prisoners, two acquitted, the others guilty. One was sentenced to receive 300 lashes[7] in the usual manner; the other to a fortnight's imprisonment.

I sat all day on the court martial. Foy's trial we got thro' & commenced Sergeant Anderson's for selling meat . . . we found him guilty of selling the squadron meat; sentenc'd him to be reduced to the rank of dragoon. But the court strongly recommended him to the clemency of the Command'g Officer; afterwards proceeded to the trial of Mahoney of Captain Clements's troop for drunkenness. Tomorrow the Court will resume its sittings & inquire into the abuses in Captain Turing's troop, when I hope we shall be released for I am heartily tired of sitting on this court. . . . the court martial ordered to reassemble this morning and to reconsider the crime we found Sergeant Anderson guilty of and the punishment we awarded him being too lenient. The court confirmed their former opinion & return'd the proceedings. The court then proceeded to the trial of Sergeant Sheridan, Armourer, for absenting himself without leave & for drunkenness. He was found guilty of the first charge & sentenced to be reduced.

The most frequent punishment was the lash:

This afternoon was punish'd McCrealley of Captain Burke's troop for selling his necessaries – he received 300 lashes. . . . Graham of Kennedy's troop punished for theft, received 250. . . . The Regiment paraded this morning at 7 o'clk when the stripes was cut off Sergeant Anderson's jacket; Foy received 200 lashes.

The arrest of one troop sergeant major, for 'drunkenness & disrespectful behaviour to his officers' and alleged fraud by another, showed the problems in keeping discipline. Sweeney of Captain Bolton's troop 'begged to be allowed to lose his stripes, instead of being brought to a court martial'. Troop Sergeant Major Duncan, of Captain Kennedy's troop had defrauded him of a large sum, near eighty pounds. It's a very serious loss to him here, where money is so scarce. I hope to God he will make an example of him.'
The other regiments in the Hussar Brigade were also suffering from the protracted stay in Lisbon and the readily available, cheap drink; four sergeants of the 10th were broken for drunkenness. The Household Cavalry had worse problems; Woodberry heard that 'the Life Guards are going on rather queer; many have mutinied and the Colonel was oblig'd to call in the assistance of the Blues'.[8]

Personal Administration

Searching for a baggage mule, Woodberry found 'exorbitant prices' being asked for the few that were in the market.[9] The shortage was not surprising as the demand for pack animals was huge. Supplies from Lisbon started their journey to the army by barge, up the Tagus, and then by ox-cart where the roads were adequate. Forward supply had to be by mule over roads that were often little more than tracks. Seven to eight hundred mules were required for each of the eight British infantry divisions; a similar number was needed to support each of the eight cavalry brigades. Woodberry eventually bought one for 150 dollars and a few days later employed himself 'arranging & packing up my clothes preparatory to our marching up the country. Had the whole of my baggage on the mule and find he can carry it well.'[10]

Twenty or thirty 'ill-constructed ox-carts brought daily rations to Luz. . . . As the Portuguese have no idea of greasing the axletree, when loaded they send forth a horrible noise.' Woodberry received 'one pound of bread (rather brown but very good), ¾ lb beef (generally killed a few hours before), 6 pounds of hay, 8 pounds of corn and 9 lbs of wood – for which I am charged three pence.' He thought an officer 'may live very well indeed in Portugal on his pay, particularly after he gets up the country. Towards the end of February he received £4 2s 6d allowance for bât forage[11] from the Paymaster, followed next month by '56 Dollars, one month's subsistence'.

The Commissary issued a pack saddle, canteen, haversack and one blanket for Woodberry's servant and he sent his 'large trunk to the Regimental Stores'.[12] On various trips to Lisbon he laid in a variety of campaigning essentials: 'two silver forks (6 dollars) & a stand of cruets for my canteen, a bedstead & several other things, a good stock of tea, sugar, coffee, hams & tongues, 'four silver forks, a dozen silver buttons' and finally, on 30 March, 'Bought a pony this day at the Mule Fair in Lisbon, price 40 dollars. I now have everything complete, don't care how soon the rout for our marching arrives.'

Prices of goods in Luz and Lisbon, February 1813

Eggs (each)	½ Vinterns	Port Wine	½ Dollar
Butter pr lb	16 V.	Porter (English)	12 V.
Cheese (very bad) pr lb	14½ V.	Tea pr lb (best)	1 Dollar
Suggar (Soft)	pr lb 6 V.	Coffee pr lb	½ Dollar
Chickens (couple)	1 Dollar 6 V.	English Hams pr lb	12 V.
Brace of Woodcocks	1 Dollar	Brandy pr Quart	½ Dollar
Do. Partridges	1 Dollar 6 V.	Gineava Do	½ Dollar
Rabbits, each	16 V.	Basket of Salt	18 V.
Brace of Hares	1 Dollar	Oranges (8 large ones)	1 V.

72

CHAPTER 8

ADVANCE TO THE ESLA

April to May 1813

With spring and prospects of adequate green fodder, operations could begin. The French, expecting Wellington to advance from the south, held the River Douro between Zamora and Valladolid. Hill reinforced that impression by driving towards Salamanca with a large cavalry screen, while Graham took the bulk of the army on a wide outflanking movement to the north. That possibility had been discounted by Joseph and his generals, unused to the flexibility of sea power. They thought the approach too difficult for supply from Portugal, but Santander was planned to replace Lisbon as Wellington's principal base.

The Hussar Brigade was in one of the three columns of Graham's force, converging on the north-east corner of Portugal between 21 and 27 May. Their route took them past the eastern Lines of Torres Vedras, through country devastated by the French after the 1810 campaign.

Benfica & Luz to Cartaxo

On 2 and 3 April the 18th set off in two wings for Cartaxo. Hughes rode with one of them after parting regretfully from 'Donna Michiella'. At Vila Franca de Xira he dined at 'an Italian's, a passable restaurateur but expensive'. At Azambuja Woodberry, transferred from Bolton's to Burke's troop, was in 'a very good billet'. His hostess, 'a young widow of great family & fortune, paid every attention to my comfort, ordered her servants to cook & wait on me'. The road on to Cartaxo was 'remarkably pleasant'; and 'the higher we ascended

73

the more lovely & cultivated & pleasant the country appeared'.

During a fortnight's halt at Cartaxo they visited 'the strong lines, occupied by Marquis Wellington'. The country round seemed 'all laid waste' and most of the houses in Santarém were completely gutted. Seven skulls were hanging up on a church tower, 'of traitors, who plunder'd the churches & assisted the French'.

On 13 April, Woodberry's twenty-first birthday, he bathed in a brook near the *quinta*[1] of Senhor Baynes, where most of Burke's troop were billeted and felt 'much refresh'd. . . . I begin to look worse than I did last week, or any time since I left England, must therefore take care of myself, will try to leave off drinking so much wine. . . . A strange fellow, this Senhor Baynes – I took little notice of his daughter, yet the old buck walk'd her off to Santarém this morning, wife and all; dam'd suspicious people these Portuguese.'

Doctors Chambers and Pulsford dined with him and 'a most tremendous storm of thunder and lightning came up; the rain fell in torrents . . . after which we took a delightful walk on the hills & mountain.'

Coursing with Baynes's older son, a Captain of Militia, produced 'little sport, the Portuguese dogs are good for nothing'. Next day he breakfasted with both sons, but that evening: 'The militia captain threatened to stab me or cut my throat on account of his sister who he said I came on purpose to seduce! What a villain; he is worse than his father, who took the poor girl to Santarém . . . when he returns I will teach him to threaten an hussar's life!'

He was 'plagued to death' with the troop:

> The men are going on very bad. Two men were punish'd this morning by their comrades, and I was compell'd to send another to Cartaxo to be tried by a court martial. I am now determined to work them right & left till I bring the fellows to a true sense of duty.

The Regiment had their first casualties. Sergeant Fletcher died after a kick from his horse and a man of Kennedy's troop was lost, 'supposed murder'd & thrown into the Tagus'.

Woodberry thought the local people 'extremely civil, but like all the lower class throughout the country, excessively dirty'. One Sunday, after mass, 'the rustics' came onto the green by which Woodberry's tent was pitched and a *fandango* was danced by four of them, while 'a very nice girl' played a guitar.

Relations must have been restored with Baynes; he and a Colonel Azeberde, of the 2nd Caçadores, supped with Woodberry. He also received a present of a fox from 'a gentleman in the neighbourhood'.

Cartaxo to Tomar

It rained the whole way to Santarém, where the wretched fox from Cartaxo was turned loose and 'occasioned much sport to all for several hours. The last I saw of him was in a parlour of a house where he had panick'd all the women.'

After some 27 miles on a very hot day to Golegã, Hughes was 'well lodged in the house of an old lady, where I fell in love with a very pretty girl'.

Arriving at Tomar, Woodberry and Chambers walked to the Tagus and saw 'the Moorish castle which stands on a rock in the middle'. A friar at the convent near the castle, 'after showing us every curiosity in the place, regaled us with plenty of good wine, cake & made me accept of a dozen oranges'. Hughes rode with Carew and Foster to bathe at some falls and, crossing a channel on the way back, 'we became muddled amongst the vineyards & fences as a result of which we plunged into the river & my horse (as I was in the lead) fell into quicksand under the water and we were in some danger; however after plunging and sweating we got out in safety'. Dining with Turing later, they were 'wreathed in roses by two pretty ladies in fun'.

Commissary Schaumann now joined the 18th. Years later he compiled entertaining, if somewhat embroidered, memoirs of his Peninsular adventures. He praised several British regiments, including the 18th, for their successes during the Coruña campaign,[2] but in 1813, 'As I had some experience of troops freshly landed from home, who were unfamiliar both with the country itself and with war conditions, and as I was also aware of the ridiculous pretensions of English cavalry regiments in general, and cordially detested them, my disgust may well be imagined.'

He regaled Woodberry and Burke with tales of the storm and sacking of Badajoz, despite not having been at the siege. But Woodberry thought well of him, writing later: 'Our Commissary is very ill, and I am sorry about this; because he is a gallant and honest fellow, well liked, and few men in his trade warrant the certificate I give him.'

75

Our troop at Quinta de Cardiga broke open a wine house & plunder'd it of near a pipe of wine before it was discover'd. I rode over with Burke & found nearly the whole troop in a beastly state of intoxication. Sergeant Eyres, Corporal Barflower & the whole guard are the principals in the transactions; they are all confined.

One man in his 'villainous troop' confessed that he had been accessory to a murder, 'which has never been found out for want of an informer'. Another was caught 'in the act of a crime at Cartaxo' and 'the whole troop has broken open several wine houses since they have been here & committed numberless depredations . . . the punishment which will be inflicted on Sergeant Eyres, Corporal Barflower & three privates tomorrow morning for breaking open the wine house at Quinta da Cardigo will I sincerely hope deter the troop from committing the like again'. Sergeant Eyres received 200 lashes, Corporal Barflower and Private Crilley 300 each; the other two privates were pardoned. Woodberry was sorry for the Sergeant who 'before this act bore a very good character'.

Several of the officers came to see a tent he had made for his servants and 'one offer'd me sixty dollars for it. I have the vanity to think my tent is better than any in the Regiment. I shall therefore keep it.'

No regiment ever moved up the country with a greater train of baggage than the Hussar Brigade and the Life Guards. Now most every one is anxious to dispose of part of those 'comforts', which was thought indispensable. An officer, who had built a tandem purposely for this country's service, sold it, with harness &c complete yesterday, for four dollars.

At a convent, looted by the French, a 'subterraneous passage' led to a burial vault of the 'monks, nuns & nobility' where Woodberry saw corpses:

apparently but a few years there, others that had been preserved several hundred. It struck me with horror on taking up a shroud on discovering the face of a beautiful nun, but more so, on attempting to raise up the head, it fell off. . . . I likewise saw another sight, not at all pleasing to me – about eight nuns looking thro' the grating before their windows from a nunnery at the foot of the bridge: they made many signs to me & one poor thing lifted up her hands & shook her head &

shew'd by her looks, more than she could have said with her tongue, her abhorrence to her present station.

Hughes swam 'in the pelting rain' and later bought for 'my love ... a ring which I presented and a kiss. After dinner I went to the wine house where Mme Regnier lives, she offered to come with me if I wished, for the moment I declined.'

The 2nd of May was the anniversary of Woodberry's joining the Regiment when every officer was 'mad for driving barouche & mail coaches. A year has made a great difference, we are all now mad to have a drive at the French.'

Tomar to Seia

It was 'raining excessive hard' on leaving Tomar and, although Woodberry thought the hilly country across which they marched 'most delightful, . . . such roads I think there cannot be worse'. At Cabaços he slept on a table in a house with no windows or beds. Six officers crowded in one room. Their march continued across the Serra Estrela to Espinhal and Hesse, sent on to find billets lost his way, 'got into a wood & was oblig'd to lay under a tree all night; it unfortunately rained all night'. Woodberry thought the 'fair sex in this town more prepossessing than any I have seen before, many uncommon pretty. . . . The French I understand rompa'd them, as well as their houses & property.'[4]

In Foz de Arouce, 'a fairly miserable village, but pleasantly and prettily sited on the banks of the river', Hughes went to bed with a bad cold.

In Lugar de Ribeira de Arouce, Woodberry found the inhabitants 'dreadfully afraid of the French advancing; in the event of their doing so they intend taking shelter in the Estrela mountains'. Hickey, of Bolton's troop, was taken ill and 'died in two hours afterwards; the doctors cannot account for it'. Woodberry was 'very sorry for poor Hickey; he was a great favourite of mine'.

On 7 May heavy rain prevented their appreciating the scenic grandeur from a road 'more mountainous than ever and almost uniformly bad'. They crossed the Alva at Marcella to S. Martinho da Cortiça, 'a complete skeleton'; in the Mondego valley where 'many severe skirmishes have taken place between the French and English.

77

. . . Not a day passes but we discover the remains of many brave men who have fallen in their country's cause, but whose bones from neglect are still where they fell.'

After a march through more open but still mountainous country, in Oliveira do Hospital Woodberry rhapsodised, 'the sweetest romantic seclusion I ever beheld, a valley of prodigious extent on either side, bounded by mountains & abounding in every luxury. My *padrone* gave me a chicken &c for dinner & behaved in every respect like a true gentleman.'

'Cursed bad interior management'

As Woodberry said, the 'interior management' of the Regiment left much to be desired and, over the next week, the 18th fell foul of Colonel Grant. Matters came to a head on 9 May. Woodberry had just written:

> we march tomorrow morning & go by forced marches till we arrive on the frontiers. Our men have commenc'd rompa'ing every place they stay in; at Cortizes they broke open a cellar & robbed it of oil & what they could not take they allowed to run waste in the cellar. Last night they got into a poor man's house & stole two shirts . . . this last has much vexed me, the whole village having shown us so much respect. We soon ascertained the thieves & had them confined. Nothing but mistakes in the Regiment, my God, what an unfit person Colonel Murray is to command the Regiment.

when an orderly arrived with orders to march to Seia immediately. 'Colonel Grant was at Maceira waiting to see us pass. Unfortunately the unsoldierlike state of our march owing to the short notice caused him to make some very severe remarks on Colonel Murray's conduct.' Told to remain at Nogueira, at 10 a.m. Hughes discovered that the Right Squadron was on the march. He galloped to Bobadilla and 'found it was true; I was fagged out, but having given orders and changed my horse, I rejoined the march . . . I discovered Murray who was waiting for the arrival of the Right Squadron. I persuaded him to march and he told me that the cause of the confusion was entirely his fault; he misunderstood the order which he received.'

Seia to Freixedas

11 May (Vila Cortês da Serra)

[JH] Murray told me that the Adjutant was not suitable for his position and, while awaiting the arrival of Duperier; Foster had agreed to undertake the duty.

Woodberry was quartered on the priest at Villa Rueira. 'I found him kind & friendly, pious without bigotry, generous without ostentation and desirous of rendering my residence with as comfortable & happy as a feeble means allow'd him. I never slept more sound in bed in England than I did at this good man's!'

As they drew near the frontiers everything was much more expensive, but 'the inhabitants are all poor & miserable, what little wheat they had in store or in cultivation, we have seiz'd upon. I pity the poor souls from my heart & feel the greater abhorrence to the Monster, who have so long been the Scourge of Nations.' Another long and tiring march followed during which they met on the road some fifty carts, loaded with sick being sent back to England. They came from Baraçal, where there was a large depot and hospital and 'a great many sick, all seem clean & neatly dress'd in flannel'.

At Gouveia, 'a very poor village, situated on a rocky escarpment', Hughes's billet was 'ruined, cold and very miserable'. He found nothing to buy, but there was green forage. He tried to speak with Grant about 'a number of regimental matters', but found him 'ill-mannered'. Ordered to come with the captains to Freixedas, he reached there too late for a lecture on 'the farrier's work'. However, 'I made a number of arrangements and said much to Murray about putting them into practice.'

Meanwhile Woodberry saw the 15th out in watering order. 'They have put me out of conceit of our own Regiment. Colonel Grant threatened to report us unfit for service owing to the cursed bad interior management and the great neglect discover'd in the shoeing department.' He confided to his diary, having 'formed acquaintance with most of the officers of the King's Hussars, should like very much to exchange into that Regiment for I really suspect our Regiment will disgrace itself before long; it will not be the fault of the dragoons, but the ignorance of our Colonel'.

His concern for the inhabitants increased:

The longer we stay in our present quarters the worse it will be for them. We are now actually oblig'd to send near two leagues for green forage. The whole produce of the fields near have already been consumed by the 15th & us; those very fields of corn, barley &c was their principal support for the summer. We are daily approach'd by the women & children with tears & moans, begging us to leave them a little to subsist on.

Review by Wellington

They were near Freineida, the Headquarters of the Army:

much such another village as this & Marquis Wellington is quartered in a wretched house, his room of audience is so low that Colonel Grant could hardly stand upright in it. He hunts every other morning. His dress is always very plain & he swears like a trooper at any thing that does not please him. He's remarkably fond of the Portuguese & listens to any complaint made against the English, but never any made by the English at them.

18 May

[JH] We marched past Lord Wellington; we acquitted ourselves well and he gave his opinion 'Best cavalry that I have ever seen, and at this moment, I think as good and better than the best in Europe'. He gave the orders to march tomorrow to cross the Douro & at last the campaign begins.

GW ... After forming line, the 18th in the centre, being the junior regiment. Marquis Wellington, general officers, and their staff came galloping on the ground. After a general salute he passed in front and inspected the line, we afterwards march'd past by half squadron &c. He express'd himself highly pleased at our appearance. The day was remarkably fine & the appearance of our Regiment was much superior to what it was expected. The men turned out in very high style & upon the whole astonish'd the two Royal regiments in all our manoeuvres.

Schaumann thought it a wonderful sight:

to behold these three regiments manoeuvring with their magnificent horses. . . . During the manoeuvres poor Colquhoun had to gallop himself almost to death, racing about *ventre-à-terre* with his brigade adjutant, Lieutenant Charles Jones. The latter was a small man with fox-red hair, a red moustache and red whiskers, and he also wore a red shako. It was very funny to see him galloping behind the tall black-whiskered general who wore an enormous three-cornered hat with a long fluttering feather; and from that day those two were never spoken of in the brigade except as the black giant and the red dwarf.

Freixedas to the Douro

Another long march to Erroghzinho and Ozzoro on 19 May took them across two mountains into delightful country. They met on the road 'the famous bridges and flat-bottom'd boats', each on a wagon drawn by fourteen horses or mules. Woodberry exulted: 'Frenchmen beware, for we shall soon be at your heels.' After a nine-hour march next day men and horses were 'completely knocked up'.

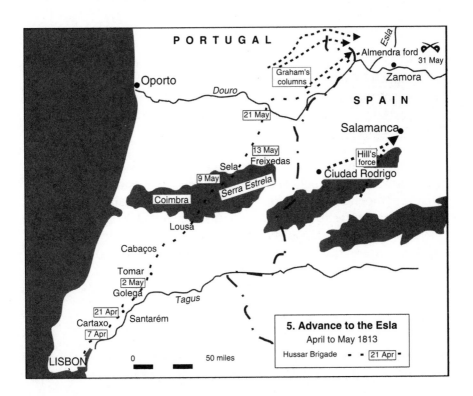

We were as much annoy'd by the dust today as we ever was with the rain and of the two would prefer the latter . . . The further we advance the more kind and obliging are the natives. Tho' I cannot boast of being in an excellent house, yet I can say I never received more civility in this country & what makes it more agreeable I have at this moment a charming young woman (knitting a stocking) sitting aside of me at the table . . . wish I could master the languages, which I am afraid I never shall.

On 21 May they bivouacked near the Douro, waiting their turn to cross by pontoon ferry. All Hughes's horses 'ran off into the mountains and it was dark before I could recover them'. Woodberry pitched his tent in a grove of cork trees and 'took some rest, being very unwell'.

Shortly after inspecting the Hussar Brigade, Wellington joined Hill. The French were driven out of Salamanca on the 26th and on the 29th he rode off to the north-west and crossed the Douro by 'a rope and basket contrivance, worked by a windlass and stretched high above the water'. By the 30th, after 70 miles across country, he was back with Graham's leading troops – issuing a stream of orders.

Hughes was 'very tired and ill' while the 'heat and fatigue' of the march nearly knocked Woodberry up. However, by 22 May, for the crossing of the Douro, he was feeling better and 'spirits began to flow this morning as usual. On this side of the river immense high mountains present themselves which we climb'd with a deal of labour and fatigue . . . several of the cannons belonging to the artillery was upset yesterday getting up and two men were killed.' Woodberry thought 'the character of the people . . . more amiable than southwards; at all events it coincides much better with the ideas and wishes of a Briton. Perhaps gratitude for the recent victories, and delivery from their enemies, inspires warmer expressions of regard. Their friendship I think is sincere and their hospitable reception of us, not prompted merely by interested views.'

Douro to the Esla

As French reconnaissance had sighted none of Graham's columns, they still thought that the threat was from the south. All enemy attention was on Hill's probing towards Zamora and the River Guareña and only cavalry watched their right flank.

The Hussar Brigade put out picquets for the first time and Woodberry was thrilled by being properly on active service. During that day's march they could see French vedettes on the opposite side of the Douro. 'Thank God we are now drawing near those reptiles the French . . . the Douro is between us or they would not sit in their quarters so quietly . . . We are all fine figures, our faces very much burnt.' Camped at Vila de Ala he delighted in:

> the enjoyment after a long & fatiguing march through a burning sun to recline on a portable bed in your tent, under a fine grown shady oak tree; how beautiful the prospect; the troop bivouacked, the horses all picketed to the neighbouring trees. The distant view of the foraging parties belonging to the Brigade. The camp all alive, the men, cleaning their horses, cooking &c.

At Sendim, the 15th had what good houses remained and Woodberry was in a wretched hovel; 'in England I would not feed a pig in it . . . Eatables of all descriptions very dear; they have the conscience to ask twenty vinterns for a loaf of bread, which we have always heretofore bought for three.' A small chapel, with 'a good painting, unlooted and undamaged . . . the subject, Christ being taken down from the cross', now held the Commissary with his staff and stores. 'This is completely making the house of God, a den of thieves.'

On the 27th they crossed into Spain and Blackett took a picquet of the 10th and 18th to the Almendra ford. Woodberry's tent was pitched by the river on a spot 'pleasing & particular romantic'. From it he could see the camps of four infantry divisions as well as the Artillery and Wagon Train, 'it look'd uncommonly pretty'. However, mosquitoes 'bite us very much; immediately after they have stung you a itching pain takes place which greatly annoys for two or three days'.

Passing through Carbajales 'the inhabitants received us with warm cordiality and joy – bells ringing – while *Viva Inglaterra! Rompa Buonaparta!* resounded from all quarters!' The Spanish and Portuguese 'dress very different; the women & men's clothes are of very gay colours, such as blue petticoats & pink gowns, yellow stockings & handkerchiefs – same variety of colour in the men's'.

The 18th camped about 3 miles from the Almendra ford, where the

French had a picquet of 100 dragoons and 'their vedettes could be plainly seen'. Next day Hughes 'made a reconnaissance & ford'd the Esla; it is a rapid stream & it requires light or a perfect knowledge to hit the ford, which is irregular & too deep for infantry'. Woodberry saw Wellington at the ford, reconnoitring with his staff, and went on picquet for the first time. The Hussar Brigade was ordered to march the following morning and 'force their way over the ford'.

CHAPTER 9

FLANK MARCH

June 1813

Skirmish across the Esla

It seemed likely that the French would make a stand at Valladolid and it was not until 2 June that they began to withdraw towards Burgos. Meanwhile the British negotiated unusually high waters in the Esla, and Woodberry exulted, 'at last I have seen a skirmish'.

31 May

[JH] The Hussar Brigade turned out at 12 o'clock at night & march'd to the ford of Almendra – a few hours before Captain Webber Smith & troop of horse artillery arrived & the pontoons continued to arrive during the night & a brigade of infantry, Lord Wellington &c march'd down to the ford. The day had hardly begun to break when the head of the column plunged into the stream, accompanied by the infantry, but the guide (Captain Clements) not having exactly recollected the direction, the confusion and distress that followed was equally grand, awful and afflicting. I endeavoured by going forward to put them in the right track, & succeeded in leading some of them over correctly; but what with the confusion, obstinacy and inattention of the men, the rapidity of the stream, its depth, & the difficulty of the passage, many of them wandered, horses got into chasms of the rocks, plunged & threw their riders, the infantry were carried off their legs, some of them drowned, & some horses, some were drag'd by the stirrups of the dragoons to the opposite banks through the water. Some fell near the banks on their backs (& the weight of their packs keeping them down) & were dragged out; the simple expedient of a rope would have saved most. Murray fell. Campbell (my orderly) on 'Percy' exerted himself & did much good. I did my best.

The infantry appreciated the help:

> A sergeant of the 18th Hussars, seeing an officer of the 51st drowning, said, 'I won't let that gallant chap go, and dashed in and saved him.'[1]

> We soon found the water was too deep and the stream so rapid that in a very short time the whole of the infantry was upset. Some sank to the bottom borne down by the weight of firelock and knapsack, to say nothing of a pouch containing 60 rounds ball cartridges. . . . But for the Hussars I should not be alive to tell the tale, they flew to our assistance and picked up as many as they could. Three regiments cavalry and two infantry plunging about in it and so dark we could scarce see each other . . . The Hussars each took a firelock the infantry soldier having hold of the stirrup.[2]

A picquet of some sixty French dragoons was taken by surprise; no more than ten escaped. The officer commanding 'was shaving himself at the time, took prisoner'. Carew and the Veterinary Surgeon took five men and four horses and Carew was seen, sword drawn, conducting three French dragoons, each holding his horse. On being asked how he had managed to conquer three dragoons, 'good sturdy fellows', he said, 'Why, as an Irishman, I believe that I must confess that I surrounded them.'

At Fresno de la Ribera the French left in such a hurry that the 18th horses could eat the forage they had cut. Hughes enjoyed 'music & dancing at Turing's quarter', but Woodberry was:

> in a poor wretched hut. . . My horses are in the parlour, my mules in a kind of sleeping room and myself in the kitchen, which is a receptacle for all kinds of animals, and amongst them, the grandfather of the family. Exposed to the hungry appetites of myriads of fleas and entertain'd all night with grunting of pigs, squalling of cats, coughing of the old people, braying of mules, squalling of children &c.

When a ' dreadful thunder and rain storm' passed over, he realized himself better off than 'our poor fellows who are bivouacked in an open field without a tree for shelter'.

'A very handsome affair'

The Brigade came up with the French rear at Morales.

2 June

[JH] The 10th were at the head of the Brigade & a troop of horse artillery was between them & the 18th Hussars; the 15th Hussars brought up the rear; after a long canter we came in sight of the enemy form'd partly in line & partly in column on the right of the town of Morales. Colonel Grant halted the Brigade sending the guns to the rear but still continued in column of ranks by threes. As the enemy was supposed to have guns, the sending ours to the rear & delaying our formation appear'd to me to be very injudicious. I therefore persuaded Murray to form open column of squadrons. I went to take the command of the left but Murray, probably distrusting his sight (which is defective) sent to me & beg'd me to remain and assist him in the command of the Regiment.

We were now order'd to deploy & take the right of the line – this was well done – & in this attitude with the 15th in reserve we advanced briskly against the enemy whose strength consisted of three regiments of cavalry amounting to from twelve to fifteen hundred dragoons. The artillery fired a shot or two, which were not returned. We advanced at this pace a long way. I observed a squadron of the enemy taking a flank movement apparently for the purpose of turning us; this I endeavoured to disconcert by obliqueing the right squadron more towards the enemy's left. The 10th had now been charged by the enemy, had repulsed and returned the charge.

I sent to Grant to request that he would allow me to go round the town for the purpose of attacking them in flank & being answered in the affirmative, I moved quickly to the right with Captain Bolton's squadron. I form'd in great haste & having arrived on their left, charged. They were at that moment advancing against the 10th, but on seeing our rapid approach they became confused, & at last went about & endeavoured to fly. I found myself in the centre of them, my horse blown & ready to fall & myself nearly exhausted, & in striking at one I nearly fell from my horse. One of them fired & others gave point, but they were closely press'd by the 10th & Lord Worcester & the foremost men of my squadron coming up at the time, they pass'd me by & the pursuit continued.

With some difficulty I now pull'd up & recover'd breath for myself & horse & then advanced – at this time Lieutenant Cotton of the 10th was kill'd by a pistol shot, having been previously sabred. We continued our pursuit over a small bridge, when the enemy open'd a battery upon us from a most commanding height. A dragoon (Job Upton) riding near me had his leg shot off, some horses were kill'd, a dragoon of the 10th lost his thigh & Captain Lloyd of the same regiment was wounded & taken. We were now order'd most fortunately to retire. I took the 18th under cover of a hill; the shots & shells began to shower about & our artillery was not up – at length it arrived and fired a shot or two, I believe without much effect. At length the enemy retired & we went into quarters at Morales, having taken 220 prisoners of which sixty were wounded and about as many horses; they were supposed to have carried off seventy wounded.

Woodberry, commanding the skirmishers, had 'much trouble in keeping my men from advancing upon their body'. They were called in when the guns came up who:

immediately fired twice & the enemy then broke . . . We now discover'd two more squadrons of their dragoons formed on the left of this town. The 10th Hussars now charged . . . all was bustle & confusion. The French tried to make their best way off, while the 10th was hacking & cutting them about in all directions . . . our right squadron moved round the right of the village while the 10th was driving them pell mell thro' it, and instantly commenc'd fighting.

Wellington arrived, well-pleased, and referred to the action as a 'very handsome affair' when writing to Graham later that day. Following up, Woodberry found it:

impossible to distinguish the enemy from our own hussars, such was the confusion. The whole plain in ten minutes presented a dreadful scene: dead, wounded and prisoners in all directions, for as fast as our men could get up with them they were cut down and out of the four squadrons a very few made their escape to the hills in front of this plain, where the enemy had eight squadrons more & a column of infantry with artillery . . . upon our closing upon them, and being in the act of following them up the hill, they fired their artillery at us. It was here our centre squadron came up with the remains of their flying force & commenced the carnage. I had a cut at one man myself who made point at me, which I parried. I spoil'd his beauty, if I did not take his life, for I gave him a most severe cut across the eyes & cheek & must have cut them out. . . of the number of prisoners we took hardly one was to be discerned without some dreadful cuts on their head & body. I never saw men so mad for action as the hussars were before & after the skirmishing and all appear'd disappointed when order'd to march into this place & take up their quarters.

As well as a horse he had taken himself, Woodberry received another in a division of captured horses. He gave Ipper his pony ('which he immediately sold') and was sent to Turo with the remaining horses to be sold. By the time he left the town, 'it was illuminated and in every street was large bonfires round which men, women & children was dancing *fandangos* & *boleros*. Bells ringing, guns firing and every demonstration of joy reign'd throughout the town. Lord Wellington gave a grand ball in honour of our victory this morning.'

Morales de Toro to Isar

Next day's march took the 18th across the scene of the action where Woodberry's 'wild Irishmen' recalled their deeds and pointed out 'the bodies they had killed'. At Pedrosa del Rey visitors to Captain Lloyd found Woodberry's old batman, Morris, who had also been wounded and taken prisoner. It was perhaps Morris when:

> we perceived a palliasse in the corner . . . A pelisse of the Eighteenth Hussars served as a coverlet, a little round head was on the pillow, and a vivid eye with a countenance of a deadly pallid hue bespoke a wounded Irishman. 'Do you belong to the Eighteenth?' 'Yes, plaze yer Honour,' the right hand at the same time carried to the forelock. 'Are you wounded?' 'Yes, plaze yer Honour' again the hand to the head. 'Where?' 'Run through the body plaze yer Honour.' 'Are you in pain?' 'I am tolerably aisy and French dacter blid me, and tomorrow I shall see the ould Rigimint." He afterwards recovered.[3]

4 June (Torrelobatón)

[JH] Don Julian Sanchez's corps of cavalry pass'd us, a despicable body of banditti . . . as cavalry they deserve no respect, & they are plunderers & really robbers, but as spies over the enemy, to plunder their convoys & escorts, & to hang upon their flanks & harass them, they are certainly useful. . . Murray so unwell that he retired to Toro & I this day took a more permanent command of the Regiment.

'The steeples of the churches of this town shook with the merry peals on our entering the town; the cheers of the inhabitants and the lively countenance of the whole on our arrival gave me a higher opinion of the Spaniards' and Woodberry 'got the best billet I have had in this country'.

At Penaflor; where 'all the columns of the Army appear'd to verge', Hughes was 'oblig'd to report the Commissary – very ill off for corn and provisions' and Schaumann wrote, 'And now the dear old troubles with the forage started afresh. Every day we commissaries were called before Sir Colquoun Grant to be reprimanded, and to listen to peremptory orders and threats. I did not get the smallest help from the Regiment. The whole crowd were like fledglings; they only knew how to open their mouths to be fed.'

Mail from England arrived but Wellington 'only allow'd the letters to be deliver'd to the officers, reserving the newspapers till a future time, thinking if the officers get to them now they will be reading the news instead of attending to their duties'.

After 'the enemy made no opposition & quitted Palencia at 8 o'clock this morn'g. We march'd thro' it amidst acclamations to Villalba.' Hughes thought Palencia beautiful and for Woodberry:

> the country about the neighbourhood . . . presents everything that can be wanted for the support of life, it bears wheat and other corn and is abundant in vineyards, game and fish. What a delightful estate would a thousand pounds English money buy in this district. With this sum, with English taste and with one honest English servant like Corporal Trim, who would act as gardener and take a hand at the plough, how happy might I close the remainder of my days.

Disciplinary problems continued to plague the 18th and the officers were summoned for a severe lecture from Grant on their men's conduct. Some had 'broke open & robbed the church and every house in the village'. In a snap check two men of the 18th and one of the 10th were found with bacon. A Brigade court martial was convened on the spot and the offenders received 'instead of the bacon, six hundred lashes each'.

At Tamora, after crossing a mountain plain through more rain, Woodberry, his servants and horses were 'stuffed into a mud cabin, the interior of which is the picture of misery'. Tamora also held three divisional generals and their staffs, 'How I dislike a general officer in any place but the field. One general & staff require as much room in a town as a regiment of dragoons would occupy, and when they are settled in quarters they are always annoying you with some foolish orders or complaints.'

On 9 June Hughes was 'obliged to put the Veterinary Surgeon under arrest; he abused me', and Woodberry prosecuted a man of Bolton's troop for leaving his picquet at Pedrosa del Rey and for 'disrespect'. 'This is the first time I ever gave evidence of a fellow creature in my life and I felt very nervous.'

That day's march, to Fromista was across swampy ground, nearly up to the horses' knees in mud. Then the road ran over 'a naked plain, where neither bush nor shrub is visible', through Santillana, an hour after the enemy had left. They crossed bridges over the Pisuerga and the 'Canal of Castile' that the enemy 'ought to have destroy'd, which would have much impeded our march'. Villasandino welcomed them with 'cheering acclamation' and every five minutes the inhabitants 'would set up dancing the Spanish *fandango* to the simple music of three tambourines'. Wine was to be had 'in great abundance' in every village.

From Hornillos on 11 June, Hughes 'reconnoitred, mounted picquets, posted vedettes &c sent a patrol to Villa Fresna'. He could see the French 'plundering about three miles off. The peasants flying'. But they were again welcomed with 'dancing &c' and, while his servant prepared dinner, Woodberry visited the church, 'which is uncommonly elegant. My guide play'd a Spanish national air on the organ; while I was in the church our Commissary came in, having heard there was some wheat hid in it. We immediately commenc'd a search – and found four barrels of flour & about three sacks of barley in a room near the steeple, which was seiz'd for our use.'

Flushing King Joseph out of Burgos

Wellington's forces were now all across the Piseurga and Hill's column attacked Reille's forward positions on the Hormazuela. While they were deploying, Grant's and Ponsonby's cavalry brigades, supported by the Light Division, appeared behind the French right flank. The enemy retreated hastily behind the Urbel.

Hughes went without breakfast that morning as his servant had not been warned that they would march at 3 a.m., 'which was the more inconvenient as a battle was expected'.

91

12 June

Met the 10th near Castillo & march'd in the direction of Burgos to some heights above Isar & here we were joined by Ponsonby's Heavy Brigade, by Alten's Brigade and the Light Division of Infantry. A small portion of the enemy occupied Isar; Alten's Brigade which was on our right advanced and were soon seen & heard on our right skirmishing with the enemy on the adjoining heights. We remain'd a long time watching them & at last were order'd to advance thro' Isar nearly straight to our front. In ascending the height, Lord Wellington join'd us shook hands with me & complimented me on commanding the Regiment. The Brigade form'd on the heights in three lines of regiments, the enemy's columns being all round us. We perform'd several evolutions, at length, the 15th was directed against one column of the enemy & the 18th against another, both columns however retired . . .

I was then directed to take a squadron of the 18th supported by the remainder of the Regiment to endeavour to cut off some baggage of the enemy, but with strong cautions, repeated by several messages, not to commit myself for that I had cavalry on my left & infantry on my right. I did take precautions & left all but the left squadron posted on commanding ground from whence they might easily retire & with the left squadron advanced throwing out a variety of skirmishers. The French return'd to us, skirmish'd sharply with riflemen & then open'd a cannonade; however I succeeded in capturing some prisoners, baggage, horses, &c. All their columns retired; we cannonaded from the heights & the heavy dragoons skirmish'd with their rear & took an officer. They blew up the bridge in the road to Burgos & set fire to three villages.

Woodberry, again with the skirmishers, 'had the satisfaction of distinguishing himself':

being on the right flank saw a party of baggage in the valley where the enemy was. I got a few men together and made a dash and took it; I just got it on the side of the hill when a party was sent after it, and oblig'd to order the men to turn about and charge them, which we did and they fled, leaving us masters of the baggage which we took quickly off; it consisted of 10 mules and about a dozen prisoners . . . we lost not a man or horse. Lord Wellington led our Regiment towards the enemy; I thought he intended to do us the honour of leading us in the charge, but the column of the enemy's on our right caught his attention.

Before abandoning Burgos, the French blew up the castle and an ammunition store. The mines were fired too early and:

> the effects of the explosion had been so badly calculated, that not only were many houses in the city injured, all the glass blown out of the splendid cathedral, but a hail of shells fell all over the surrounding quarter, and killed 100 men of Villatte's division, who were halted in the Plaza Mayor, and a few of Digeon's dragoons who were crossing the bridge. There were casualties also, of course, among the unfortunate citizens.[4]

Woodberry, returning with the picquet, was:

> astonish'd by the shock occasion'd by a dreadful explosion. The ground really appear'd to shake for the moment and we were struck dumb & motionless with the horrid roar. Immediately suspected what had happen'd, and which was confirm'd by the Prince of Orange who brought us orders to march, that the enemy has blown up Burgos Castle . . . The prisoners I took yesterday gave us some history of what was intended to be done, but none believed them. . . . I never saw a man so busy in my life as the Prince of Orange was yesterday; he carried the orders to the different troops and was galloping about the whole day.[5]

Across the Ebro to Vitoria

After a long march on 14 June, over high mountain plains, they camped at Cernégula, three and a half leagues from the Ebro. The weather was 'excessive hot, & having about every two leagues to mount still higher, we were all very much fatigued when we arrived here'. Next day the Puente Arenas was 'one of the strongest passes' Hughes had ever seen and 'one of the wildest and grandest scenes; a most dreadful and craggy descent, the bridge narrow & a rapid & deep river winding its way thro' a cleft in the most gigantic rocks'. A very cold morning was followed by a very hot day and another long march to Medina, during which they saw enemy columns moving along a plain in the direction of Miranda de Ebro. Hughes was 'fatigued & Mr Russell the Adjutant *hors de combat*'.[6]

On the march Woodberry 'took a sheep from a flock on the roadside, killed him in the hussar style – with my sword – and divided him with Mr Barrett of 15th Hussars. I dined off a part and I think I never

enjoy'd a dinner more in my life.' He was very sorry for 'the unfortunate infantry, who I saw today on the march, such numbers
laying on the roadside unable to stir a step further, it is impossible for
the poor fellows to march thirty-five to forty miles a day, two days
running, but Lord Wellington was anxious to cross the Ebro today'.

16 June (Villarcayo area)

[JH] by a good deal of exertion I produced a little activity in the
Commissary & he procured supplies. . . . Bad news that the Russians
have suffer'd a severe defeat.[7]

17 June (Medina de Pomar)

[JH] March'd at 5, the 18th in front, by the most extraordinary cross
& bad road in an easterly direction. Turing's mules fell into the water;
march'd about four leagues & encamp'd in a fine wood.

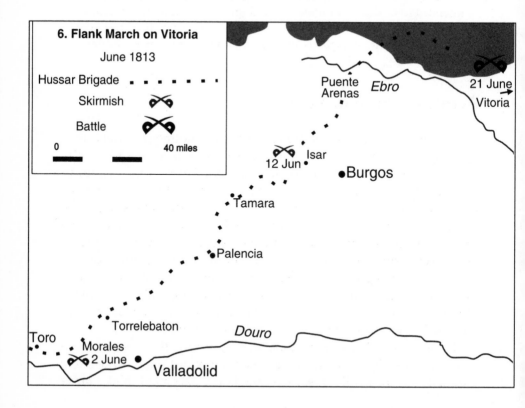

6. Flank March on Vitoria
June 1813
Hussar Brigade
Skirmish
Battle
0   40 miles

Puente Arenas   Ebro   21 June → Vitoria
12 Jun Isar
Burgos
Tamara
Palencia
Torrelebaton   Douro
Toro
Morales
2 June
Valladolid

[GW] Upwards of seventy thousand men are encamp'd within four miles of us, we having the outposts. My friend Smith is the dullest young man I ever knew. At this time, being a dangerous one I own, every one is in spirits or else appears so, as they ought and show a good example to the men, but he is very sad about something. Being absent from Mrs S. may be the cause of it, if so it is a very frivolous one for an hussar. . . . Robert Curtis, who was left at Santarém ill, still remains so, and there is not the least prospect of his joining the Regiment again or at least not till after the campaign. This is the fruits of bad company; the females have ruin'd him.

The French at last realized from which direction the British could be expected. Reille was ordered to bring his three divisions across the mountains to a position near Miravelles, to cover Bilbao from the west. But he had gone only a short distance when he encountered Graham's main column joining the road he had intended to take. Then the British 4th Division descended from the hills and he retreated hastily. A few miles south, nearer the Ebro, Maucune's column was caught between two brigades of the Light Division.

18 June (Berberana, Villalba de Losa area)

[JH] the Brigade was halted & we found that there was a partial engagement in front . . . on my arrival on some commanding ground, I saw some strong columns of French in the greatest confusion, making formations only to unmake them while some British light infantry were pushing on their right flank & engaged with their tirailleurs in a wood. The result was that the enemy retired and about three or four hundred prisoners were taken.

19 June

[JH] we marched for Subijana by roads or lanes that were even worse than the worst of Portugal; near Subijana we found our infantry engag'd . . . The enemy were driven from Subijana & the line of country near it without much loss on either side. . . . The narrow & hilly roads were clogg'd by infantry, baggage &c. It rain'd & there was much delay & confusion in encamping the Regiment. At length, having received contradictory orders, I took it on myself & encamp'd in a wood near.

[GW] When the Brigade got about half way here, we heard the report of guns . . . We ascended a high hill & descended into the valley and saw our army following up the enemy. Where my troop is encamp'd we found four dead Frenchmen; a great many prisoners are taken and tomorrow we expect to get clear of the mountains & then the Hussars will do a little to rid the earth of a few more, we are panting to have another touch at them.

. . . the Spanish never will be conquer'd. They strongly resemble the English . . . They may be defeated a thousand times, but they will never be subdued. The English newspapers & people are wrong when they exclaim that they have nothing to fight for, and say: 'Give them a Constitution! Give them Liberty!' . . . they have their country to fight for, their soil, their home, and against foreigners and invaders, surely this is something, and as to liberty, they have as much as they want, as much as they are really capable of. With respect to constitution, you might as well say, give them English roast beef, they have no idea of it, they know nothing about it, and therefore neither know the want of it nor desire it. . . . I believe there is a great deal of nonsense in the party refinements at home. They know nothing about this people . . .

Kennedy told his brother that the enemy:

never imagined we could go over such as country as we did, and were consequently not a little surprised and dismayed to find that we were across the Ebro before them and were on their flank. . . .

The British Army had this evening arrived within three leagues of the enemy and being most extremely fatigued we halted next day to take some rest . . . Never did an army travel worst roads, which with the worse weather, cold night bivouacs, without any cover, but the sky, you will allow were nearly sufficient to damp our military ardour. However, the Hussars surmounted all difficulties . . . the great Lord as he is called, (and certainly no-one deserves the appellation more justly) established his head quarters on the 19th in a village close to my bivouac, and thus two great personages reposed their bones near each other, I had the good luck to find a dinner laid out which the French in their hurry had been obliged to abandon, no less than seven of their sheep fell into my hands which I distributed among my hungry host . . . [any] description of the delightful spot we bivouacked in this evening would fall short of the reality. The most beautiful part of Wales would sink in comparison . . . I cannot describe the magnificent prospect of the whole allied army encamped on such a spot, the town of Vitoria in the distance with the French camps and as night came on the fires and lights of such an enormous host quite illuminating the country for leagues formed such a sight as I have not frequently seen . . . merely observing *en passant* that, in coming down a very high hill . . . I forgot that it was getting dark, and nearly broke my neck tumbling down a precipice—so much for the picturesque!

20 June

[JH] Received a melancholy letter from poor Murray . . . The French in position near Vitoria & Lord Wellington determined to attack them tomorrow.

[GW] The remainder of the French prisoners taken yesterday was march'd into this place a few hours back. Four hundred of them was took yesterday & about 100 killed. They have took up a strong position a few miles from us and appear determin'd to stand a battle. God send they may, for I feel confident of the issue.

CHAPTER 10

DEFEAT OF JOSEPH

Battle of Vitoria 21 June 1813

Wellington was now poised for a decisive stroke against Joseph with an Army eager for battle and confident of victory. Many, lured by recruiting sergeants with extravagant promises of glory and riches, were savouring the prospects for plunder, having heard that the enemy baggage was stuffed with years of looting in Spain and Portugal.

The French army deployed to the west of Vitoria and Wellington's operation began with Hill attacking the Puebla heights, dominating the road to Burgos and Madrid. Battle was joined at 8 a.m. and raged for much of the day. Despite heavy losses Hill secured the heights and the key village of Subijana and held them against a series of counter attacks.

In the centre, Graham's force was late arriving over the mountains, but, at about noon, Wellington heard that the bridge at Tres Puentes was unguarded and ordered Kempt's brigade to secure a bridgehead. Picton's 3rd Division arrived on the scene from the north and he carried out the attack, intended for 7th Division, on Tres Puentes and Puente de Mendoza. This was the flank of a substantial French position, but French attention had been on Hill, and Picton and Kempt soon had the French retreating. Further Allied troops arrived over the Zadorra bridges and, by 3 p.m., after a fierce fight around Arinez, Wellington personally commanded the storming of the knoll and village. The French retreated on Vitoria, halting along a ridge near Armentia in the hope of giving the refugees and baggage wagons time to get clear. Meanwhile Graham had advanced from the left and attacked the hills overlooking Gamarra Mayor and Menor, Abachuco and the Zadorra bridges. The Anglo-Portuguese stormed the ridge and soon took Gamarra Mayor and Abachuco, beating off a desperate French counter attack on Gamarra Mayor. Two French divisions prevented their crossing the Zadorra bridges for most of the afternoon, but Longa's guns closed the 'Royal Road' towards Bayonne. The retreat towards Pamplona became a rout and, by late afternoon, after inflicting some 7,500 casualties on the French at the cost of 5,000 of his own troops, Wellington had a glorious victory.

Sadly for the 18th Hussars, the day for them ended with accusations and rumours that were to cast a blight for months to come. Kennedy did not mention them to his brother:

the possession of Vitoria was now become indispensable as our Commissariat could obtain no more bread in the wild part of the country we then occupied, and thousands of our soldiers had been many days without bread. . . . it was cold attended with drizzling rain and more like a morning in November than in June, the army however moved forward in three grand divisions towards Vitoria, Sir R Hill on the right, Sir T Graham on the left, and the centre (to which we belonged) led by Lord W. in person; the 18th followed Lowry Cole's Division which was one of the centre grand divisions. About an hour after we marched from our bivouac, Lord W. with Beresford, the Prince of Orange and his staff passed us on the road, . . . it struck me, at the time, how much he must have had on his mind; it must have been to him a most anxious moment indeed, the fate of Spain in a great measure, all his former laurels, all his future glory, rested on the issue of the gigantic contest we were about to commence. . . . he had scarcely passed us to get in front of the centre when the weather cleared up and becoming fine, the immense line of the enemy soon presented itself calculated from 60 to 70,000 strong. The position they took up was about a league in front of Vitoria a river ran along their front, and on their right flank which was also supported by two villages whilst their left rested on a high hill wooded to the top, and much more steep than that opposite Cultra; near their centre rose a high conical hill, on which stood the King—which however afterwards gave us but little trouble to drive them from.

General Hill with his corps and Murillo's Spaniards (who bye the bye behaved admirably) began the battle on the hill which supported their left between 7 & 8 in the morning; at the same time Graham was to attack their right, but owing to some delay did not get up time enough to come into play and in consequence ('tis said) Hill made a feint of retreating in order to give Graham more time to come up; here the French were completely taken in, and it flew along the line that the

100

day was their own, they were soon however undeceived when the attack was recommenced with redoubled vigour. About 11 o'clock our right was very warmly engaged especially among the woods on the hill; it was soon however apparent that the French were getting the worst of it, and their *tirailleurs* were falling back on their main body, whilst our riflemen advanced after them in the most cool, steady manner. The whole of the ground at this time was unfavourable for cavalry and we were consequently spectators for several hours. On arriving near their position on the hill, the guns on both sides were opened and upwards of 100 pieces of cannon played on both sides.

. . . meantime the battle raged most furiously on the left, and about one o'clock the centre was ordered down to break through their centre, soon after both flanks began to give way and the centre retired from the conical hill they occupied as soon as they observed us passing the bridges over the river. At the back of this hill, we found three solid squares of infantry retiring with cannon on the flanks of each, one of which our Brigade was called forward to charge. To get at the enemy it was necessary to leap a very broad ditch which it was ten to one if

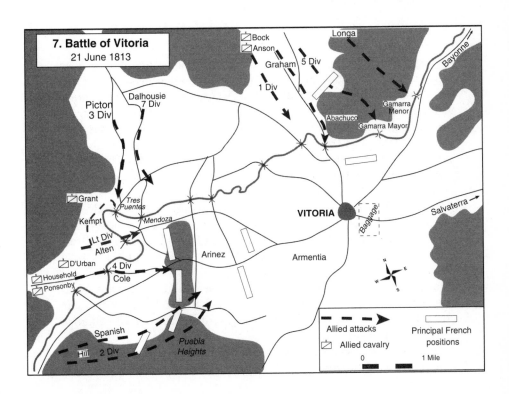

101

one half of our squadron got over safe, and afterwards we had to charge over deep ground and up a hill. Scarcely had the leading squadron leaped into the field, when they were almost annihilated by the most destructive volley of shots, shell and musketry that ever an unfortunate squadron of cavalry was exposed to, Captain Turing, Cornet Foster and many men fell instantly, the former completely riddled with shot, poor Foster was shot through the knee but will recover I hope without losing his leg.

Colonel Grant now found he had done rather an imprudent thing in thus exposing his cavalry and we were ordered to retire until the artillery and infantry came up, and broke the enemy's columns. I commanded the centre squadron of the Regiment and had already leapt the ditch to follow when we received orders to retire. Such a cannonade as we were exposed to for some minutes you have not idea of, I thought the whole regiment must have been destroyed without a chance (from the unfavourable nature of the ground) of being of the least use. Shot and shells together with every delicacy of the season were dealt out among us in profusion, one of the latter burst over my head, and almost stunned me for a short time and broke the sword in my Cornet's hand, who was by my side.

Hughes had been with Turing:

When the Hussar Brigade & the Light Division was order'd by narrow passes round the mountains to force a bridge on the enemy's right this was done & it had an immediate effect in causing a change of position which movement was so rapidly press'd by the British cavalry & infantry that much confusion ensued amongst the French. But they were very strong in artillery. The Hussar Brigade advanced rapidly over ground that they abandon'd, but the arrangements of Brigadier Grant being highly imperfect or rather he having made none, the rear of the column of the Regiment was halted while I advanced with the left (Captain Turing's Squadron). There appear'd nothing for us to do, but to take artillery & this we were about to attempt under a most heavy fire when we were halted. I then wheeled half squadrons to our left & a column of French infantry being in front on an abrupt hill I order'd out skirmishers but Captain Turing waved his sword, cheer'd and charged; it was a most unfortunate business; I tried to stop it but it was too late & on we went; poor Turing was kill'd & Foster with some dragoons was wounded. We then were order'd to retire & infantry advanced against these men.

[AK] On the infantry coming up the battle raged nearly as violent in the centre as it had done on both flanks. It was the expiring effort of

102

the enemy who was retiring on all sides disputing the ground by inches although to little purpose, for who could withstand the impetuosity of our British and Portuguese who rivalled each other. In about two hours after their centre had been attacked the enemy's infantry had completely given way, their cavalry which had been below the town of Vitoria during the day moved out to the right of their position in order to cover the retreat of their columns of infantry. At this time their centre was flying in disorder and now the Hussars were brought up in their proper place, to pursue the fugitives. As we galloped over the field in pursuit the scene was horrid in the extreme, the wounded, the dying and the dead of different nations were lying in groups indiscriminately, guns, carriages, and ammunition tumbrels, scattered about broken, the mules or horses having been killed they were of course obliged to be left behind.

On arriving within half a mile of the town (owing to the blunder of a sergeant who carried the order) the Brigade was divided, the 15th with one squadron of the 18th went down to attack the enemy's cavalry which had formed on the right of their position, whilst the centre and right squadrons of the 18th followed by the 10th, were ordered to attack the town, rather a hazardous undertaking you will allow . . . however as it happened we succeeded in our attack and we entered Vitoria pell mell with the enemy, amidst the acclamations of the delighted Spaniards, among them some beautiful women who waved their handkerchiefs from their windows. As I commanded the leading squadron I had the honour of first forcing the gates, which were quite blocked up, with cannon, carriages broken down, and the fugitives of the enemy half dead with fright. It was consequently some time before we could all gain admittance, and never did I expect to see many of the Regiment come out alive; however the enemy were so closely pressed, they had not much time for defence, and although many of them occupied the houses in their flight and fired on us as we galloped through the street, we had only a few men wounded.

On reaching the outward gate of the town on the Pamplona road . . . such a scene presented itself as I never can forget . . . the whole of the Royal and French generals' equipage consisting of many coaches, some with 6 & 8 mules, and horses, each. Treasure chests, wagons, carts, numberless servants, in the Royal livery, the finest horses and mules every species of animal, in short Noah's Ark, seemed here assembled: even King Joseph himself . . . had been in this same spot but a few minutes before we made our appearance through the gate; he had remained here to the last minute never supposing we would attempt to send cavalry through the town, the consternation consequently which ensued on our appearance had the effect of striking all with a panic and the whole of their immense collection quickly fled or attempted to fly in all directions, thousands making their escape for want of a sufficient number of our men to secure them, for at this time not one quarter of my squadron had succeeded in getting through the outward gate of the town owing to the numerous obstacles we met with. The Guards, which had been about the carriages, instantly fled with Joseph. Several French ladies . . . were to be seen crying out for mercy, their servants, horses, mules running about in all directions and abandoning every-thing, carriages of all sorts, tumbling over each other whilst the Spaniards were taking advantage of the general confusion and immediately set to breaking open the treasure chests, travelling carriages, etc, etc, literally strewing the ground with bags of doubloons and dollars, not to mention jewels, watches, trinkets and all sorts of plunder which the portmanteaus and band boxes of the ladies afforded. . . .

It was some minutes after I succeeded in getting through the gates before the men could follow and by the time I got about half my troop through and attempted to form among the crowd, I was charged by a body of Joseph's Guards who surprised us by coming suddenly round a rising ground, and consequently we did not see them till they were close up with us. They seemed to have made this *dernier* effort to cover the retreat of their master whom they supposed we should follow, and probably overtake. Resistance with such a handful of men (for at this time they were so occupied seizing prisoners, I had not half a dozen of my men near me) was unavailing, and to retreat into the gates was equally impossible – from the crowds of people in our rear. In short we were surrounded on all sides with friends and foes, Spaniards and French, I therefore saw there was no alternative but to leap a large ditch which was close by. I forgot however that I was mounted on a French officer's horse, which I had just taken and mounted (my own having been blown on the gallop through Vitoria) and accordingly the brute refused the leap; when I abandoned him I escaped over the ditch on foot and mounted a troop horse in the next field, whilst the French unable to follow me ineffectually fired a volley from their carbines. I was scarcely off the horse when he was re-taken by the enemy. For a minute or two I was something like Richard and would have given 'my kingdom for a horse' when a dragoon of my Troop at his own risk dismounted and gave me his and by this time our rear squadron having come out of the town, Joseph's guards were obliged to decamp in haste . . .

We had nothing now to do but scamper after them in all directions. Guns, tumbrels, wagons, prisoners, everything fell before us like magic, and the pursuit continued until it was quite dark, the army then

104

bivouacked about half a league from Vitoria on the Pamplona road . . .

The loss of the enemy would have been much greater but for the very unfavourable ground for cavalry, the close intersected country, the numerous ditches and woods favoured their escape, whilst on the other hand they prevented the escape of their cannon and carriages, every piece of which with one solitary exception fell into our hands before they reached Pamplona, they say 152 in number. Joseph escaped on horseback, with a single attendant and without any clothes but those he wore. . . .

You will observe that our gallant Brigadier made no less than two grand blunders with our Brigade on that day, the first was charging a solid column of infantry, a thing scarcely ever attempted by light cavalry except in the greatest emergency when every other method of breaking the square has failed, and the second was sending us through the town of Vitoria which although it fortunately succeeded, might have been attended with most fatal consequences and that we should have done more, much more, than was done had Stewart or Lord Uxbridge commanded us. . . . All the infantry movements were like clockwork, nothing could be more beautiful. I had an opportunity of being near Lord W. at the middle of the day, we were halted near a hill from he directed the operations, he was dressed in a grey frock and gave his orders with so much coolness watching all the movements with the sangfroid of an indifferent spectator. The quantity of treasure taken must be immense. But at least one half of it fell into the hands of the Spaniards, the French say 40 millions of francs which was Joseph's private purse. If it is ever divided it will be something for the army.

At the end of the day, Hughes wrote miserably:

The French fire being silenced we once more advanced & were proceeding on the left of the town when the 18th were order'd to charge thro' the town leaving the Left Squadron under Captain Carew & with the Right charged thro' the town. This is no place to describe the extra-ordinary, wild, confused & shocking scenes that took place here. We took all King Joseph's baggage & almost captured him. But the Regiment was utterly broken & fit for nothing. I could only collect a handful of men with which I advanced against the French when we took some guns.

and subsequently told his brother:

A circumstance occurred to me, which will illustrate the confusion. Some dragoons, who had surrendered to me and thrown away their

105

arms, were dismounting from their horses, when some sort of officer (a Portuguese dragoon I think), dressed in green, galloped furiously at them and began to sabre them. I interposed my sword and cried out 'You scoundrel, why do you cut at these men? Do you not see that they are disarmed and are my prisoners?' He instantly turned and aimed a blow at my head, which I parried, said 'Scoundrel? I am an officer of the 95th Regiment. They wounded me as I lay on the ground.' So saying he rode off.

We succeeded in driving the enemy through the town, while women were screaming and jumping on balconies, Frenchman firing from others and Spaniards stabbing them in the streets and we were followed by the 10th. As the men had followed the French through the different streets, we got there in a very broken state. On the other side stood a crowd of carriages, horses and carriages. To skip a variety of incidents, we pursued the French till dark.

Woodberry's journal entry began: 'Field of Battle. Victory of Vitoria'; 'O God dispose my heart to return thanks for thy goodness for withholding the sword that was pointed at my existence from having the effect it was intended.' When Grant ordered the Hussar Brigade to withdraw, after the charge against French infantry, he was sent out with skirmishers:

and found poor Cornet Foster, laying under a tree where some men had left him, shot thro' the left leg. I instantly rode towards the infantry lines & procured two surgeons and took them to him. It was now the battle become general. We advanced along the Roman paved road towards Vitoria, we was several times halted, and remain'd under the range of the enemy's fire. Every position the enemy took up they were drove from; we saw the cannon laying about as we advanced, which they were compelled to leave. At last we came to the town and when opposite it two squadrons of the 18th & the whole of the 10th were order'd to charge through the town, which they did. I was with the Left Squadron and the 15th; we went to the left of the town and found the whole of the enemy's cavalry was formed to protect the retreat of their King and the infantry.

It was here the Hussar Brigade was damn'd for ever. Colonel Grant, who knew nothing of part of the Brigade being order'd into the town, order'd a charge, we advanced upon them riding over a column of infantry. I know nothing more that occurred till I formed up the Squadron upon the ground we moved from. I saw Carew in the hands of the enemy & saw the Squadron & the 15th Regiment retreating; I

106

was the last that arrived being pursued (and wounded) by a whole squadron of the enemy. Poor Captain Carew, the last words I heard him speak was, 'come along Woodberry and the left'. . . . They were just preparing to charge us, when two pieces of artillery arrived and put them to the rout. We now advanced — but their brigade never charg'd again.

After pursuing the enemy until dark:

We were order'd to bivouac in a wood about a league from Vitoria. I lay'd myself under a tree, so did Carew's troop round me; our horses, poor things, fared as bad as us, for we got nothing to eat. After the battle was over, I saw a mule with baggage on its back laying in a ditch. I got him out & took it to our camp. The mule was stolen from me, but the contents of the boxes I had under my head all night or I should have lost that; it proved to be a little of Joseph's baggage. One man took a wagon of roast legs of mutton & chickens; we got them in time for breakfast. Turing was buried immediately after the battle by some of the men, near where he was killed. Foster was carried to a village; Carew, the enemy took with them. I hope to God he is well.

[JH] About half a league from Vitoria a surgeon of the Royals came to me & told me that Captain Carew lay in a village near mortally wounded. I took him back with me & at the entrance of a house found him on a rug groaning mournfully . . . He acted like a hero & heard his inevitable fate like a Christian, his hands were in mine while the surgeon attempted to perform an operation, the success of which he despair'd of. I left him & it being nearly dark & the business of the day over I return'd to Vitoria much fatigued. I tried to get the 18th (who I found in great numbers posted as guards) relieved. A squadron of Life Guards[1] were here, I gave them some directions for posting sentries over the gates & they wished me to take the command of the town, which I declined. . . . I saw Pulsford & sent him to Carew; at last, much exhausted I got a billet where they gave me a supper & I retir'd to bed.

When the general *débacle* began King Joseph and Jourdan took their post on a low hill half a mile east of the town, and endeavoured to organize the departure of the Park and convoys – a hopeless task, for the roads were blocked, and no one listened to orders. . . . Presently a flood of fugitives were driven in upon the staff, by the approach of the British cavalry in full career, who had turned the town on its left, and galloped down on the prey before them. . . The King and his staff had to fly as best they could, and were much scattered, galloping over fields and marshy ravines, mixed with military and civil fugitives of all sorts.

107

Some of the British hussars followed the throng, taking a good many prisoners by the way: more it is to be feared, stopped behind to gather the not too creditable first-fruits of victory, by plundering the royal carriages, which lay behind the scene of their charge. The French stragglers had already shown them the way.[2]

The Allied Army had totally defeated Joseph's Army, which had 15,000 casualties against their own loss of 5,100, as well as capturing the bulk of their guns and baggage. 'If the prisoners were fewer than might have been expected, the material captured was such as no European army had ever laid hands on before, since Alexander's Macedonians plundered the camp of the Persian King after the battle of Issus.'[3]

The Hussar Brigade had the bulk of the cavalry casualties, the 18th losing eleven killed and twenty-three wounded.

CHAPTER 11

UNDER A CLOUD

June-July 1813

Regiment in 'a shocking state'

Kennedy's letter to his brother continued:

> the Gazette will inform you of our having continued the pursuit to Pamplona, where the greater part of the enemy fled. General Graham pursued the remainder on the Bayonne road. We remained with Lord W. and reached Salvatierra, the first night the rain fell in torrents and the roads, if such they could be called, were strewed with dead horses, men etc. We pressed them so closely that they only had time to break down one bridge between Vitoria and Pamplona where their remnant arrived in a most wretched state . . . Here they have left a garrison of 2,500 and the remainder we have never since seen, they left Pamplona in a most scattered manner making the best of their way to the Pyrenees.

> ### *22 June (Salvatierra)*
>
> [JH] I collected the men & sent them off & after a few other arrangements I went myself, but first I brought Quincey to Carew. He was still alive & even seem'd better but there was no hope. I parted with him forever. I join'd the Brigade which I found on the march, Grant attack'd me for charging into the town. We arrived late at Salvatierra, the Regiment in a shocking state. . . I gave orders about plunder & got under cover.

Woodberry went back to Vitoria with the casualties and sick and the Regiment had moved on by the time he returned, with stragglers he had found. His party spent the night in 'a most miserable hole' where, as they were nearly starving, he seized a sheep for supper.

On the 24th Grant visited Hughes and, 'an explanation took place at my quarters'. Soon after his return Woodberry was called out on parade 'for the men to deliver up their plunder & be searched. A great deal was found on them, which of course was took, to be equally shared amongst the Regiment. On one man was found seven hundred & forty quarter doubloons.' Later in the day he, 'had some words with Smith and am very sorry for it as I feel a great friendship for him'.

Major Hughes took about £2,600 from the men, besides jewels and clothes; this he gave to the Paymaster for the general benefit of the Regiment, and, during the halt at Olite later on, employed the money in equipping the men.[1]

Next day, with the men in 'a shocking condition', they marched through villages burnt down as the French retreated. Woodberry heard that some of the officers 'got a deal of plunder. Burke, near two thousand pounds, Dolbell as much.'

Pursuit of Clausel

[AK] General Clausel, with 12,000 men, having come from the north to reinforce Joseph but being too late and having been cut off from the Bayonne road by Graham's corps, and by us from Pamplona, he had no alternative but to push forward to the Ebro, in the hope of joining Suchet . . . In consequence of this his Lordship set out from the neighbourhood of Pamplona on the 26th with 4th and Light Divisions, our Brigade and General Ponsonby's brigade of heavy cavalry to try and intercept him.

Before the pursuit, Grant summoned the officers and told them:

[GW] his Lordship was very much displeased with the insubordination of the Regiment, particularly of the conduct of the men in Vitoria on the 21st. Numbers of them he saw plundering in the streets; he was likewise very much displeased with several of our officers who was there likewise, instead of being in the field, and to finish he had to inform us that his Lordship was determined if he heard any complaint against the Regiment he would immediately dismount us, and march the Regiment to the nearest sea port and embark us for England.

Looting had been widespread after the battle, with officers often just as involved as other ranks.[2] The 18th were perhaps unlucky that

110

8. Pamplona Area
June to October 1813

BAYONNE

N
W   E
S

St Jean-de-Luz

Hasparren
• Urcuray

Hendaye

SAN
SEBASTIÁN

St Pée-s-Nivelle

F   R   A   N   C   E

• Pasajes

Sare

• Renteria

• Hernani

Lesaka •

Etxaler

Maya

St Jean-P•
de-Port

Oitz •

Santesteban

Tolosa

Donamaria

Roncesvalles

Olague

Ostiz

Irutzun

S   P   A   I   N

Errotz

Sorauren •

Asiain

Huarte

PAMPLONA

Noain

Unzué

Mendivil

Tafalla •

0   10 miles

Olite

Wellington came across them himself, but it *was* when they were needed for the pursuit and the general indiscipline of the preceding months must have told against them.

Woodberry was greatly upset. 'O God is it come to this! I want language to express the grief I feel on the occasion; to think I should have come out with a Regiment, who have contrary to all expectation acted so differently.'

At Tafalla on the 27th, they 'had just got snug into quarters' when the bugle sounded for a march to Olite. There and at Tafalla: 'We being the first English who ever enter'd . . . was received with the greatest demonstrance of joy and kindness by all. We get excellent feeds, abundance of fruit & wine.'

Woodberry, recovering from his wound, was sent forward with Woodhouse of the 15th to reconnoitre Tudela, which the French were said to have left that morning. However:

> upon entering the gates, near a doz'n shots was fired at us by the French sentries, we immediately turned about & gallop'd off, being pursued nearly two miles by a dozen dragoons who was ready mounted & prepared to dash out after us, but the superior metal of our horses set them at defiance. We after got upon a rising ground & saw the enemy withdraw from the town and it turned out that the army was actually gone but had left their rear guard in the town, which upon their leaving, they blew up the bridges.

They returned to Valtierra:

> amidst the cheers & acclamations of the inhabitants, who forced us off our horses into the principal house where we was regaled with dinner . . . The bells rang, the people danced all about the streets, the clergy offer'd up prayer for our success; we were took to the church by the people & heard their organ, several of their most joyful airs was played & a *Te Deum* was sung. On my way back I was meet by near an hundred men, women & children who came out on purpose to give any English they might meet wine, cake &c. I was detain'd nearly an hour by them and was oblig'd to drink two good bumpers of wine before they would allow me to depart.

> [AK] on next day towards Tudela, where Clausel was, we received information of his having destroyed the bridge over the Ebro there and proceeded to Zaragoza, he had that morning intended coming by the same road we were then on, in order to get to Pamplona but unfortu-

nately he heard we should meet him and went off to Zaragoza from whence it is thought Suchet and he will escape to France . . . Finding they had escaped and his troops uncommonly fatigued Lord W. ordered us to return and halt there. The Hussars in Olite and the heavy cavalry in Tafalla, where we are likely to remain in some days to refresh the horses and men.

Wellington had 'not yet got in touch with his new bases of supply at Santander and on the Biscay coast, so that for the moment he was a little short of ammunition, and also living on the country, a practice which he disliked on principle . . . his army was tired and sulky . . . many of his stragglers had not yet rejoined'.[3] His principal concern, however, was that Napoleon might secure a separate peace with Russia and Prussia. That would free substantial forces to oppose him in southern France. For the moment, therefore, his aim was limited to securing the approaches to France, by besieging San Sebastián and clearing the north-west corner of Spain of enemy. The Spanish were to blockade Pamplona.

Refreshing Horses and Men at Olite

In Olite Woodberry at first felt 'very unwell . . . All my limbs pain me and am sure if I was oblig'd to march tomorrow & next day it would kill me' – but he had a good billet:

1 July

and the *patrón*, a civil obliging old gentleman, gave me yesterday my leather bucket full of wine. Poor Captain Carew's baggage was sold yesterday; it was too ridiculous to see the prices given for the eatables; 2 bottles of sauce was sold for 35/-. Cheese of about 7lb weight sold for 73/6d. – two tongues for 27/-. The principal purchasers were Lord Worcester, Hill & Mr FitzClarence & Lord W. gave 34/- for a pr. of brass spurs. I bought a bridle, which cost me £4, a monstrous price & cloth for a pr. of overalls.

2 July

[JH] A Brigade court martial upon Russell of the 15th Hussars for striking me when I interfered to prevent his assaulting a woman.

[GW] I have forbear before to mention . . . The day of the Victory of Vitoria, after the 18th & 10th had charg'd the enemy thro' the town, Major Hughes directed Mr Dolbell to take charge of twenty men who were placed sentry over the carriages, baggage &c of the nobility & French officers & he immediately, so is the report, commenc'd plundering. Many of the prisoners & persons of rank belonging to the enemy dined with Lord Wellington, at dinner in course of conversation, Madam Guizl say'd that if it had not been for a private hussar, an officer of hussars would have plunder'd of every thing. That after she had deliver'd up her husband's sword to him and likewise a beautiful double barrell'd gun, he took by force off her finger a ring. Lord Wellington was in a great rage . . . He sent for Colonel Grant the next morning and . . . desired him to make immediate inquiry that he might bring Mr D. (whose name he had learnt) to a court martial. Mr Dolbell wrote a justification to Lord Wellington & the officers of the Brigade. It utterly denies the ring business, but owns that he took the gun & sword; here the matter stands at present.

Woodberry was:

happy to understand the Hussar Brigade will be broke up, immediately, by Lord Wellington who is not at all pleased with Colonel Grant's manoeuvres at the Battle of Vitoria; they all allow this officer to be possessed of courage and resolution, but all say he wants judgement. The 10th & 15th are to be brigaded together & Lord Fitzroy Somerset will command it. The 18th will be brigaded with the German Hussars under General Bock.[4]

3 July

Opposite to my quarters is a convent and in it twenty-two nuns. I was talking to several last evening thro' a thin partition of wood. . . . There were several young women amongst them, but none handsome. One who have been in the convent thirty-two years, was the most engaging of the whole; she enter'd it very young and her countenance bespeaks she was once beautiful. I asked them if they would like to live in a *casa*, instead of the convent, which was answer'd immediately by the Lady Abbess in the negative. They appear'd particular happy in the sight of an Englishman and . . . I made them comprehend that I was an hussar and that in England we are the pride of the fair sex which they were not at all astonish'd at. They said they liked us better than those they had seen from their windows in red coats.

I am now quite recover'd from the fatigue of the march, and am

1. James Hughes of Kinmel C.B.
Lieut. Colonel 18th Hussars.
Born 12th Nov 1778.
(Courtesy of the Trustees of the
Kinmel Estate.)

2. Sergeant John Taylor and French Cuirassiers at Waterloo.

[A Storm came on] during the night which was most dreadfull.

13th. I distributed an extra quantity of rum & gave quantities of corn to the Horses, the day did not clear up but the storm on the contrary continued, it was impossible to act in any way & all operations were suspended. Spent the principal part of the Morng. in writing, sketching &c with the exception of the Intervals necessary to Military duties. Our Dinner the same as yesterday except that the party was increased by the arrival of the new Brigade Major, and that as the wind & storm continued to encrease our habitation was less comfortable; this Habitation deserves a description, it was a large Shed or Barn intended for sheep during the Winter; it had no Doors, but was divided into two by a low wall & again divided by a little Hedge & the low Beams kept our Horses & Mules from encroaching on us & having cover'd the Door by canvas & lit a large fire in it we made ourselves very comfortable & the candles were fortified from the wind by a contrivance of mine]. The Portico served for our Kitchen, others had Tents but most of the Men & Horses were quite exposed. We sent another Picquet to the Front, an order arrived for the Brigade to go into Cantonements, it was too late, so we had another dreadfull [night].

3. From the Hughes diary: see transcript in italics, left. (Courtesy of the Trustees of the Kinmel Estate and the Department of Manuscripts, University of Wales, Bangor.)

4. A silver beaker taken from Joseph Bonaparte's travelling carriage at Vitoria. (Courtesy of Sir Anthony Weldon Bt.)

5. Cavalry pistol 1802-35. (Courtesy of the Trustees 13th/18th Royal Hussars Museum.)

7. A private of the 18th Hussars.

8. The Hon. Sir Henry Murray C.B.
(After R. Cosway R.A.)

. Light cavalry sword 1796.
Courtesy of the Trustees 13th/18th
Royal Hussars Museum.) '... the hilt
was absurdly inadequate, insomuch
as it afforded no protection to the
hand. Hence during the campaigns
of 1810-15 wounds in the hand
were very frequent. The swords of
the officers were similar in shape,
but lighter in every way.' (*History of
the XIII Hussars,* C.R.B. Barrett.)

Yeneste, — Monday 31st May. At last I have seen a Skirmish — The Brigade passed the Ford of Almandra. — supported by the 7th & 8th Divisions of the Army & Bottons Squadron of Flying Artillery. — we passed about 2 oClk. then very dark. the Enemy did not expect us so early. was taken by surprise and out of about Sixty Men, that formed the Squadron in charge of the Heights & Ford. not more then 10 Escaped. The officer Command of the piquet was a shaving himself at the time. took prisoner. some of the Men made great resistance but was most horribly Cut & hacked about by the Men of the 15th Hussar. who had the honor of passing over first & was thereby obliged to act. — Capt. Carew or the Veterinary Surgeon. saw a party of the flying Enemy enter the Village Almandra. gallop'd there immediately & took five Men & four Horses — I was ordered to return to our Camp & bring the Baggage of the Brigade over the River. — by the time I arrived with it. the Ponton Bridge was put across the River which I passed over; it was made with 9 Boats. with Boards across them. —— when the Baggage Mules &c. had advanced about 2 Miles on the Road to this place from the Ford. an Orderly Man from a Piquet under Capt. Grammont. of 10th Hussars. came Galloppping past. & inform'd us. that Two Squadrons of the Enemies Dragoons — was advancing towards us, — I halted the whole. & desired an officer. of the Kings Hussars. who had charge of their Baggage to remain with the whole while I went forward & reconnoitred. On my return. I observed all the Baggage Mules &c &c —

The Duke of Wellington and his staff 1813. 'How I dislike a general officer in any place ut the field. One general & staff require as much room in a town as a regiment of dragoons ould occupy, and when they are settled in quarters they are always annoying you with me foolish orders or complaints.'

). (Opposite) Page from the Woodberry ary; see Transcript below. (Courtesy of the irector National Army Museum, London.)

1este, – Monday 31st. May. At last I have seen a Skirmish. *e Brigade pass'd the Ford of Almandra, supported by the* *. & 8th Divisions of the Army & Boltons Squadron of* *ying Artillery. We passed about 2 o'clk. then very dark, the* *emy did not expect us so early, was taken by surprise and* *of about Sixty Men, that formed the Squadron, in charge* *the Heights & Ford, not more than 10 Escaped. The officer* *nmandg. the piquet was shaving himself at the time took* *soner. Some of the men made great resistance but was most* *rribly cut & hacked about by the Men of the 15th.* *ussars, who had the honor of passing over first & was there-* *e oblig'd to act. Captn. Carew & the Veterinary Surgeon* *v a party of the flying Enemy enter the Village Almandra,* *llop'd there immediately & took five men & four Horses. I* *us order'd to return to our camp & bring the Baggage of the* *igade over the River. By the time I arrived with it the* *ntoon Bridge was put across the River which I passed over;* *vas made with 9 Boats with Boards acrosst them. When the* *aggage, Mules &c had advanced about 2 Miles on the Road* *this place from the Ford an Orderly Man from a Piquet* *der Captn. Grammont of the 10th. Hussars came* *allopping past, & inform'd us that Two Squadrons of the* *emies Draggoons was advancing towards us. I halted the* *ole & desired an officer of the Kings Hussars who had* *arge of their Baggage to remain with the whole while I went* *ward & reconnoitred. On my return I observed all the* *aggage Mules &c &c ...*

11. The silver trumpet: 'Purchased by desire of the soldiers of the Eighteenth Hussars, with part of the prize money arising from the enemy's horses captured by their brigade, under the command of Major-General Sir Hussey Vivian, KCB, etc, at the battle of Waterloo, 18th June, 1815.' (Courtesy of the Trustees 13th/18th Royal Hussars Museum.)

DIVISION.

BUREAU

ENREGISTREMENT

Préfecture des Landes.

2. Extract from Kennedy's letter.
(Courtesy of Sir Anthony Weldon Bt.)

Mont-de-Marsan   6 March 1814
Préfecture de Landes

*My dearest Mother, The date of this will show you that
we are so far on our way to Bordeaux. We arrived here
on the 1st and we have been in such an settled state
since the Battle with pursuing the flying foe that till now
I have been unable to command any time to give you a
detail of our proceedings, of which I conclude the
Gazette will have informed you long before this reaches
you. I am at present left here with my squadron to keep
up the communication with the rest of the army. It is an
uncommonly nice town and I am quartered in no less a
house than that of the Prefect of the Department who
thought proper to take himself off on our approach and
such a Palace as it is I have not often seen. He was the
greatest man in this part of the country and you can't
conceive any thing more elegant than his mansion is. I
do him the honour to drink his fine claret which is really
delicious and I am obliged to make use of his letter
paper as you may see.*

*I believe my last letter was dated the day or two after the
campaign recommenced, but lest it should lead you
astray for the circumstances of the army being in motion
and the post consequently irregular I may as well
recapitulate some of our achievements. Know therefore
that on the 15th February the army took the field. We
marched from Hasparren, crossed the Joyeuse river and
the French, after but little resistance vanished. On the
16th were at Ayherre, the 17th at Bardos …*

*groaning under. At Bordeaux the people are waiting
for arrival with the greatest impatience and they say
6,000 men there are ready to join us. Soult however
has retreated towards Toulouse where we hear Suchet is
to join him so I suppose we shall not advance much
further at present. Bayonne is not yet attacked but the
Citadel is surrounded I hear, and as St. Jean Pied de
Port also holds out, we can't well advance further till
they both fall. The day after our Brigade arrived here
General Hill again attacked the enemy near Grenade
where they had formed to cover their retreat and
defeated them with great loss; I have not heard the
particulars as yet. The remnant of Soult's army therefore
that will reach Toulouse cannot be very considerable I
should think. The weather, which had hitherto favoured
us so much, changed on the 1st and we came into this
town like so many drowned rats; such torrents of rain as
we had for two or three days you can't think. It is
however now fine. The heavy rain however has in some
measure prevented our further pursuit.*

*You will see by the papers that Lord March is among
the wounded. He is aide de camp to Lord Wellington …*

13. Robert Bolton who 'charged the French
with the 18th, drove them back, but brought
his squadron too near a wood from wherein
their infantry mortally wounded him & took
him prisoner.' (Courtesy of John Mollo Esq.)

14. The porch of the English church at
Biarritz 'dedicated to the memory of
the officers, non-commissioned
officers and men of the British Army
who fell in the south-west of France,
from October 7 1813, to April 14,
1814'. It was 'erected by their fellow-
soldiers and compatriots A.D.1882'.
(Bolton's name is under 'Eighteenth
Hussars'.)

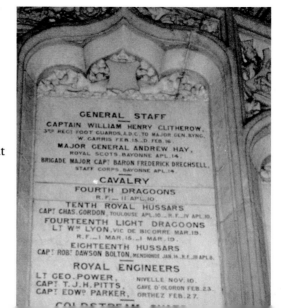

GENERAL STAFF
CAPTAIN WILLIAM HENRY CLITHEROW,
3RD REGT FOOT GUARDS, A.D.C. TO MAJOR GEN. BYNG.
W. GARRIS FEB. 15...D. FEB. 16
MAJOR GENERAL ANDREW HAY,
ROYAL SCOTS, BAYONNE APL. 14.
BRIGADE MAJOR CAPT BARON FREDERICK DRECHSELL,
STAFF CORPS, BAYONNE APL. 14.

CAVALRY
FOURTH DRAGOONS
R.F.—II APL. 10.
TENTH ROYAL HUSSARS
CAPT CHAS. GORDON, TOULOUSE APL. 10...R. F. IV APL. 10.
FOURTEENTH LIGHT DRAGOONS
LT WM LYON, VIC DE BICORRE MAR. 19.
R. F.—1 MAR. 15...1 MAR. 19.
EIGHTEENTH HUSSARS
CAPT ROBT DAWSON BOLTON, MENDIONDE JAN 14...R.F. III APL.16.

ROYAL ENGINEERS
LT GEO. POWER,   NIVELLE NOV. 10.
CAPT T.J.H. PITTS,   CAVE D'OLORON FEB. 23.
CAPT EDWD PARKER,   ORTHEZ FEB. 27.

15. Private James Ayres (or Eyres): enlisted by a recruiting party in Trowbridge, received the General Service Medal with clasps for Vitoria and Toulouse and served – as a private – until the disbandment of the Regiment. (From a contemporary painting.)

16. Elizabeth Kennedy (née Cole): 'Tell somebody to write to me as I never hear from a creature but yourself.' (Courtesy of Sir Anthony Weldon Bt.)

ready to begin again tomorrow morning. What a silly fellow Smith is, he will not be friends with me . . .

4 July

[GW] I went this morning to the convent and heard my friendly nuns sing, I was most gratified. . . . I don't care how soon we move now I am now tired of this place, tho' I am so well put up.

5 July

[JH] went to the ball of the Heavy Dragoons in the even'g. I diverted with Cotton's *patróna,* my partner, did not leave the room 'till near four in the morn'g.

[GW] What a despicable person is our Captain Burke. There's not a grain of a gentleman in him; . . . Sergeant Taylor, he has brought to a court martial this morning, merely to annoy me . . . He yesterday took away from me my second batman and offer'd me the choice of two of the most notorious rascals in the Regiment in his place.

Went out this morning at 6 with the foraging party of the Regiment, it was a delightful morning, what a shame it is to lay abed after that hour. . . Sergeant Taylor is acquitted of the charges brought against him, and Major Hughes order'd Captain B. to send me the second batman he took from me.

6 July

My desk has been robb'd of four doubloons . . . I valued my servants for their honesty & don't know whether to blame them or no. However I am much to blame myself on leaving the key of my desk about . . . I hope to God John Ipper has had no concern in it for I really respect him & think he is the most faithful servant in the world.

Sir Stapleton Cotton inspected the Regiment on the 7th; they 'got off better' than Hughes expected and Woodberry said, 'the men turned out remarkably clean and neat'.

Burke had not given up a diamond cross, 'but the officers insist upon having it . . . some say its worth two or three thousand pounds, if so it ought to be divided amongst the Regiment'. Rowlls talked of resigning 'on account of ill health' which would be 'a step' for Woodberry.

115

Lord Worcester's ball 'would beggar all attempts at description. There was all the respectable and all of another description in the town present, the scene was beyond anything. The surprise of many finding themselves in such company who left the room in disdain, caused laughter to many of the bucks who brought the latter company. *Fandangos* was the rage, the women danced them and many behaved in a very immodest manner.' Woodberry left 'rather early, not at all pleased with the evening's diversion'. But he thought 'very laughable' that the Band, having been engaged to play, 'at the appointed time, they never came. A non commissioned officer was sent in search of them & found the whole in a room dancing, completely naked except having their pelisses slung across their shoulders. I understand there were some women present, but have not heard whether they were stripp'd or not.'

Robbery and Murder

A man of the 15th was found 'with his brains knock'd out & his mouth stuffed full of rags'. The victim had been seen with a woman walking outside the town, the evening before he was murdered. Woodberry feared that, when the Brigade moved on, they would 'leave some dreadful mementos of their revenge for their murder'd comrades'.

Another day, he became separated from the foragers and 'heard a cry of distress at a distance. . . I saw a poor fellow on the top of a hill holding up his hands and begging for help; I likewise saw another running away. I rode up and found him nearly dead, having been stabbed in the back part of his head; it bled profusely and I assisted him on his mule & brought him to this town . . . Doctor Quincey dress'd him and I believe the wound will not prove mortal.'

Next day, 'More murders; McNorton, one of the bandsmen, was discover'd in a field about a mile from this place murder'd and a man of the Artillery with him.' Another man of the 15th was found murdered in a wood. McNorton, an 'excellent player on the clarinet', was the first man of the Band to have been lost and Woodberry gloomed: 'I don't expect one will return . . . It was one of the first bands in England . . . I cannot think General Stewart was justified in ordering them out with the Regiment.'[5]

A billet-doux came from 'a lady in the town, who signs her name Isabella Lucinda' inviting Woodberry to a party, no other officers were asked and he declined, 'it may instead of a party be a *tête à tête* – the consequences of which may be on return to my quarters a knife in my side. No, no, my Dulcinea, no intriguing with any of you, I don't want to be murder'd; I have seen what your creatures will do.'

12 July

[GW] to be halted so long in such a murderous place as this is very annoying, a few English books would make one's case better.

. . . the officers of the Regiment assembled to investigate the dispute between Captain Burke and Mr Dolbell; when after deliberately & maturely weighing the whole affair, came to the unanimous resolution that they ought to be requested to resign immediately, but Major Hughes recommended a milder course & proposed that they should be reprimanded in the most strongest manner before the officers of the Regiment, which was according done by both being instantly called in; Major Hughes told them of the sentiments of the officers & that tho' want of courage was not proved against either yet the language made use of by both was such which ought to have oblig'd gentlemen to have had immediate recourse to arms & that death alone ought to have settled it between them & that it ought never to have been referr'd to him; however as Commanding Officer he now strictly forbid them proceeding to any but conciliatory arrangements. They immediately begg'd each other's pardon . . .

Orders given out this evening that no man leaves his quarters without his side arms.

Kennedy told his mother:

I have been on the doctor's list for some days, which I attribute to the change of quarters, bed, etc. to our late severe sort of life, which we had for such a length of time. I am now however convalescent.

. . . Our horses are fast recovering and we shall soon be fit for anything again. I suppose Lord W. will now be Duke of Vitoria, he certainly merits any title. I only wish the fate of Europe was to be decided between him and Bonaparte with any thing like equal numbers.

How unlucky I was not to catch Joseph . . . had we been five minutes sooner through the town we should have taken him. . . we unfortunately went up the wrong street; had we taken the street leading to Pamplona at first I really think his escape would have been impracticable. . . .This is a very good town but the natives have already contrived to murder some of our men.

117

Woodberry bought a black Andalusian horse, taken at Vitoria from 'a French general who received him a present from Joseph.' When next out with the foragers he practised 'Vitoria' in the 'necessary exercises of a charger & found him well broken'.

Repercussions from Vitoria continue

14 July

[GW] this day last year the Prince Regent review'd us on Hounslow Heath, and gave the Regiment great credit for its appearance that day. Good God how the Regiment has fallen off since then.

Gossip had it that 'near half the officers are implicated . . . respecting the plunder & remaining in the town of Vitoria and will be oblig'd to exchange, resign or perhaps before either can be done, they may be cashier'd'. Hughes wrote later:

> The truth is, the Army was jealous of the riches that we had acquired. For my part, I cautiously avoided ever to accept the diamonds, crosses and jewellery which were offered to me, and which, without inconvenience, I might have put in my sabretache. As it is, my poverty and abstinence enables me to be strict.[6]

Woodberry felt 'more than happy when I think of that day and of my not going into the town. . . I dined with Kennedy; he, poor fellow is very unwell, fearful that his name may be brought in question with the above. . . Burke gave up the diamond cross which is supposed to be worth about a thousand pounds.'

'Tir'd of this idle life'

15 July

[GW] Captain Carew's troop presented me yesterday with a most beautiful poodle dog, that they took at Vitoria, for my conduct with them at that glorious battle. It was a gift from the whole troop . . . Captain Kennedy dangerously ill, Smith in high spirits because he is the next for a troop and thinks K. may die.

16 July

Employed myself making a foraging cap having obtain'd a piece of embroider'd cloth.[7] It is a very dashing one & much admired amongst all the officers.

In another visit to the convent the nuns gave Woodberry a cup of chocolate and sweet cakes. He thought they told him that 'about two years back a nun escaped with an officer, but he was oblig'd after a very short time, to give her up to the convent, where she was condemned directly to the punishment of immuring. She surviv'd about a fortnight after.' However he had 'the vanity to think the youngest nun would leave the convent and share the fate of the 18th Hussars in defiance of her vows'. Next day he was 'most cursedly annoy'd; I went as usual to see my nuns, when the old hag of an Abbess told me she orders from the *Alcalde* to deny me admittance and requested I would come nigh no more . . . I wonder what can be the reason of it. It must be those rascally friars.' A week later, however, he 'got admittance again into the convent; I am likewise inform'd I may come as usual. I spoke rather free upon it; the *Alcalde* therefore withdrew his order respecting the admittance of officers.'

Foster had died at Vitoria after his leg was amputated. His servants arrived with his baggage and soon afterwards Hughes settled his and Turing's affairs. Turing's will left his property to his young nephew and Foster's 'gives a horse to Carew & another to — of the Blues; all his mules, baggage &c to his servant'. Woodberry bought one of Foster's double-barrelled pistols and a tongue.

Hughes thought the Regiment 'began to show strong symptoms of recovery' and on 18 July they turned out well for an inspection by Somerset.

Bolton, Dean, Kennedy and Curtis dined with Woodberry when he gave them: 'soup, two roast fowls, two rabbits (boil'd with onions), beef steaks & onions, peas, potatoes & a rice pudding; not a bad set out'. Although 'very tir'd of this idle life', he enjoyed the Tafalla annual fair, 'unlike in some respects to the English fair, yet from the number of females, I began to fancy myself at Greenwich'. Meanwhile, 'Smith and self are getting better friends, though both rather shy of each other.'

Hughes often dined with fellow Welshman Edwin Griffith of the

15th and clearly regarded him as a friend. Yet Griffith wrote to Hodge of the 7th Hussars:

> The 18th I am happy to say no longer form part of our Hussar Brigade, but are removed to Altero; they are a very loose lot, to say the least of them. Had they behaved as they ought at Vitoria we should have all shone in the Gazette upon that occasion but by their stopping by dozens to plunder in the town instead of pushing through to support the 15th we were placed in a most critical situation surrounded by five times our numbers, and that we were not annihilated I attribute solely to the good countenance the Regiment put on upon the occasion. Ld Wellington has threatened to dismount them and send them home the next time he has any fault to find with them. I don't think Grant was quite justifiable in ordering us to charge till he had a support at hand; but however the thing is over & there is no use in talking.[8]

'Enemy under Soult are coming down upon us'

24 July

[GW] News arrived this morning . . . that the enemy under Soult are coming down upon us and intend to relieve San Sebastián.

25 July

[JH] Duperier arrived with a letter from Murray who is still very unwell.

[GW] Mr Duperier, our new Adjutant arrived this morning. He was originally Adjutant to the Tenth Hussars and was before that a private and rose thro' merit. I can only account for the wretched insubordinate state of the Regiment to the want of a good adjutant.

Last night Kennedy and self meet two nice girls walking. We dismounted and walked with them some time and then came to their homes & found we had got acquainted with two of the most respectable ladies in the town. Kennedy, who is more brazen than me, walked into the house with them; of course I follow'd and was entertained some time with wine and cake . . . I shall give up the nun, no more my religious fair shall you see me at your grate.

I had a dinner party today . . . Smith sent Blackett to me this morning and on his arrival to dinner we shook hands and became friends again (each saying how sorry he was any words had escaped him that should have led to this disagreement).

26 July

[JH] A sudden order arrived to march by daybreak tomorrow to Pamplona.

[GW] Huzza, a rout is arriv'd and we march tomorrow morning where I don't yet know. I am not particular whether it is towards England or France, so that we are on the march is all I want for I am heartily tired of this idle life.

CHAPTER 12

BATTLE OF SORAUREN

July 1813

On 25 July, in a drive for beleaguered Pamplona, Soult suddenly launched attacks on two of the passes over the Pyrenees from France.[1] The British withdrew from Maya after ten hours of fierce fighting. At Roncesvalles, Cole held up some 20,000 French for a complete day, but a thick fog came down and Cole, concerned about losing touch with his troops withdrew to Sorauren. Wellington, who did not hear what was happening until late on the 26th, hurriedly issued orders for his forces to concentrate. Infantry reinforcement could not reach Sorauren until the morning of the 28th, but Soult did not launch his main attack until that afternoon.

'Duty completely to my heart's desire'

After a 'long & tedious march' in hot weather, the Hussar Brigade halted near Pamplona. They then 'marched and counter-marched', before Wellington ordered them to Huarte to support Picton's 3rd Division.

Kennedy wrote to his mother:

We arrived within half a league of Pamplona by 5 in the evening and found the garrison and the investing Spaniards firing on each other. We now met the Prince of Orange from whom we heard of Lord Wellington's arrival from San Sebastián, seventeen leagues in one day . . .

. . . towards the close of day came up with our infantry who were retiring gradually before the French, disputing every inch of ground. The heads of our cavalry columns had scarcely presented their mustachios on the heights opposite the enemy when with the additional persuasive arguments of a few long 9-pounders their career was stopped and they formed in a position exactly opposite from us. It was now nearly dark and the most tremendous thunderstorm came on . . . for the space of an hour; all this time the cannonade of the enemy's columns continued together with the fire of our skirmishers and our riflemen, which lasted till near 9 o'clock, when the firing ceased on both sides and all was silent. The French garrison in Pamplona making signals to their friends on the hills with blue lights and the thousands of fires which were lighted in all directions altogether made it one of the most awfully magnificent night scenes you can possibly conceive. The vedettes of both armies were within pistol shot of each other.

27 July

[JH] A hill on our left covering the road & town of Huarte was the bone of contention & some contest was going on our right, the weakest part of our position. It grew very rainy & night came on. At last we were order'd into a village, Govita, on the heights where the R. of our position was . . . The village besides being miserable in itself was to be occupied by General Colville.[2] There was neither fire nor light to be procured . . . as I had only order'd my small canteen up when it was late. I lay down rather gloomy in my cloak. At last Jean Row arrived with my canteens . . . I received orders from General Colville to be in the low ground on his right at daybreak.

Woodberry's troop spent the night, 'all prepared and ready to turn out at a minute's notice . . . I slept near my horse in a shed, wet to the skin, but drank plenty of brandy, which was the only thing I had since the morning.'

28 July

[JH] I was not call'd & did not awake before day began to dawn. I was feverish & uncomfortable & had not time to breakfast or do more than hastily mount my horse. However I made the best dispositions in my power . . . I patrolled & the French drove back our patrols.

About 2 or 3 the 10th relieved the 18th at this post & we went to the village near, where I had just time to wash myself when we were hastily order'd out to support the 10th. We took the first position we occupied in the morn'g . . . We were order'd forward to protect the guns & afterwards to support the 10th, the Right Squadron took a patrol round the heights to our right while with the others I went to support the 10th who suffer'd something in skirmishing. They used pistols & the French carbin'd at them. The 18th took their places & drove back the French. We were cantoned for the night in a village on the rocky height near our picquets. Most difficult to get at & full of peasants who had fled from the plains, but very hospitable & comfortable.

[AK] several of our divisions had not yet come up . . . we were obliged to act on the defensive and had orders to form the line of battle at 3 in the morning; soon after which, long before day broke, their attack recommenced with a very smart skirmishing. We formed on the right of our lines, which was the weakest point, and as the day broke the battle was becoming pretty general, when it slackened a little and was again renewed towards noon with very great exertion on both sides. Four times the French attempted to drive us from a hill and as often were they driven down with dreadful slaughter. Here the Portuguese and Spaniards behaved admirably and cheered each other on; the latter at one time feigned a retreat and the French came on with great confidence when to their no small astonishment a strong body of British infantry who had been concealed purposely near the summit suddenly jumped up gave them a volley and then a charge as I believe they have seldom experienced, and they consequently were not long shewing their backs and the whole division of them tumbled down the precipice and the few that escaped the shot or the bayonet, are said to have broke their necks.

About 3 o'clock . . . their cavalry, about 3,000 in number, began to show themselves and were seen filing down the hill into the valley towards our right flank which I supposed they meant to make an attempt to turn, and to get in our rear. Their cavalry now formed in column under cover of villages in front of us and one squadron of the 10th was sent towards them to skirmish with the enemy whose skirmishers shewed a disposition to advance over a river which ran between us. . . . The 10th attacked them with their pistols whilst the French used their carbines and by coming too close to each other the enemy hit several of our men. They fired at our officers principally and had very nearly killed several of the 10th owing to the advantage their carbines had over the pistols. They continued firing at each other till the 10th had expended their ammunition when a squadron of the 18th was sent for to replace them and your humble servant being next on the butcher's list I set off to the right flank but instead of pistols I ordered my rifles[3] to be used. The French soon discovered the difference and the second or third rifle shot drove them about and they quickly recrossed the river, faster than they came over and kept a most respectful distance the rest of the day. We had the honour of tumbling over one or two of them without being allowed to pursue them over the river . . . both parties sat on their horses looking at each other for an hour . . . The French who are very expert with their long carbines, singled me out at the head of the skirmishers, having been unluckily mounted on the Spanish bay horse I borrowed from King Joseph at Vitoria and one or two shots came by me in a very good direction but none took effect. Lord Worcester of the 10th was knocked off his horse by a shot, Captain Harding had another; another officer had his horse shot, and a private fell into their hands, through the imprudence of using pistols against their carbines. My loss, although longer engaged than they were, consisted in nothing more than wounds from their tongues, after they recrossed the river, one of them in very good English called us all manner of names, saying 'Come over the puddle after us you very fine officers of the Hussars as we wish to have revenge for Vitoria', together with many other witticisms which made them all laugh most immoderately; at the same time whenever we shewed the least disposition to cross the river they soon fell back to join their columns in the rear. Our Paddys were not as you may suppose very backward in blackguarding them and you can't conceive anything

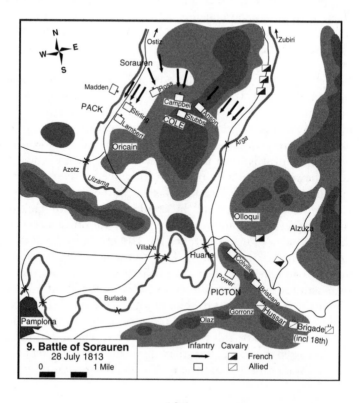

9. Battle of Sorauren
28 July 1813

126

more ridiculous than the war of words from both parties from each side of the river, which was occasionally enlivened by a shot or two.

All this time our infantry were driving theirs about in famous style and, finding their attempt to reach Pamplona to be quite hopeless, the firing ceased on both sides soon after sunset, and after a most desperate contest which lasted so many hours under a burning sun, both armies seemed inclined to rest.

Woodberry was up before daylight, after 'not two hours' sleep'. After Stapleton Cotton placed the Brigade on 'a most strong piece of ground about half a mile distant from the enemy', he was sent to reconnoitre a large wood on which Hughes 'expected the enemy had thrown a column'. He found none and Burke then sent him to drive in the enemy's picquet and vedettes in front of their position and 'take possession' of the villages.

[GW] I crossed a ford with ten picked men; the vedettes & picquet instantly fled. After I had search'd the first village and found it deserted by enemy & inhabitants, I left two vedettes on the point opposite to the enemy's left, then march'd to the second village, Ibeisua, with eighteen men, which was about a quarter a mile distant. On our arrival I found a party of the enemy's infantry, about fifteen running away in high style. We galloped after them, one I must have killed or wounded but they made their escape over a bridge, we gallop'd thro' the village and finding no more, was about leaving two men as vedette there, when I discover'd Captain Burke's signal (an hussar galloping round a circle)[4] the signal fixed on if any element of danger. I therefore trotted with my hussars to the other village from which I saw a strong column of the enemy light dragoons galloping down with the intention of cutting me off, but I had not reconnoitred in vain, I had another road to return. I therefore withdrew the whole of my men that way and left one end of the village as the enemy arrived at the other and walked quietly over the ford, arriving at our position in safety. One of my men was wounded, Sergt. Harrison, but very slightly. This was a duty completely to my heart's desire.

. . . After we had relieved the 10th it was discovered one of our men had sold his carbine. He was instantly tried by drumhead court martial, & punish'd in front of the enemy. At the same time, and which saved him from receiving the whole of his sentence, our attention was taken up by the advance of the enemy in a strong column on the mountains, driving our men before them; on a sudden we saw a division of ours rise up, who before was hid purposely to draw the enemy after the skirmishers. They first gave them a dreadful volley, being within ten yards of them, nearly half fell. The English then rushed on them with the bayonet & the carnage was dreadful. About 7 the enemy withdrew . . . and we retired to a pretty, romantic mountain village, Ratenath, when I took about two hours' rest in a good house & bed but with my clothes on. I was oblig'd to have the door broken open, but when I did get in the old lady made much of me, excusing herself for barring her door, by saying she thought I was a Portuguese.

Soult had failed in his attempt to reach Pamplona. On the 29th he marched west in an unsuccessful attempt to drive a wedge between the main British force and those besieging San Sebastian.

On the British right flank overnight reports of French movement alarmed Picton's staff.

29 July

[JH] At daybreak we resumed our old position, everything very quiet. The French on the old ground, but seem diminish'd in number. We were order'd into the same village we occupied on our arrival to cook; scarcely any firing all day except from picquets or riflemen . . . I went to sleep on straw in a very dirty room, but had hardly slumber'd when I was awakened by Major Arbuthnot Dep. Adjt. Genl. who told me that Sir Thos. Picton had received information that the French had two battalions on the outside of the walls of Pamplona & as he had observed some movements on the left of their centre he apprehended that they were about to execute a combined attack upon our right flank & beg'd to know what were my orders. I told him that my orders were to resume our old position at daybreak and at the same time said that no movement from Pamplona could well take place unknown to the cavalry under Sir Stapleton Cotton who were in our rear & that if they attempted to move round our right they must make a great detour as I had patrolled that country, that our horses were saddled, our men with them & that I could turn out very quickly upon the least alarm, that at all events I would turn out the Regiment before daybreak. . . . Once more I attempted to take a little rest, when I was again disturbed by the arrival of Major Stovin, a Brigade Major. Being more intimate with me he spoke more familiarly, restated what Major Arbuthnot had mentioned, express'd his assurance of being attack'd before daylight & beg'd me to mount immediately & be on my guard. I told him I was sufficiently on my guard & repeated to him what I had said to the other, but said I would send a patrol to the battery directed on the side of the position on Pamplona. When he left me, however, I sent for the Adjutant & order'd the men out in half an hour it being then one o'clock.

[GW] Last evening while with the Regiment on our position, we saw in front of us, near the rivulet, some of the 95th – about a dozen – skirmishing with the enemy; they were at it till near dusk, when they left off. Three of the Frenchmen advanced and met several of the 95th, each without arms – and entered into conversation, shook hands &c and after a short time withdrew to their post, where they are today, looking at each other but no fighting.

Soult driven back to France

On the 30th Wellington counter-attacked, driving the French back everywhere with heavy losses. Foy took the disorganized remnant back to France. When Hill repulsed Soult's westward drive he too withdrew to France.

30 July

[JH] At 2 we turn'd out, Sir Thos. Picton pass'd me, I spoke to General Colville's aide-de-camp who I inform'd of what I had heard from the Hussar Brigade Major, viz that the enemy had but one battalion out of the town, that the 15th had a picquet at the battery & that Pamplona was very quiet. Sir Thos. Picton wish'd to hear this from me & I repeated it to him. He desired some additional arrangements to those I had order'd which however were not necessary. We went to our position & when day dawn'd found the French had retired from the left of their position. Our squadron said that their fires had disappeared at eleven in the night. They were at that moment apparently retiring from their right, but it was represented that their object was to get round our left, from all I knew & thought, I did not believe it, nevertheless we had hardly got into quarters . . . when I was informed by the Adjutant their cavalry began to appear on the left of Pamplona & that an order was on its road to me to move the Regiment. Tho' I could not believe this account I order'd the Regiment to saddle & went to reconnoitre, I saw the French retiring & press'd in a manner that left me no doubt. Being convinced of the falsehood of that account I unsaddled the Regiment & order'd the more quiet but necessary occupations.

When Woodberry was woken and ordered to bridle up and every man to stand 'to his horse's head', it was a beautiful night with the stars shining 'very bright'. French campfires were burning 'very dim' and Woodberry told Kennedy he thought they were off:

Half past 12 o'clk – Thank God the enemy are off; they are retreating in the greatest confusion towards France. The artillery are now playing on them in all directions.

6 o'clk evening. We have just receiv'd accounts of the enemy; our Army have gain'd a complete victory, after fighting four days, the victory is now certain, and glorious. Huzza! Eight thousand prisoners are taken!!

I am in my old quarter, the old lady, who before barred her door, sent to me the moment I enter'd the village & invited me to her house.

31 July

[JH] march to Ibeisua, a village occupied by the French the preceding day, I order'd the Regiment to forage after which I took up my quarters. I rode after dinner towards the contested height, met many peasants laden with arms & plunder, night commencing I returned to Ibeisua calling in my road on Griffith.

Aftermath of battle

1 August

[JH] I rode to the position which was cover'd with kill'd, wounded & the melancholy traces of war. From the contested height I soon discover'd its importance, it commands the road, the river & the bridge, nevertheless it was much too strong to attack when defended by British troops.

[AK] I have just returned from the field of battle . . . The sight was incredibly horrid. The ground literally strewed with dead and dying French, who have been lying there for three days without any food or any sort of medical aid. The poor wretches abandoned by their General and his surgeons crawled down the hills and collected as well as they could together in groups, some without arms or legs, others dying every moment and hundreds among them lying dead all under a scorching sun which had the most extraordinary effect of completely roasting the body the moment it expired. All the dead were completely black and swollen with the heat most enormously although not more than five minutes dead. . . . Our loss has been great, the 4th Division suffered severely . . . The weather is turning hot in this valley at present, you can't sit out in the middle of the day, so you may conceive the wretched state of the helpless wounded French. The numbers of our men wounded has been so great that we were not able to collect those of the enemy till yesterday evening. To-day the spring wagons are at work collecting as many as they can but hundreds have died for want of care. . . .

You might send this to the Governor when you [have] read it.[5]

. . . Should the war in this part of the world soon be over I wish you would ask Lady Londonderry or at least sound her if it would be possible for me to get on Stewart's staff in some capacity or other in Germany; I should like much to see that part of the Continent . . .

(3rd August) Lord W. says it is one of the greatest victories he has ever gained and is highly pleased with the business. . . . I have been for some time a *Chef d' Escadron* which in the French services ranks very high and should any untoward accident befall our present Major and one Captain who is above me the command of the Regiment would devolve on your most obedient Very Humble Servant.

A 'dreadful dull life'

Woodberry's legs had been 'much swollen . . . owing to sleeping in my boots and never changing my linen for several days'. He too visited the battlefield and on the side of one hill, saw 'no less than three hundred slain, and many more poor wounded fellows, who begg'd in the name of the Almighty for water and victuals. They were being moved into nearby villages, one of which, Urdeniz, was crowded with wounded British officers. . . . many brave fellows is there, who will never see the land of Liberty again.'

After 4 August, when the Brigade marched to villages near Pamplona, it was once more: 'a dreadful dull life, we have nothing but the sound of the cannon before Pamplona to amuse us'. The heat made it impossible to ride out, except in the evening.

Peasants who had fled to the mountains were returning home; Woodberry's landlord found 'every article in the house rompe'd, the beds and furniture cut & broken to pieces and every thing of value carried off'. The French had also 'carried off their priest, an old man, after stripping the church of everything of value & destroying what

131

they could not take'. Woodberry was struck by:

> the violent animosity which prevails between the French & Spaniards; indeed the conduct of the enemy is really painful to think upon. Every house broken open, every piece of furniture destroy'd, every cask of wine which they could find taken away or stav'd in, all the fowl, pigs & cattle killed & taken away and afterwards they set fire to four villages, three of which are completely destroy'd.

However,

> the mirth and pleasantry of the Spaniards very much resemble an English, more than what we usually conceive of a Spanish scene. Jesting, loud laughing, pettishness in those who have drank to freely and pleasant reproof from their companions, made me many times fancy myself at an English harvest home. The French and English of course, the standing topic of their discourse. Everyone freely abuse the former and seem to think the latter had no other faults than they were not Spaniards and were heretics.'

One evening he was attracted to a neighbouring house by the sound of music. 'I have been dancing *fandangos* with all the women there that look'd pretty and am now as happy as a prince.'

> Mr Dolbell got another dreadful fall smack into a dirty pond. Never did Sancho Panza on his embassage to Dulcinea make such a out-of-the-way figure as he did. This time last year, I was figuring away at Brighton, much intoxicated with foppery. I think if I should ever live to return, I shall be not be the puppy I was at Brighton: but quite debonair. To be perfect in horsemanship is a necessary part of a gentleman's accomplishments; that a military officer should be an accomplish'd horseman is a position scarcely necessary to be stated. A man who every moment fears to be divorc'd from his saddle cannot properly possess that undisturb'd recollection, that cool and undeviating attention, which ought to be given to the troops under his immediate command.
>
> Burke, from what reason I know not, has alter'd his behaviour towards me very much of late; he is very obliging & polite & appears to court my company, but he is a deceitful knave and one I must ever despise.

Hughes, who was passing much of the time reading, finished the *Medicin Malgré Lui* and was pleased with the turnout and performance of the 'whole of the troops' in marching order. Woodberry was afraid he would have to record the younger Curtis's death before the campaign was over:

> I never beheld a young man who looks so dreadful; he is wasted away to skin & bone, fretting, I am confident it is nothing else. On the other hand, his brother who had been left ill at Santarém, is now at Salamanca . . . he has written for leave, saying he is unable to proceed further owing to a rheumatic complaint in his back & arms; it is all my eye & Betty Martin. . . . I am sorry the army is disgraced by such beings who study nothing but dress, frippery & debauchery.

Another Sunday came, with 'no service performed before the Regiment'; he thought it would 'surely be better for an officer to read the church service by which many of the men would know that it was Sunday and might devote a part of the day to devotion'.

Return to Olite

Orders came for a return to Olite and Kennedy wrote to his mother:

> it is really astonishing, the more one looks at the position to conceive the daring intrepidity the French must have possessed in four times attacking a hill from which they were as often repulsed. The smell of the half buried wretches is now most offensive. Various legs and arms are visible above the ground, which is even yet literally strewed with arms and all sorts of accoutrements which both armies lost in the attack.
> . . . Our cousin Lowry did not shine in defending the Roncesvalles pass. It is said he was surprised. His talents are not thought very much of with the army *entre nous*.
> . . . I find since I began there is a chance of poor Foster's servant going to England so I send this by him to save you postage. He goes home with about £500 in his pocket, his master having made a short will before he died leaving him all his baggage, horse etc. Should I die I have ordered mine to be sent to you which I beg your acceptance of although probably not worth much. Tell somebody to write to me, as I never hear from a creature but yourself. You can't think how great a luxury a letter is here.

10 August

[JH] Watering order; symptoms of the Vety. Surgeon's return to his senses.

[GW] Every one seems anxious for Peace. I begin to wish all the fatigues of war over; I wish some of my London friends would inform me how Ministry goes on and what the good citizens of London think of the present state of affairs?

11 August

[JH] March'd at six o'clock . . . The Regiment turned out better than any in the Brigade, quarter'd at Noain in a house without doors or windows, nevertheless a good stable & for the season & place not a bad quarter. . . .

[GW] This village is entirely deserted and contains not one tenantable house in it; the famous aqueduct contains no water now, it being cut off in the mountains where the spring is. I dined with Conolly in a most wretched house without windows, doors &c. but had a good dinner. We both had our beds put up and slept in the same place. Some ungrateful rascal in the Troop during mine & my servants' absence took the whole of my brandy out of my keg. . . . I suspect it was Flanagan who I thought the best man in the Troop. . .

12 August

[JH] We were too late at the place of assembly of the Brigade. . . principally owing to the neglect & inattention of Captain Kennedy; the baggage & led horses march'd execrably.

[GW] a very fatiguing march, about six leagues, the burning sun nearly overpower'd me. On arrival here I got a fresh quarter, a much better one than I had before, and not only that, but the young ladies I had got acquainted with before I left this town, live in the house.

CHAPTER 13

SEEKING VINDICATION

Olite August to September 1813

Troops given out of the Regiment

Normal practice would have been for vacancies, caused by death and postings, to be filled from amongst the junior officers. The 18th were appalled to hear that Wellington had ordained otherwise.

> [GW] I am quite astonish'd; the troops that were vacant and which every one expected Russell and Conolly would succeed to are given out of the Regiment. Conolly sends in his resignation this afternoon. I think I shall resign if my leave of absence don't arrive in November. Smith thinks of resigning his commission too. I am very sorry for poor Russell. He must feel the disappointment very severely indeed, having given up the appointment of Quartermaster &c under the idea of his being gazetted to one of the troops.[1] Hesse is very much disappointed; he wrote to the Duke of York for one of the vacant troops.

Hughes spent much of the next ten days worrying about 'the troops given out of the Regiment'. Russell was 'in great distress of mind; his whole dependence was upon it, in fact the existence of himself, wife and six children'.

Meanwhile Woodberry:

> was getting quite desperate in love with Señora Zacarias. But it is not the kind of love that attacks a mortal in England; here it only lasts while in sight of the object, while the English version pierces the heart so deeply that only death erases it; and I actively think nothing of telling a dozen females here the same tale.

On 15 August, the Assumption of the Virgin Mary, 'a grand procession paraded round the town and then to the large church'. In the afternoon Woodberry and the others went to Tafalla to see a nun invested, 'the ceremony was very grand', but, 'poor miserable creature, I dare say compell'd to that life by a cruel father or mother to enrich some more favourite child'.

That evening he gave a ball 'to the fair ladies of Olite', but, as at Worcester's, 'there was a few of the immodest among the numbers'. Hughes brought 'one of the most notorious of the country round', a dancer from the theatre in Pamplona. However, 'she was a beautiful dancer.' Woodberry thought it 'beyond doubt the best English ball given in Olite' and would have been proud of being a favourite in Olite were it not for 'their cursed cutthroat husbands'.

Next day he discovered his desk had been broken into and sixty-eight pounds taken from it (in doubloons). More worrying, he found Van Voorst had neglected his affairs in England and he was anxious to return home. Nevertheless he had another dance that evening with 'the Miss Murphys and my *patróna* aided by the assistance of a flute; we kept dancing till near 11 o'clk.'[2]

17 August

[JH] All these days occupied with Regimental business & the distressing business of the promotions going out of the Regiment.

[GW] a court of inquiry respecting the robbery . . . firmly of opinion McDougal my batman broke open the desk and took the money. . . I had another visit from my female acquaintances, six of them; the doctor play'd the flute and we danced. Doctor was drunk and created such mirth the ladies got him on the ground and nearly tickled him to death and I was oblig'd to drive them away from him.

19 August

[GW] I rode this evening towards the Ebro, which I saw from the top of a hill. The view was heavenly; a most delightful valley and immense chain of mountains with the river running beneath. I had my dog 'Vitoria' sheared today likewise one of my mules. 'Vit' looks all the better for it. This day four years my brother William died at Surinam.

On 20 August Hughes received a letter from Lord Fitzroy Somerset[3] saying that Wellington was 'discontented with the disorderly conduct

136

of the Regiment at Vitoria & stating that he had in consequence procured the promotions out of the Regiment'.[4] This news convinced Woodberry that he would send in his resignation, but that day, 'being Orderly Officer' he walked round the town, 'visiting the señora and had some prime fun at Kennedy's *casa*'. There was 'more fun' in the evening at his quarter, when 'the gentlemen were all so, so and the *señoras* did nothing but cry out "Mucha drunkie"'.

Hughes wrote a 'very strong' reply to Somerset which he showed to Palmer of the 10th, 'who approved of it, the officers also approved of it'. However, the Brigade Commander, Lord Edward Somerset 'detained it thinking it too strong'. Hughes also found that the letter which Dolbell had written 'in justification of himself respecting the affair of the ring of Madam Guizls', had not been forwarded by Grant.

'to explain and vindicate the character of the Regiment'

On 23 August, 'after a restless night much depress'd', Hughes made arrangements to go the following day to headquarters at Lasaca. He assembled the officers for 'a general explanation' before setting off to seek an interview with Wellington. He wanted, as Woodberry put it, 'to explain and vindicate the character of the Regiment to him'.

Hughes had first to persuade Cotton that he had a reasonable case and it was the 27th before Cotton returned from a trip to Bilbao, but then 'he agreed to do what he could'. Elley, his adjutant general, drafted for Hughes a letter to Wellington.

It was still several days before he finally made contact. The immediate concern was the siege of San Sebastián and, although it was stormed on the 31st, Hughes's attempts to contact Wellington over the next few days were fruitless. Until the 5th he was busy writing dispatches, but, at last Fitzroy Somerset 'presented my papers' and Hughes was bidden to dine, before which he had 'a conversation during which I contrived to communicate the substance of what I had to say. He seem'd in common with everybody else to admit the gallantry of the Regiment, but justified the steps he had taken on the score of its indiscipline. We both got warm. However I believe my journey & explanation did some good. Colonel Taylor, Ponsonby &c spoke to me about it.'

Travelling home via San Sebastián he found it a 'heap of ruins with the exception of the church & a few houses which I entered, part still on fire'. The French still occupied the castle and Hughes 'had some escapes' as well as visiting 'a fine library' from which he brought away one book. It was the 9th before he arrived back at Olite, 'to dine at Blackett's, a great assembly of the officers who seem'd well pleased with my embassy'.

Meanwhile, at Olite —

Woodberry had told Hughes 'of the accounts I had received from England and that I intended, on his return from Headquarters, that I should apply for leave of absence to return to England'. But he still wanted to distinguish himself, 'The French are said to be coming again. I trust the 18th will recover all their former glory and add new lustre to it. I am determined if I get near them again I will fight like a hero . . . Anything I will do to regain our former character.'

He was sure Burke had 'made himself despised by all his brother officers owing to his crafty methods he has adopted to get clear of all blame respecting the Vitoria plunder business; all agree his character is "noxious"'.

26 August

[GW] It is very strange that I should have written above some remarks respecting Burke, whose conduct last night fully proved to me that any name but that of gentleman belongs to him . . . I am very anxious to get to England to arrange my affairs and I am afraid the Marshal will not grant me leave.

29 August

All the discourse of the town was respecting the diversion of bull fighting to take place this afternoon. Every entrance to the square was block'd with carts &c early in the forenoon . . . About a dozen oxen was at last brought into the square & put into a stable . . . and they were then brought one after another to be baited by a set of brutes collected on purpose. . . . I have not laughed so much before, since we left Lisbon. Some of our men who were anxious to see & more anxious to shew the Spaniards they were not afraid of a wound was hurt, one seriously . . . after dinner the ladies began to collect and my ball commenced about 8 o'clk; we kept it up till 12. I opened it with Abereta. I afterwards danced a fandango with Fermina and attempted to waltz with several others, so did Hesse, but they don't waltz like the English.

30 August

I dined with Kennedy and a large party; afterwards went to Captain Burke's quarters and was drinking brandy & water, & smoking segars nearly the whole night. I must leave off two things, which have grown on me lately: drinking & swearing.

He went to Tafalla with his 'memorial for leave of absence' and played billiards there with Pulsford and Quincey. 'A very considerable part of the officers of the Regiment was at my quarters this evening, smoking segars & drinking mulled wine.' Teaching his friendly *señoras* English created 'lots of laughter . . . I can never think of my doings in Spain but it must cause instant laughter, if it was fifty years to come.'

More bad news

Turner of Woodberry's troop shot himself one evening 'in a drunken fit':

> [GW] the ball went through his belly & out of his back and is considered a mortal wound. . . . The surgeon open'd the vein of his right arm and left it open to bleed all night. He appears in great pain, but is so insensibly drunk, has no recollection at all of his dreadful situation.

Woodberry had one of the friars to pray for him who arrived 'with attendants with wax torches &c and after reading some Latin prayers to him, he rubb'd oil on his temples, cheeks & feet'. The following morning he was still alive and was moved to the hospital. It appeared that, after two men had been punished, Turner had said 'he would see no more cruelty in the 18th and immediately got drunk purposely to commit suicide – how horrid'. He died next day.

Croker brought 'some very unpleasant intelligence from England':

[GW] nothing less than that the report of our disgrace having reached England and that rascal Captain Dundas, who Croker saw at Vitoria, told him the 18th Regiment run away at Vitoria and that the 66th Foot fired at us; what a villainous liar. A meeting of the officers will take place immediately and Master Dundas will suffer for his falsehoods.

News also came that Rowlls, sent to Bilbao 'for sea bathing', had sailed for England without leave. As Woodberry said 'disgraceful – everything goes against the Regiment. I hope to God he may be advertised in the *Hue and Cry*'.[5] He was now 'not at all anxious about going home, now I find the Regiment has so bad a character in England. The men are good; the fault lies in the officers. Had they been well led, they would have done their duty.'

7 September

Every subaltern officer of the Regiment, that is out here, seems anxious to leave the service; all disappointed – I may say disgusted – having entered the service in a Regiment that all Ireland & England looked to for something great, by which means we become the envy of the Army, but all would have been well, had we had another colonel in the place of that great ass, Colonel Murray who knew no more how to command a regiment than I do. We are beholden to him for every misfortune or disgrace attached to the Regiment. My dear friends in England you will think all are equally blameable, but my conscience tells me I have done my duty. . . .

Progressive Improvement

However, Hughes was pleased with the state of the Regiment on his return. Satisfactory inspections by Somerset preceded their being sent to join their new brigade.

9 September

[GW] Major Hughes return'd this evening from Headquarters. He saw Lord Wellington and explain'd every thing respecting the Regiment to him; the Marshal told him he thought the men of the 18th at Vitoria behaved more like rebels and a *banditti*, than a regiment of hussars. Major H. asked him if he had any thing to say against their bravery –

'O no, certainly not, I think them very brave but too impetuous'. Thank God we are not stigmatised with cowardice, if we are with plundering. Colonel Grant of the 15th has behaved towards the 18th like a villain; to him we are indebted for all, he never forwarded Conolly's or Dolbell's statements they drew up in vindication of their characters.

10 September

[JH] The Regiment was inspected in watering order by Ld. Edwd. Somerset; pass'd muster well & I found that the Regiment upon the whole had progressively improved under the system establishing.

[GW] No answer to my memorial; betting in the Regiment three to one that I do not get leave, indeed I have given up all thought of it and must therefore trust to those friends in England I have, to do their my best for my interests. Smith and Blackett sent in their resignations this afternoon, . . . I really think I shall be tempted to send in mine if the Marshal refuses me leave.[6]

11 September

[JH] dined with Ld. Edwd Somerset, lost my money at whist to Berkeley of the 10th, rode home, a very cold night, caught cold & cough'd all night.

12 September

[JH] By no means well; . . . Divine Service, addressed the Regiment relative to Ld. Wellington, rather nervous, but acquitted myself very tolerably.

13 September

Felt much better this morning & with a few exceptions the Regiment appear'd to advantage, manoeuvred well & obtain'd very full praises from Ld. Edwd. He gave me a route for the march of the Regiment.

Woodberry too thought that, on the whole, 'the Regiment conducted itself very well'. He was sent in advance to find quarters on their march, which came none too soon for Schaumann. He thought the inhabitants of Olite, 'gloomy and ill-natured. . . They were so jealous that no hussar was safe whom they saw joking with a girl. . . . When our adjutant, Duperier, and the officers of the Brigade were returning home at night . . . they frequently had to fight their way through this mob with their swords and compel their respect.'

Hughes:

14 September

had the *Alcalde* before me in consequence of the people of the town, with some of Mina's men having shot one of the Commissary's men, & violently attack'd Mr Duperier &c. Threatened to fine the town & confine the *Alcalde* if he did not discover the men. The men were found & imprison'd. The *Alcalde* issued a proclamation which was singular, he directed that everybody should go to their houses after 8 o'clock (by my desire as 'Commandante') or give a good account of themselves to the Patrol, that they should carry candles, that the young should not play tricks with the women, as they were accustomed to do on such festivals &c.

After taking leave of his favourite *señoras*, Woodberry left Olite with much regret and marched with his men to Mendivil – and 'a most pleasant village in the mountains called Unzué'. He found 'all the young *señoras* are remov'd to the south, out of the way of danger' but in any case did not feel inclined:

to look for more beauties after leaving Olite. Angaletia wanted much to leave home and parents to partake of the fortune of 'Gorgio', but no, it would not do. Thank God, I can say, my conscience is clear. I am not inclined to make myself unhappy for the momentary pleasure of seduction, no, no. . . . My men romp'd for me several fowls – and my pero – 'Vitoria' killed one pretty chick; I was much surprised in finding large stores of wheat, barley and straw in the village.

CHAPTER 14

FOOTHILLS OF THE PYRENEES

September to November 1813

A Fresh Start

15 September (Fornes)

[JH] Jean Row deserted. . . . After dinner mounted a high & rocky hill to visit a hermit's cell, the reverend father had however quitted his mortal habitation & had become a saint. . . . I wrote JAMES HUGHES on the door; my road back was dangerous & tedious & it was past nine before I return'd after several falls.

[GW] Was there ever so unlucky a dog as poor me! Lord Wellington refuses me leave to go to England. Well I must either send in my resignation, or run the chance of losing part of my property, besides the disgrace of having many accounts unsettled, which that rascally fellow Mr V. will not attend to. I never slept so bad in my life as I did last night. . . . expected before morning to be half eat with the bugs & other annoying vermin.

16 September (Errotz, Irurtzun)

[JH] a very hot day, Mr Woodberry had taken Noain &c for our cantonments, but as it did not divide the march I moved on to the villages occupied by Ld. Wellington, Genl. Beresford &c immediately after the Battle of Vitoria.

17 September

Kennedy's troop acted in a mutinous way. Walk'd after dinner to a most magnificent & romantic pass.

[GW] the prettiest village I have seen in this country. I got a billet in the pastor's *casa*, who was most kind and attentive to my wants. . . . Major Hughes, Dean & myself bathed together today in the river it had a surprising effect on us and I feel quite another being.

18 September

[JH] order'd a court martial on the mutineers & Corporal Edwards; Burke President. Bath'd. Did not approve of the court martial on Edwards. Walk'd to a high hill, nearly kill'd some Spaniards by rolling down a stone, gather'd what resembled mushrooms.

[GW] My host is very kind; I shall never forget him, he appears as much pleased with me, as I am with him. I have to ask for nothing, for all my wants he anticipates. This is the second kind priest I have been quartered on.

19 September

[JH] The court martial was [stood down] & another appointed, order'd Sergeant Major Duncan under arrest; punish'd the mutineers, Edwards &c.

[GW] A rout is arrived and we march to villages in the Pyrenees tomorrow morning and join the 1ˢᵗ Regiment of German Hussars.

Six Weeks in Ostiz

20 September (Ostiz)

[GW] The road was alternately ascending and descending the whole way, and became steep & rocky, but as we ascended we were amply repaid by the grandeur of the prospects . . . Conolly intends going to England immediately . . . and as this book is nearly full of 'nonsense' I shall send it to England with him for the perusal of Donna Maria & Flora Amelia.

21 September

[GW] I hired Mr Curtis's late servant – Porter – this day. I agreed to give him 100 pounds per annum; he finds himself in clothes, victuals &c, but when in England I am to find him a bed . . .

22 September

I went over to headquarters this morning and am just returned and dined, having been a member of a court of inquiry upon Sergeant Major Duncan of Captain Kennedy's Troop.

23 September

The 18th Hussars is now brigaded with the 1st German Hussars: General Alten's Brigade – he sent a very handsome letter to the Regiment yesterday, saying he felt himself highly flatter'd & honour'd by the Commander of the Forces, in having so gallant a regiment as the 18th added to his Brigade and strongly recommended to the officers not to relax in the discipline of the Regiment, but to bring to punishment every man who committed the most trivial crime; that the fate of the whole Army is often entrusted to an hussar regiment and strongly reprobated drunkenness in an hussar. He concluded:

'The duties of hussars in the field are so various & require so much practice & experience that too many opportunities cannot be taken, even in cantonments to instruct the men in them, and the Major General will find great pleasure in giving that assistance which his experience may enable him to do.'

I am order'd upon a patrolling party to Santesteban; and am to go into France. Huzza, I am much pleased because I shall see something of the borders & the peasantry of France. I am quite delighted with my duty for I am to remain & make observations seven days and I likewise feel pleased because it is a post of trust and I am appointed to it out of my turn . . . I bought a small pig this evening and a couple of fowls to take with me. I am to have twenty men. I should much like to pick up a few straggling prisoners; it would do famously to begin my new book with the account of the capture.

24 September

Smith left me this morning on his way to his troop; he dined with me yesterday, I gave him for dinner – soup – pigeon pie – a roast fowl & a rice pudding – and Dutch cheese; a famous dinner I think for hungry subs. I always like to provide well for to entertain Smith, for I actively think he half starves himself, now he messes alone.

. . . The following 'Military Notice' was discovered stuck against 'Shiny' Burke's door this morning. 'Captain Burke, having been deprived by the fortunes of war of the society of his dear FRIENDS in the Regent's Hussars intends graciously to condescend to associate with the 18th 'fellows'. Burke was certainly heard to say words nearly to the above effect, I believe only in joke, but the fun is that he threatens vengeance against the writer who he and every else well knows; but he pretends he do not, and if any one was to tell him, he would not believe them!

I start for Santesteban tomorrow morning at daybreak; intend taking two horses and John Porter with me. This book Ipper takes to Vitoria, this night.

A list of his 'household' (see Annex B) was the final entry in the first volume of Woodberry's 'Idle Companion'. (Subsequent quotations from the 'Companion' have been translated back into English from Georges Helié's translation.)

25 September

[JH] Court martial on T. Sergt. Majr. Duncan.[1] Communicated to Smith that he was free to go to England.

27 September

General Alten inspected the Regiment in watering order, went round the quarters, the Regiment look'd worse than usual. A great deal of conversation with him, . . . General Alten very kind.

Alten clearly thought that the horses were not as they should be and Hughes was invited to visit the 1st Hussars KGL. Their horses were 'in excellent condition', but by then he thought those of the 18th were improving.

Wellington now advanced across the Bidassoa and into France. Soult's defences stretched along the whole line of the river, leaving him vulnerable to the concentrated Allied attack launched on 7 October.

News reached the 18th of the successful crossing on 7 October and Luard arrived from the 4th Dragoons, to take over one of the troops 'given out of the Regiment'. The 7th Hussars were on the march to join Somerset's Brigade and Vivian, their commanding officer, asked Hughes to meet him. He ordered 'a Dress Foraging Party' to meet the 7th.

146

11 October

[JH] Sent off the party ordered last night; Blackett, Duperier & I rode to Irurtzun & overtook the 7th just on their arrival, the scheme of the Foraging Party succeeded admirably. . . Had a long conversation & explanation with Vivian about the 18th Hussars, he thought us very ill-treated.

Kennedy wrote to his mother:

The infantry in front have been fighting a good deal last week. . . Our horses are in fine condition and I believe the cavalry never were in better order in general, so that I think if we have a meeting with the foe on the plains of Gascony he will be very lucky not to have the worst of it.

. . . Love to Miss Betsy, Mandurt etc. tell the latter I saw Wm. Vernon pass by here with the 7th the day before yesterday, they are gone to our old quarters at Olite.

. . . I almost forgot to tell you that I am become parson and offici- ated last Sunday for the first time as chaplain to the troops with great *éclat*.

Hughes set off with Blackett for a visit to San Sebastián, but had gone only two or three miles before being overtaken by the Sergeant Major, at a gallop, with a letter saying that Cotton was on his way to inspect the Regiment. On Hughes's return he had a sheep killed 'in expectation of the General & staff kill'd a sheep & arranged every-thing for his reception'.

16 October

[JH] Sir Stapleton arrived at eleven, Regiment turn'd out strong & well, manoeuvred a little & received applause with a promise that a favourable report would be made to Ld. Wellington & a hope that it would do away all disagreement. Invited the whole party to some cold meat &c prepared for them; having eaten & drank plentifully they all departed for a place near Pamplona. Part of the remount arrived, troop'd them & rode to Buinza.

Leave to San Sebastián

The excursion resumed and over the next week Hughes had his usual mix of adventure and mishap. They reached their first halt, Tolosa, after negotiating 'a pass of the mountains & a considerable distance over one of the worst & most dangerous roads I ever saw'. Having obtained a billet they went 'to the *posada*', but as they could get 'little food & no civility' returned for some bread and wine at their billet, where they were 'flea bitten for the rest of the night'. At Hernani, Hughes renewed acquaintance with a 'little friend' he had met when in search of Wellington. She was 'delighted to see me; I promised to visit her on my return.'

At San Sebastián 'the trenches were now fill'd & the batteries & approaches levell'd. . . . The same few houses still existed but some . . . were now occupied & they sold wine &c.' They crossed by ferry to Pasajes and found Clements and Conolly who were to sail home that night – and therefore vacate their lodging, but taking it over proved difficult. 'We exhausted entreaties, insinuations & threats, these people were immovable; at length I sent Nahan to the *Alcalde* for a billet on them which he procured but even this they resisted & at length they themselves procured us one on the other *posada* where we were more fortunate & got a supper & tolerable beds.'

Next day they walked on 'the heights', getting 'a fine view of the country & the sea' and 'a most magnificent view of France & that part of the country lately the subject of contest', but, after a visit to Irun and Hendaye, Hughes had caught 'a violent cold'. He was still unwell the following morning when, in 'dreadful' weather, they needed a boat to cross the river. After a long delay and 'much squabbling' they succeeded in:

> pressing a boat, the rowers of which (women) abandon'd it . . . I got my horse in who fell to the bottom & threw me as well as the dragoon. . . . My two Irishmen knew nothing of the management of a boat & began to abuse one another; I made one of them come to the horse's head & myself began to scull in the meantime; we were taken in tow & safely landed.

He continued on his own over 'the most horrible road', lost his way in search of a short cut, but eventually ferried over the San Sebastián river and arrived at Hernani. Here he 'found my little friend very glad to see me'. He left on the 24th, after he had 'kissed and tickled Madalena', and went on at a fast pace. By now 'my horse knock'd up & obliged to come on slow. Met a pretty & kind girl in the woods, arrived in good time, my horse tired.'

Welcome news and preparation for advance

A letter from General Alten greeted Hughes on his return:

October 23rd, 1813.
My dear Major,
I should and would have a long time come to see you and the Eighteenth Hussars, but the bad weather has prevented me from it, my health not being quite as it should be.

I cannot omit to acknowledge that I find the horses of the Eighteenth so much improved as ever it can be; at least, all what I can see here on guards, and also that detachment which went with Lieut. Hesse towards Pamplona. It is certainly to your highest credit, and the officers and Hussars also, that the horses improved so very much; likewise to the credit of the Commissary, and it shows what can be done when everyone does his duty and works, as it must be . . . your men behaved on guard in a most excellent manner in every circumstance. You may depend upon it that it gives me a great pleasure, and I beg that you will be so good as to make known to everyone how much pleased I am about it. As soon as I can I shall do myself the honour to call upon you.
My dear Major, yours faithfully,
(signed) Victor Alten M.G.

Orders went out from Wellington's headquarters 'to be acted upon after the surrender of Pamplona, and when the troops of the right of the army have reached their destination'. Of the light cavalry:

Colonel Grant's brigade of cavalry[2] is to move up into the valley of Batzan, immediately as each regiment becomes apprised of the surrender of Pamplona . . . Major General Victor Alten's cavalry brigade (immediately on the surrender of Pamplona) will move forward to the valley of the Bidassoa; one regiment occupying Sante-Esterban and Sumbilla, the other regiment Yanci and Lesaca. Major General Alten will keep up a communication with letter parties with the cavalry, which will succeed his brigade in the cantonments which it now occupies . . . Lord Edward Somerset will move the Hussar

149

Brigade from its present quarters, and will canton it in those now occupied by Major General Alten's brigade . . . The main object of the proposed movement is to place the centre of the army, in the first instance, upon the heights which lie between the villages of Sare and Ascain: and those which form the left bank of the Nivelle river in the neighbourhood of the village of St Pée.

Detailed instructions followed for the attack across the Nivelle:

When the heights beyond Sare have been gained, the corps employed against them . . . will establish themselves firmly on these heights, pushing forward at first detachments only in pursuit of the enemy; and in that situation of things these troops will receive fresh instructions as to their further movements.

Major General V. Alten's cavalry brigade will act with this part of the army.

Hughes was warned on 26 October 'to be ready to march immediately' and, when he walked with the *padre* to call on his friends, news had been brought by a peasant that 'Pamplona was to capitulate instantly.' Next day, there was official notice that the Regiment was instantly to march to Santesteban and Lasaca on the fall of Pamplona. Riding back from seeing Alten his mare was taken ill with staggers, 'bled her copiously & she appear'd to recover'. On the 28th she seemed much better, but she died next day and when Hughes had her 'open'd, lungs gone'.

The surrender of the Pamplona garrison was at last confirmed and the Regiment marched early on 1 November, in wretched weather. It continued next day and the sleet and snow made 'the roads & passes execrable'. After a 'tedious, broken & winding march amidst the obscurity of woods & snow we received the order to halt & return to our quarters, operations being for the present suspended'. Hughes now felt 'very unwell' and retired to bed after taking 'remedies for cold'.

Wellington issued 'Memo of orders to be sent for movement on 8th November upon Sare':

Supposing Sir R. Hill to put his troops in motion on the 6th, attack should take place on the 8th. . . . Major General V. Alten to be instructed to move the 18th Hussars into the valley of the Bidassoa on

150

6th instant and to canton the brigade in Yanci, Etxalar, and Lesaca. Lord E. Somerset to be directed to occupy the quarters quitted by the 18th Hussars, together with such other cantonment in the valley as may place the brigade most á portée to pass into the Bidassoa valley should it be so ordered. One squadron of the brigade is to be established at Santesteban, on 7th, from which letter parties are to be sent to Vera and Etxalar, and also to an intermediate point between these places and Santesteban.

On the move for the frontiers

The march resumed on the 6th when they reached Oitz, Donamaria and the neighbouring villages. After dining at Santesteban with Alten Hughes 'rode home a very cold night, frosty'. His cold was worse when they marched for Etxalar, by a 'bad & tedious road along the Bidassoa, the pass choked by bullocks, mules &c'. Etxalar was crowded with 7th Division and Hughes 'turned out some Brunswick officers'.[3] They were to march next morning by the Pass of Etxalar towards Sare – and he ordered newly arrived overalls to be worn. However, after dinner a message arrived from General Le Cor to say that operations were again postponed.[4]

Kennedy wrote to Grace:

after the fall of Pamplona we are on the move for the frontiers. We moved off in such weather as I suppose was never seen since the time of Mr Noah. The miserable goat paths through the mountains were consequently impassable and the waters of the Bidassoa having over-flowed their banks we were obliged to halt some days and did not reach this place till yesterday. . .

The French completely run to earth are entrenched strongly about three leagues from this village on their own dunghill, so we may expect pretty warm work to dislodge them. . . . The army had orders yesterday to advance by daybreak this morning. But late at night we received a countermand and are now in momentary expectation of orders to advance. It is supposed the deep snow at Roncesvalles has prevented General Hill from advancing by the enemy's left flank which it is supposed Lord W. means to turn previous to our attack on their entrenched camp at Sare, a village in our immediate front. There is no doubt of our driving them the first day behind the Nive river, and then 'tis thought they must retire behind the Adour, in which case we expect to become masters of Bayonne and winter on the Adour.

. . . Such a series of rocks and mountains as we have scrambled over on our way here from Pamplona you can have no conception of and yet the mountains are but small compared with the full grown Pyrenees in the neighbourhood of Roncesvalles and St. Jean Pied de Port on which town the left of the French rests.

. . . As soon as we pass the Nive we shall have a good country for the cavalry to act in and as we are the foremost brigade shall no doubt have an opportunity of being distinguished or extinguished. We are fortunate in having a most excellent officer to command us, Baron Alten. He is Lord W.'s favourite outpost officer, so that we shall have severe work during the winter doing the outpost duty.

The garrison of Pamplona were reduced to the last extremity having ate all the dogs, cats and rats in the town. One of our officers, who carried in a flag of truce a day or two before it surrendered, was told by the French officer at the advanced post he was sorry he had nothing to offer him to eat but a '*Fricassee de Chien ou un ragout de Cheval*'. . .

Should any of the mischances of war befall me in these perilous times Hugh will write to W Deane Esq. our Paymaster here who will arrange my domestic affairs.

9 November

[JH] A warm but cloudy day; received a confidential communication that the suspended operations take place tomorrow. The official order arrived for the march tomorrow by the Pass of Etxalar.

PART IV

INTO FRANCE

CHAPTER 15

OVER THE PYRENEES

November to December 1813

Attack Across the Nivelle

On 10 November the 18th marched under 'a beautiful moonlight', without which 'it would have been impossible to have proceeded, the road was so bad & the precipices so dangerous'. A provost marshal guided them down one of the steepest Pyrenees, where 'there was neither pass nor road'. When the attack began the Brigade 'follow'd closely the movements of the infantry but there was no opportunity to act. All the heights & redoubts were carried, with comparatively inconsiderable loss . . . the day closed with every advantage on our part.'

However, Wellington caught an 18th chasing a sheep 'and the Regiment got another row'. While halted a long time at Sare Pass and being soaked in pouring rain, Hughes 'read Ld. Wellington's orders & address'd the Regiment'. In view of the sheep-chasing, the orders were probably those of 2 November:

I have it in command to recall to your attention the expediency of your taking every possible step to impress on all ranks the necessity, as well as the policy, of preserving good order and discipline on the army entering France. General order of the 9th July is to be read on the first three parades after the advance.

'It is His Excellency's wish that you should take a favourable opportunity of assembling officers commanding brigades and regiments, and expressing to them His Lordship's peculiar anxiety on this subject, and it is expected that you should explain that measures of precaution are to be preferred to those of remedy, as there is hardly a possibility of redressing injuries committed by an uncontrolled soldiery, who, once let out of control, cannot easily be brought under subordination.'

Eventually the 18th bivouacked in a wood; Hughes shared a shed with Alten and his staff. 'Between us we made something of a dinner, but there was no wine. We took some tea, which kept us awake all night, laying on our blankets on the ground.' He spent 12 November, his 36th birthday, 'reconnoitring everything and found all going well'. The storm continued, all operations were suspended and Hughes distributed 'an extra quantity of rum & gave quantities of corn to the horses'. The 'large shed or barn', which he shared with the Brigade Commander:

> had no doors, but was divided into two by a low wall & again divided by a little hedge & the low beams kept our horses & mules from encroaching on us & having cover'd the door by canvas & lit a large fire in it we made ourselves comfortable & the candles were fortified from the wind by a contrivance of mine. The portico served for our kitchen.[1]

Most of the men and horses were in the open and, although an order arrived for the Brigade to go into cantonments, 'it was too late, so we had another dreadful night'.

Hughes sent a squadron to relieve the one on outpost duty and took the remainder to St. Pée-s-Nivelle where, with great difficulty, he got them under 'inadequate' cover.

Senior Officers in the Swim

After a tour of quarters and outposts he visited Cotton:

16 November

the country scarcely passable. He mounted his horse to ride with me to Ascain (Alten's Qrs.) & St. Jean-de-Luz, but the rain came on violently . . . We return'd to Colonel Elley's, once more we started by another – and a most difficult country we encountered . . . Cotton & I having left the others in the rear got into a narrow road which more resembled a river; there was however a broken causeway which for sometime we kept, but Cotton finding it impossible to proceed suddenly turn'd, his horse got into a hole & after a variety of plunges, the General began to think it better to quit his horse; this however, he had hardly done & dismounted up to his throat in water, when the horse in his efforts to mount the bank tumbled over & knock'd the General under water, where they both

156

flounder'd together, at last Cotton made his appearance & after some hard knocks we got him out, but it seem'd almost impossible to retrieve the horse whose violent throes & efforts only served to exhaust him; the zeal of the orderly & Major Dicken made matters worse, it sunk twice & got away from us, at last he recover'd & swam out.

Soult withdrew from the Nivelle to the east bank of the Nive, upriver from Bayonne, keeping a bridgehead in front of Cambo-les-Bains. That was driven in on 16 November, but soon afterwards the Nive flooded, and operations were again suspended.

Kennedy wrote to his mother after returning from picquet, 'within pistol shot of the French lines':

I mentioned our having had a skirmish with their outposts. Yesterday we had another and drove them back before us in great state, so that we have now taken up a good position close to Bayonne . . . The weather is now become fine but the roads still bad for the guns to come up. . . . You can't imagine a finer climate than this, it appears quite like May to-day. At one side, we have a fine view of the Pyrenees, which appear almost touching the sky, and on the other the Bay of Biscay and the coast beyond Bayonne.

. . . When does Forbes become a Benedict? I think next to Bonaparte and Paris, the best thing worth seeing must be Forbes making love – Most conjugal. It must be capital. Love to Betsy and all your neighbours; write frequently as it is my greatest consolation on earth.

After a General Court Martial found a Private Conway guilty of 'quitting his post as vedette for plunder'; Hughes was sent for by Alten and they agreed that 'the finding & sentence of the court shew'd ignorance & that the infliction would be cruelty'. After pursuing the matter at Headquarters Alten 'believed he had succeeded in favour of Conway'.

Operations remained suspended for the next fortnight, during which Hughes made several visits to St Jean-de-Luz, keeping an eye for female company. He thought 'on the whole the Hd. Qrs. Grandees were cool' and wrote to his brother:

We are now, as you see, in France, about two leagues from Bayonne, doing outpost duty; and, from the beginning of the campaign to this hour, they have not once failed to avail themselves of our services, when cavalry service was practicable, and have ever given us the post of honour when other regiments were in the rear, though on pretence of 'plunder', they gave three vacant troops out of the Regiment!

Hill and Beresford crossed the next river barrier, the Nive, Hill by the fords at Cambo, Beresford a pontoon bridge at Ustaritz. Hope advanced on Bayonne along the coast.

On 7 December an 'Immediate Service' letter arrived, ordering one squadron to Ustaritz and the rest of the Regiment to be ready to march the following day. Kennedy's squadron went to support Beresford and on 9 December the others followed up Hill's divisions. At a ford over the Nive near Halsou, 'the road & the ford were very bad, but had not much difficulty as the passage had been previously forced by the infantry under Sir Rowland Hill. . . . It became very rainy, the ground did not admit of cavalry acting; we patrolled &c.'

After drawing lots with 'the Germans . . . the latter bivouack'd' and the Regiment went into Halsou, where 'the inhabitants received us well'. But next day:

> whilst we were dining, a complaint arrived against men of the Regiment who had been stealing from and ill-treating the inhabitants; the Adjutant and I immediately mounted and took ourselves to the scene, here we discovered that they had had opened a commode and stolen handkerchiefs. I paid for them, as I could not discover who was guilty. In another house they had killed a pig, fired a pistol and otherwise mistreated the inhabitants.

Later, 'much cannon fire on our left. An order arrived . . . for the Brigade to retire again to St. Pée; it was almost dark before we could cross the ford, the consequence was great confusion, several falls & much wandering in the woods.'

It was 13 December before they were on the move again, on 'a fine moonlight morn'g, a frost & very cold'. They recrossed the Nive and joined the 13th and 14th Light Dragoons, 'whom we found in position, the 14th having suffer'd some loss & the brigade a good deal harass'd by the cavalry & infantry of the enemy who had driven them from Hasparren. We push'd forward some patrols, the enemy with their infantry skirmish'd with the Spaniards the whole day; Major Brotherton of the 14th made prisoner.'[2]

A few days later Kennedy wrote to his mother:

for the last five days there has been most desperate and bloody battles in this neighbourhood, all of which have terminated in our favour . . . The advance of the army towards Bayonne was fixed for the 9th and, the day before, a squadron of our Regiment was ordered to march to support the centre column at Ustaritz under Marshal Beresford. Mine happened to be first for duty and I marched from St. Pée on the 8th.

. . . at daybreak next morning the army began to cross the river, the infantry by a bridge which was thrown over on the right and my squadron by a ford. We soon drove in the enemy's picquets at all points and Sir R. Hill having crossed the river at Cambo he drove forward the enemy's left flank and they retired the whole of this part of their line close to Bayonne on a hill near the town on the right of the Nive, they collected their forces after we had pursued them for a league over hills and through woods and making a number of prisoners, and on their left flank they shewed a very great force with which we had continued fighting the whole of the day without either party gaining much advantage. . . . Towards the close of the evening the French under General Darmagnac advanced in great force to drive us from a hill which our infantry had gained. The contest was most obstinate and bloody; three times they were driven down with great slaughter and we finally succeeded in keeping our ground. . . .

We had advanced more than a league and had taken the town of Villefranque near which our centre column remained till next morning. I put myself up in a most excellent house occupied by a French colonel the night before, and the delight of the people at seeing us was only to be equalled by the hospitable reception they gave me. I never met anything like it . . .

The numberless acts of kindness and attention we have met with from everyone makes one quite forget any hardship we have endured and renders our march more a tour of pleasure than anything else. You can have but little conception of the high regard and esteem they all have for the British although the Spaniards they naturally detest and dread.

. . . On the night of the 9th Soult withdrew his whole force from his left, into Bayonne when he crossed the Nive which . . . divided our right wing from the left, and early next morning (supposing that we could not readily reinforce our left in consequence of the river dividing our wings) he in a most masterly manner brought his whole force to bear upon Sir John Hope whom he attacked most furiously . . . as I was with the centre column I can't give you any particulars of this day's battle, but that the cannonade and firing was really tremendous all day and did not cease till long after it was dark. On this evening the centre division was ordered to return to Ustaritz in order to recross the river

159

to support the left if necessary. We halted there during the night and the morning of the 11th was ushered in with a renewal of the contest on our left flank, which now in turn attacked, and drove the enemy towards their entrenchments near Bayonne. The firing ceased towards midday and about 3 in the afternoon again recommenced with redoubled vigour. I never saw so heavy a fire for two hours when night once more terminated the battle.

Next day being Sunday, both armies seemed to observe the Fourth Commandment . . . I had accordingly turned into bed to take a little repose when I was suddenly awaked about one in the morning by the bugle and an order for our Brigade which I had rejoined that day to advance forthwith to this village to check the advance of above 2,000 of the enemy who were attempting to steal round us on our right flank, to get in rear of Sir R. Hill, whilst Soult once more recrossed the Nive with his whole force to attack him in front. We arrived here in good time and met the French General Paris with his corps who seemed rather surprised to find we were beforehand . . . He had four regiments of cavalry and two of infantry with which we had been skirmishing all day which terminated so much to his disadvantage that he fell back and disappeared in the night; the 14th Dragoons in pursuing them through a village lost their Major and one officer whom they carried off with them.

. . . Soult having failed in his attempt on our left flank . . . resolved to make a grand attack on our right and accordingly brought his whole force across the Nive on the night of the 12th once more to make an attack on Sir R. Hill. Severe as all the other attacks had been, they appeared but preludes to the battle of the 13th. It was apparently their last effort and was consequently furious in the extreme, the contest was most obstinate and sanguinary and although our loss was of course severe, British valour was once more triumphant and I understand the enemy went back faster than they came, minus nearly 10,000 men, 6,000 of their prisoners and eight pieces of cannon.

. . . Our loss in all these sanguinary battles must be great, that of the enemy immense. The result at present is we have closely invested Bayonne on this side the Adour and the enemy are confined to their redoubts . . . the weather is horrible and the roads almost impassable owing to the continual rain . . .

Almost all our cavalry still remains in Spain . . . We have here at present only two brigades of light cavalry besides ours, for the country is not adapted for dragoons and forage scarce in many places. Our horses have been for days without corn or hay, and feeding on leaves or whatever they could pick up among the woods and hedges. However since we advanced we have got into a fine rich country with a good deal of corn and which the French army were civil enough not to destroy previous to their departure.

... I am just about to attack the enemy in the following advantageous positions. A boiled knuckle of veal on the right, a roast shoulder of lamb on the left, and an apparently good looking dish of calves head hash in the centre. Each flank covered with a bottle of champagne and same of claret, not forgetting some Irish potatoes, my usual attendants. The whole commanded by a most civil landlady who quite oppresses me with her extreme attention and probably expects to carry me by a *coup de main*. But although a late hour for attack (being 5 o'clock) it is to be hoped from the enormous appetite which the air of France gives me, I shall completely at all points and 'swallow the enemy up quick so wrathfully has he displeased us'.

Soult now established a defensive position with seven divisions on the line of the Adour from Bayonne. In case of a British assault across the river another two divisions and his cavalry were positioned on the flank, but Wellington had no intention of undertaking major operations until the winter rains had eased.

The Affair at Mendionde

On 14 December the Regiment moved into Urcuray – and 'many Spaniards arrived'. The latter were a small Spanish division under Morillo, which remained with the main Allied army after Wellington had sent back to Spain the bulk of his Spanish troops. They were not only half-starved, 'owing to the neglect of their own government, so that they must plunder or die, but also inspired by bitter resentment at the treatment which their own land had suffered at the hands of the French for so many years'. The 18th soon found themselves all too closely involved with Morillo.

On the 16th Hughes was warned that an attack was 'expected in our quarter . . . the Regiment turned out. I made a reconnaissance as far as the enemy's picquets, there appear'd no reinforcements & all was quiet . . . Nevertheless the enemy push'd forward a strong reconnaissance of cavalry & infantry, which, after skirmishing with our picquet, retired with some little loss.' Next day, he visited the *curé* of Mendionde who 'gave intelligence & much civility; he cautioned me not to advance further in that direction'. Returning to his quarter he found an order from Alten to take two squadrons of the Brigade to support Morillo in an attack he proposed to make on the French at Mendionde:

> On December 18th, Morillo, on Wellington's extreme inland flank, made an excursion against Mendionde and Hélette. . . He had borrowed two squadrons of the 18th Hussars from Victor Alten, who had not been authorized to lend them. After driving in the French outposts, and pillaging the countryside as far as the Joyeuse river, Morillo found himself beset by all Pierre Soult's cavalry, and turned back in haste. The British Hussars, covering his retreat, were badly mauled and lost some prisoners. Both Morillo and Alten received vigorous reprimands from Wellington. As a punishment for plundering the Spanish division was ordered to be kept under arms for five days in bitter weather.'[3]

In fact one of the squadrons came from the 1st Hussars KGL, but it seems extraordinary that Alten should have allowed them and the 18th to be involved in such an expedition. He was due to return to England shortly afterwards and perhaps, in later parlance, was 'demob happy'?

18 December

after a considerable time General Morillo arrived & having placed myself under his command we advanced, cavalry in front with company of riflemen on the flanks . . . General Morillo gave no orders or even communicated . . . at a turn of the road which was conceal'd he halted his troops and withdrew them to the heights he had left, without any notice, with the exception, only, of the company of *caçadores* . . . we drove in their vedettes, picquets & cavalry on their infantry . . . nevertheless the *caçadores* abandon'd the posts I had directed them to, & which it was necessary to sustain, by which the enemy's infantry was enabled to bring a heavy fire upon the cavalry which could act no farther . . . the *caçadores* retired & while I was in the act of ordering a retreat I received a shot under my arm which lodged in my right breast.

I left the field, Captain Bolton withdrew the 18th & the Germans had already retired, but the *caçadores* being in the rear were charged by the enemy's cavalry upon which Captain Bolton charged the French with the 18th, drove them back, but brought his squadron too near a wood from wherein their infantry mortally wounded him & took him prisoner. Croker & Woodberry were slightly wounded with three men, two prisoners & ten horses.

My ride home (for I did not dismount at all) was very painful; at Mendionde my friend the *curé* gave me some wine, which refreshed me. On my arrival Pulsford soon came, who at my request & in presence of Captain Kennedy began to extract the ball, but his knife was bad & it was tightly lodged. Chambers arrived & completed the operation which was rather tedious, but not, perhaps, so painful to me as to the spectators. My wound was pronounced 'severe but not dangerous'; I wrote a note to General Alten & found myself wonderfully well, however I could not eat much, but had a very tolerable night.

Kennedy added a postscript to the letter to his mother:

Dec. 18th. . . . I was sent out on picquet on the morning of the 16th to watch General Paris's movements, as it was reported he was again advancing towards us from the road leading from St. Jean Pied-de-Port. I had scarcely reached my destination about a league from this town in front, when three squadrons of their cavalry and a battalion of French infantry came on to attack me. I happened to be at the moment at the advanced post where there was only ten men with which I retired as soon as the enemy came up within musket shot. I then joined my next party on the road consisting of as many more and with my strong force of twenty Hussars I formed across the road and awaited their approach. They came on very regularly and in order to check them I advanced at a gallop a few men to skirmish with them, which had the effect of checking their advances for several minutes so as to give time to the Regiment and Morillo's.[4]

19 December

[JH] I found myself so well that I got up for the purpose of writing my report to the General . . . a flag of truce went to the French on behalf of poor Bolton, in the meantime I received a very handsome letter from the Colonel of *Chasseurs à Cheval*, stating that every attention had been paid to our Captain, who was '*grievement blessé*', demanding at his request one of our surgeons & his servant & promising that they should freely return if he died & stay always by him until he recover'd if he should be so fortunate; this letter was brought by a peasant to our outposts, who received it from a *chasseur à cheval*. I returned an answer in which I endeavour'd to express myself in terms suitable to the occasion, such as I thought became the character I wish our Nation to sustain. I had a very bad night & was obliged in the middle of the night to take an opiate.

Pulsford returned later from Hélette to report the death of 'poor Bolton'.

Leaving Hughes at Urcuray, the 18th marched under Kennedy to Hasparren. While recovering from his wound Hughes remained in touch with both Regimental and Army affairs – and alert to opportunities for dalliance.

'The Baton Catchers'

Kennedy wrote to his mother:

I wrote you a long letter by an officer who is to go home today . . . His name is Curtis, brother of the man who purchased my cornetcy. After I had sealed my letter, which he carries, a squadron of our Regiment was sent to assist Morillo's corps of Spaniards in attacking a village where the French were strongly posted. The result was the brave Spaniards ran away and our men were obliged to fight to cover the retreat of the runaways in a place where cavalry could not act to any advantage in narrow lanes and roads lined with hedges. Their infantry of course could do anything they pleased against cavalry and in consequence in a short time Major Hughes who commanded was badly wounded, Captain Bolton next in command mortally, and died next day, almost every other officer in the squadron hit slightly and many men and horses . . . in consequence of the Major's wound the command of the Regiment devolves on me. Therefore should anything occur in the way of promotion whilst I am the senior it would be a good thing if you mention the circumstances to Castlereagh in any way to bespeak his interest with the D. of York, for although Clements and Milner are both senior captains now, yet they were both junior cornets to me in the Regiment formerly, having entered the army after me, but by good luck and money have got above me. . . . Clements is at present hunting in Yorkshire and Milner is fagging at the Court of Palermo as aide-de-camp to Lord W. Bentinck, whilst here am I leading the Baton Catchers to glory. For you must know it has been discovered by chance that it was a corporal of the 18th that took the famous baton of Marshal Jourdan at Vitoria. The gold ends of that baton were yesterday found in his pocket . . . a friend of his in the 87th Regiment stole the wooden part with the case containing it, and gave it to his colonel who

164

presented it in the name of the 87th to Lord W. However the ends which are solid gold and which the corporal has been keeping till he should go to England are to be sent to Lord W. to undeceive him about the 87th having taken the baton.

Corporal Fox, 'the real person who took the baton of Marshal Jourdan at Vitoria' brought Hughes its golden ornaments. One end bore the legend: *'Teror Belli, Dicus Pacis'* and the other *'Jean Baptiste Jourdan nommé par l'Empereur Napoleon Marechal de l'Empire Floreal'*. Hughes sent them on to Wellington, who asked him to give ten dollars to the corporal.

[AK] We are today going to advance a little under Sir Stapleton Cotton. . . . I think you mentioned knowing his sister, I wish you could get me an introduction to him as he commands the cavalry and might be of great use to me. I think you had better write to Lady Londonderry to use her influence with Castlereagh in the event of a vacant majority in the Regiment; you might mention the circumstance of the Major being wounded and in case of anything happening to him I should have a good claim . . .

The trumpet just sounds to turn out . . . I think your prayers have had good effect; I am now with two more the only captains alive that left England with the Regiment. How singularly unfortunate we have been in losing officers you will allow.

165

CHAPTER 16

WINTER OUTPOSTS

January-February 1814

Hughes Convalescent

'Soult tried to molest Wellington's right flank beyond the Nive'[1] and the Portuguese brigade in la Bastide-Clairence was driven back to Briscous. Two days of incessant rain frustrated any counter-attack until 6 January when three divisions pushed the French back across the Joyeuse.

By Christmas Eve Hughes was recovering well and he 'pass'd the day as before with the addition of more company . . . Burke was put under arrest by Sir S. Cotton for foraging contrary to order, which gave rise to great agitation & bother on his part & great laughter at his expense.' Vivian took over from Alten as Brigade Commander. Before leaving for England, Alten undertook to see the Duke of York and the Prince Regent about the Regiment's affairs. He also took back a note from Hughes for his sister, Mary Hester, with the bullet that had wounded him. The convalescent began to 'walk out a little':

> after being dress'd by the Surgeon, I shaved, wash'd, put on clean things &c had my bed made to which I return'd, took my breakfast, read my book, received my visitors, of which there were many, rose an hour or two before dinner, dined with Kerrison the Dr. & sometimes one or two others, conversed with the people of the house & then retired to rest.

He found the locals 'disaffected to their Government', wishing for nothing more than 'peace, commerce & good fellowship':

The conscription has been resisted & in many instances utterly fail'd. The French Army has lost its discipline & its spirit, they are two years without pay & being in their own country cannot so readily pay themselves at the expense of the natives.

The English have been expected since the Battle of Vitoria & had they follow'd the French up . . . would have found Bayonne without a garrison & the people waiting for them with a mixture of inclination & terror . . . The remembrance of old times & families is still preserved & they retain their old prejudices about rank.

Riding for the first time, on 1 January Hughes visited the mayor – and his 'pretty daughter', Gracieuse – before visiting the Regiment. He thought Gracieuse 'very friendly and pretty; she undertook to teach me French and I to teach her English'.

Woodberry, again 'tired of this monotonous life', resumed his diary and pasted in it a newspaper cutting:

We are happy to learn that that gallant young officer, Lieutenant Woodberry, of the 18th Hussars, who was seriously wounded on the 18th December during an engagement with French cavalry near Mendionde, is sufficiently recovered to rejoin his regiment.

There were also copies of certificates for the medical board in London signed by the Regimental surgeons, 'Lieutenant George Woodberry, of the 18th Hussars, was wounded in the hand by a musket ball facing the enemy between Urcuray and Mendionde (south of France) during an outpost action' and, 'the index finger of the right hand is very weakened'.

After shooting 'two rabbits and a plump chicken which had strayed' he was afraid that 'the poor devils of inhabitants, who bless us as liberators' would soon have good reason to curse them for eating all their supplies.

A trumpet call mustered the Brigade on 3 January; the French had driven back picquets at la Bastide-Clairence and Bonloc, and advanced on Hasparren. Woodberry went with Croker's troop to cover the approaches to Hasparren. The infantry exchanged fire all day, and 'little progress was made'. Come evening:

[GW] General Picton is with us, and we have our new commander, Colonel Vivian, of the 7th Hussars. A squadron of the 18th, and one of the 1st Hussars are on picquet, with two guns, on the heights; the remainder are in quarters. The men are resting by their horses, which are saddled up, and ready to move at the first alert.

On 6 January, when the British advanced, Hughes 'went fully fit to take command of the Regiment, well received by the officers'.

At midnight Woodberry took twenty men 3 miles on the road to Bayonne. His patrols 'found a camp' which he thought could be the enemy, but turned out to be a battalion of Brunswickers. Two divisions, camping behind him, moved off along the hills 'until one mile from the enemy where they halted until the arrival of Lord Wellington. Towards ten o'clock his Lordship passed in front of my picquet and, about two hours later, ordered the attack . . . the enemy withdrew beyond a stream, to la Bastide-Clairence.'

Fraternization at the Outposts

A major preoccupation for both sides was keeping their horses fed. Mutual self-interest led to a good deal of fraternization and General Harispe complained that the English picquets were firing on his people every time they went to fetch water. 'He asked that both sides should agree to remain quiet and have equal right to the stream; la Bastide-Clairence would be occupied on the right bank by the French, and on the left bank by the English.' Each side was to give an hour's notice before starting hostilities. Vivian's Brigade picqueted the stream between la Bastide-Clairence and Bonloc and British and French sentries almost met on the bridge.

Both Hughes and Woodberry seem to have suffered after effects from a ball given by Cotton, where 'we met about fifty officers and nearly as many ladies, really pretty . . . After the quadrilles, there were several waltzes, then a *fandango* and finally supper, with lots of toddy, which we did not spare. No one left before two in the morning.' Next morning when he went to the outposts, and conversed with the French picquet at Bonloc, Hughes had a 'wretched headache' and a fall from his horse. Woodberry blamed the 'hard and unyielding' floor of the ballroom for 'completely' exhausting them.

His troop's quarters were changed so they were better housed and 'more under my eye'. His own quarter had a fireplace only in the kitchen, 'I quickly remedied this by building a hearth and making a hole in the ceiling and the roof: I will stop it up tomorrow after having fixed a chimney flue.' At Ayherre, in the house where they were billeted on picquet, he met a pretty girl, whose company was 'most agreeable . . . She knows how to read and write.'

Kennedy reported to his mother:

We all remain here stationary in winter quarters; such horrible, stormy, wet weather, we can't attempt to move. . .

We are on this part of the line quite close to the French, separated by a small stream about three or four yards wide, their sentry and ours within twenty yards. It is quite ridiculous to see the friendly terms we are on with each other. I was going the rounds as Captain of the Day last week and had a long conversation with a French officer of one of their picquets who gave me some excellent French brandy from his canteen. You have no idea how civil they are, will give you anything but forage, which is now becoming very scarce indeed. . . . Nothing can equal the civility and attention of the natives in this part of the country and their fright the other day when they thought the French were going to advance here is not to be described; they were in as much terror as if they had been Spaniards.

Major Hughes has quite recovered from his wound and has now taken command of the Regiment, which was much improved of course under my government! . . . I believe I asked you to get me a letter to Sir Stapleton Cotton from Lady Londonderry in my last; it might be of use. I have just had an invitation to dine with him to-day, but I think a letter of recommendation would make him still more civil, for you must know he is a great personage here, 3rd in command of the army besides General Commanding the whole of the cavalry.

Tell Betsy if I return by Paris I shall bring her some kid gloves. In the part of the country we now inhabit nothing of the kind is to be had, we have eatables enough but everything of course immensely dear in consequence of so large an army being here.

Woodberry thought highly of Kennedy. Referring to him as an officer 'full of merit and a brave man' he wished he could outdo him in some act of bravery.

After a fruitless search of all the houses in Bonloc for forage, Woodberry took three troops out and 'chased away the enemy picquet at the gallop'. In ten minutes, 'my foragers had their fill. . . . They will probably do the same to me; there is such a lack of forage.' They heard guns every night; 'to begin with we thought there was an alert and stood the Regiment to; but we became so used to it that the noise scarcely wakes us up; it is our batteries on the

170

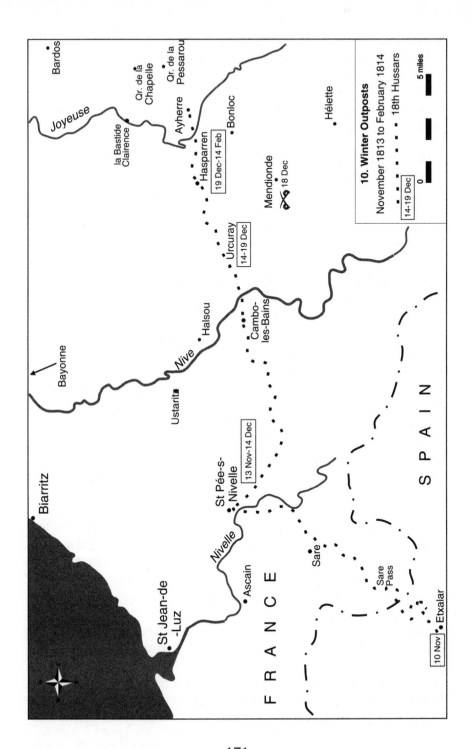

10. Winter Outposts
November 1813 to February 1814

······· 18th Hussars

14-19 Dec

0   5 miles

Bardos

Qr. de la Chapelle

Qr. de la Pessarou

Ayherre

Bonloc

Hélette

la Bastide Clairence

Joyeuse

Hasparren
19 Dec-14 Feb

Mendionde
18 Dec

Urcuray
14-19 Dec

Halsou

Cambo-
les-Bains

Bayonne

Nive

Ustaritz

St Pée-s-
Nivelle
13 Nov-14 Dec

Biarritz

Nivelle

Ascain

Sare

Sare
Pass

St Jean-de
-Luz

F R A N C E

S P A I N

10 Nov

Etxalar

Adour firing on enemy boats carrying supplies to Bayonne'.

After dining with a large party at Cotton's, Hughes 'danced with Jeanne Marie &c; they kept me up 'till about 2 o'clock in the morn'g by playing at cards in my bedroom'. The same day, when Woodberry arrived at the Bonloc outpost, he was called to the bridge to talk to an aide-de-camp of General Pierre Soult:

> He wanted to have some English papers and gave me in exchange the latest ones from Paris. I promised to send him some tomorrow. . . . He asked how we passed the time: I said that we had balls at Hasparren and that there would be one that evening at Sir Stapleton Cotton's. He wished he could be there, as a beautiful woman of Hasparren, his friend, was expected.

That evening he asked the officer of the enemy cavalry picquet if he would send him 'some of the excellent wine' from the other side of the village; he did and refused to accept payment. 'The French officers take all that they want without bothering to pay.' He was visited by Vivian 'who I begin to like a lot, as he seems to be happy to explain outpost duties to young officers'.

Pulsford went to St Pée 'to examine Mr Morris, who left England some time ago with the remounts and has fallen sick at Bilbao, where his wife and child join him before long.[2] Major Hughes believes that Mr Morris's state is not as bad as his letters make out.'

Woodberry was soon on picquet again as there were so few subalterns and heard from a peasant, from Pau, that Soult and Clausel had been reviewing their troops. They were said to be training about 15,000 recruits, whose 'number reduces by ten to twenty a day through desertion . . . there are several thousand deserters who live with the inhabitants among our lines'. Meanwhile the local French troops tried to prevent the British being brought provisions, but high prices in Hasparren encouraged the peasants 'to risk a lot to attend the markets and every night they cross the stream with huge baskets of eggs, chickens and bread'.

The shortage of forage was increasingly worrying. One morning Woodberry checked all the beds in his quarter. 'The mattresses, stuffed with straw, have been emptied and I shall keep the contents for my poor horses. The woman is very angry, but all the officers have done the same.' They now had neither hay nor corn and had to send foragers to the hedgerows, 'the only place where one might find some'. Others were employed cutting gorse and fern, which could be crushed with a mallet and then chopped. 'The horses are famished; it keeps them alive but does not give them much strength.'

They had to pay five shillings for 'one pound of poor quality sugar' and eighteen pence for coffee. Tea came from English sutlers 'for which they have the effrontery to charge thirty shillings a pound'. One sutler, a one-time servant of Woodberry, had been beaten 'by order of the Provost Marshal of Cambo for having bought meat from the locals at the market and resold it at twice the price'.

Kennedy's next letter vented unusual spleen on the 'Head Butcher':

It is said the Spaniards are to be left to watch Bayonne whilst we advance towards the Garonne . . . What a glorious termination the war appears likely soon to have. I think nothing short of the dethronement of Mr Boney will now do. We appear completely to have the ball at our feet, if the Austrians are only kept together, but there appear some doubts of the Emperor of Austria. . . . One thing is certain if they ever let Boney get his head up again, he will be like a fire half quenched only to break out worse than ever and destroy all within his reach. . . . I think a march to Paris now most highly probable. I can't think the population of France will offer much resistance, at least if they are all like the people here, Bonaparte is most cordially detested. . .

(They had heard that when Curtis went home his goods were seized at Falmouth by the Customs House officers 'who were disgustingly familiar enough to search his trunks and found some stockings or contraband articles therein'.)

This deterred me from sending you any gloves or such like articles. However, if I live and do well I shall try and bring you some articles from Paris if we go there. What a great man Lord Castlereagh will be if he is the means of keeping the Allied powers together just now and terminates the war as every one must wish. They have been certainly a most lucky family so far. I suppose the old peer is not a little proud of his progeny . . .

A man gets no thanks for getting his head broke now-a-days. It is as common an occurrence now to be shot as it was formerly to sit down to breakfast and you are no more thought of. This has been amply veri-fied with us, never did a Regiment lose so many officers with so little thanks from the Head Butcher as he literally is. He is a good officer I believe, but without very much feeling or regard for the feelings of any of his officers. He gratifies his own ambition by the gallantry of his troops and that appears his principal object and although he must be acknowledged a good and clever General he is I believe no great friend to either officers or soldiers.

Woodberry met 'an old friend from Olite, the Spanish Captain Murphy; he threw himself into my arms and embraced me. I learned that all my friends from Olite are well and that Zacarias is married.' Out with a party to collect the day's forage, he came unexpectedly on the French picquet, which saved itself by galloping in the direction of Hélette. 'I crossed the stream and occupied the high ground opposite; but I got a poor harvest, scarcely enough to feed the officers' horses for one day. We were engaged by a squadron of the 21st Chasseurs, but no shot struck either side.'

Woodberry suspected that promissory notes on the Paymaster General, with which the Commissaries paid the inhabitants for rations and forage, were being redeemed several days later for a twentieth of their face value. 'These poor people know nothing about these notes.'

On 3 February Hughes heard from Vivian, 'we are to march in fourteen days & requesting that the Regiment may be immediately got into order. Great talk of Peace.' Woodberry and Hesse visited the hospital at Cambo, 'full of the sick and wounded in the army. There I saw my old servant Bentley, who was wounded a few minutes after me, the day that poor Bolton was killed. At first it was thought the unfortunate lad would lose his arm, but that is no longer a threat.' On picquet next day at Ayherre, he watched a review by General Harispe. 'There were about three thousand men in good order, well clothed, all with whitened gaiters. They had three eagles. I long to take a French eagle, and if ever I reach the centre of the enemy infantry during a charge, I will try to take one or die.'

A French officer, under a flag of truce, handed over Southwell of the 14th at Bonloc; two French cavalry lieutenants having been sent in exchange:

Southwell said that immediately after he was taken prisoner with Captain Brotherton, both were taken to Pau, where they dined with Generals Harispe and Soult; in the evening they were taken to a ball, and everyone showed great interest in them. Next day they were transferred to Bayonne by an aide-de-camp; there they dined with Marshal Soult, and stayed for several days. . . . Brotherton remains a prisoner, because Lord Wellington and Soult cannot agree on his exchange.

Issue of the Vacant Troops Unresolved

One of Murray's letters caused Hughes fresh disquiet; he took it to Cotton, 'and began a conversation on the subject of the troop which the letter said would not go in the Regiment 'till Ld. Well.'s sanction had arrived'. Cotton became heated and 'circumstances indicated that he was not so innocent of unfairness as he wish'd to be supposed'. Hughes 'spoke my mind' – and Elley came in, 'in the midst of it'. They 'parted friends' but the thoughts of their injustice disturbed Hughes's evening. Next day Cotton came to inspect the Regiment and Hughes rode round the cantonments with him, finding 'everything better than I expected except the Right Troop, which was shocking'. Cotton entered into 'a long explanation abt. Ld. Wellington & the troops, *je le ne crois pas*'. However, something must have been achieved, either in France or Horse Guards, as Russell was appointed to the remaining vacant troop.

The Campaign Resumes

Woodberry's horses were now in 'a really bad way'; they had to go 4 miles away even for gorse. One day the mare fell, that he had taken at Morales and who carried some of his baggage, and he had to put her down.

There was no escaping the routine of administration and on 9 February the annual inspection began under three captains and next day Hughes 'order'd an inspection of the books of C Troop'. He continued his pursuit of Gracieuse; calling one day he found '*beaucoup de monde*, Gordon, Thornhill &c but I thought I was preferred'.

> [GW] The Basques are up on stilts like the ones, which I myself made and used when I was a child. Our adjutant, Mr Duperier, who is, I believe, a native of the department of Landes, has a pair and walks in the village as quickly as the most nimble of the peasants.

By arrangement with the French, on the 11th the Regiment foraged at Ayherre. 'The infantry moved off at the same time; we warned the enemy of our move three hours in advance. The French were ready to leave at five o'clock in the morning. Their chief of staff gave the signal to our advance posts at Bonloc by waving his hat. They left the village immediately, bugles playing and drums beating.'

They now found forage for several days, and the horses ate so much that Woodberry worried they would make themselves ill. He found Ayherre 'very lively' and thought, when the army left, 'the women will all accompany them'. On outpost duty he met the 'lovely Maria again', who seemed sad and lonely. He asked her to follow him on campaign, 'but she replied: "Marry me" But no, Maria: I want to play and amuse myself with you; I want to embrace you – but I'll be hanged if I will marry!'

Kennedy wrote to his mother:

Fine weather having at length made its appearance . . . the campaign recommences tomorrow. . . . You need not be 'in the fidgets', as the country is not likely for some time to admit of the cavalry distinguishing themselves and we have not much to do with storming the works of the fortresses. The French have collected some of the peasantry near this but it is thought they will all take advantage of our advance to desert most gallantly . . . You may imagine their civility when they sent us back a horse of our Regiment that had strayed away from one of our picquets into their lines a few days ago. They sent to say that we should have it by sending for it and they gave the officer who went a good lunch and were as polite as possible, so you see how completely humbled are the hitherto haughty Gauls!

. . . our cannon commence a firing every night on the Boats attempting to pass with provisions down the river to Bayonne, which tends very much to disturb my nocturnal slumbers. . . . At the present moment (in the evening) they are firing away great guns and musketry; although pitch dark I see every flash from my exalted habitation. I hope you have not been buried in that deep snow I read of in the papers. How different is the climate here. We have scarcely had any snow although rain in profusion. A few days ago I saw a butterfly and the thermometer was up to 80 in the sun.

I don't know if Sir Stapleton received any letter about me from our friend in Mt Stewart[3] but he has been civil to me. He inspected my Troop some days ago and asked me to dine. Charles Manners, Edward Somerset and a few other grandees were invited to meet me; we had a most splendid feast, quantities of champagne etc.! Sir Stapleton goes home I hear after the campaign to be married to a very young girl although he is no chicken himself.

When you write to Hugh tell him not to be giving the public any more extracts of letters from an officer to his friend near Belfast, as I observe he has been doing lately! I suppose the editor bribes him for the most authentic and earliest intelligence from the seat of war . . . You of course know the Duke d'Angoulême has arrived here, and I suppose will declare himself soon. . . .The French Empire seems to be as fast on the decline as the Roman one of old, and I think we shall very soon see the ancient order of things re-established and a long and secure peace will be most probably the result of this wonderful twenty years' war which England has carried on with a constancy and perseverance certainly unparalleled in the history of the world. To the army of the Peninsula Europe is in no small degree indebted for the glorious change which has taken place; it has been the spark which has kindled into a flame such as the tyrant is now unable to extinguish and I think bids fair to destroy him and his Dynasty.

CHAPTER 17

FIGHTING THROUGH GASCONY

Advance to Orthez

Wellington's manoeuvre . . . consisted in the turning of Soult's left wing by the persistent advance of a large flanking column under Hill, which got well south of Harispe's division, and by dislodging it in succession from the lines of the Joyeuse, the Bidouze, and the Saison, forced the other three French divisions, which lay north of Harispe, to conform to his retreat, and abandon those river-lines, under pain of being taken in flank and rear by the turning column. But lest Soult should take the offensive with these divisions, when Harispe began to fall back, the English general kept three divisions in front of them, so as to contain them. . . .. Soult was driven to successive retreats from river-line to river-line, till, when he had been drawn to a very great distance from Bayonne, and had lost his communication with that fortress, he finally massed six of his seven divisions, and stood to fight at Orthez.[1]

Across the Joyeuse and the Bidouze

With his position at Hélette threatened by Hill, and Morillo likely to get behind his flank, on 14 February Harispe abandoned the line of the Joyeuse and retreated halfway to the Bidouze. Picton's division, supported by Kennedy's squadron, advanced on Bonloc, which Villatte also abandoned. Somerset's brigade and the rest of Vivian's were with Beresford, containing Soult's main body.[2]

[AK] the French were attacked to-day at 12 o'clock and took to their heels most manfully. . . . I am just returned after being at their heels for a considerable way. The cavalry with Sir Stapleton expected to move to-morrow. The infantry are advanced a good way to-night. . . . I have

179

been with Sir Thomas Picton to-day following his division of the army, commonly called the Fighting Division.

15 February (Ayherre)

[JH] Received an order at 7 o'clock to send one squadron to Bonloc, at 8 received another order to march the whole Regiment to Ayherre; sent a patrol under Captain Luard . . . on arriving at Ayherre found the troops in quarters, wrote a note to Vivian who arrived before I finished it . . . Luard's report arrived with prisoners.

Beresford's advance made the French evacuate their line along the Joyeuse and take up positions behind the Bidouze. On the near side, Harispe tried to fight a rearguard action on the Motte de Garris, but he had only 7,000 men and there were 12,000 men in front of him, as well as Morillo's division working round his flank. Pringle's brigade took the Motte, a general retreat was ordered and Harispe's troops suffered badly in getting away. Many were cut off and the whole division poured back across the bridge at St Palais. It was blown ineffectively at the last moment and Hill's engineers had it repaired by noon next day.

Beresford was now ordered to push on beyond the Bidouze, with the hussar brigades in front. Vivian's patrols discovered Villatte's division at Sauveterre.

Operations notwithstanding, the 18th had a variety of domestic problems:

16 February (Qr. de Pessarou, de la Chapelle)

[GW] A man has been brought before a court martial for having lost his breeches, and he will be punished this morning if his wife has not come to swear that it was she that sold them.

17 February (Bardos)

[JH] Morris, who went on picquet to the heights, by a blunder was some leagues in front yesterday & did not return 'till today; a court martial, much villainy in the Regiment; a sudden order to march to Bardos, did not get the Regiment into quarters 'till night, lodged myself at a small house belonging to two sisters, for which purpose turned out some muleteers, very bad quarters, dreadful cold weather. . .

[GW] marched about five leagues on a bad track. I am in a good house, at the foot of a hill; my hosts are very obliging and they have plenty of forage. This horrible Mrs Morris, the wife of the Lieutenant, has followed the Regiment here on foot. I could not bring myself to have pity on her, because she is a real bitch. I offered to take her child on my horse and to carry it here: she refused with an oath, cursing the whole world and the Regiment in particular.

18 February (Bardos)

Kennedy's squadron rejoined the Regiment and he added another postscript for his mother:

The French fly pretty quick in all directions . . . Some smart fighting yesterday and to-day our vanguard has crossed the Gave . . . Nothing can exceed the delight of the people in general at our successful advance. The weather most propitious to military operations and the country improves so much as one advances that one is quite enraptured with this country and climate. We are in the midst of plenty once more & I hope shall continue so. You buy a fine lamb here for half a crown and all sorts of eatables inconceivably cheap. . . . I saw to-day the famous Château de Guiche, the former seat of the Duke de Gramont

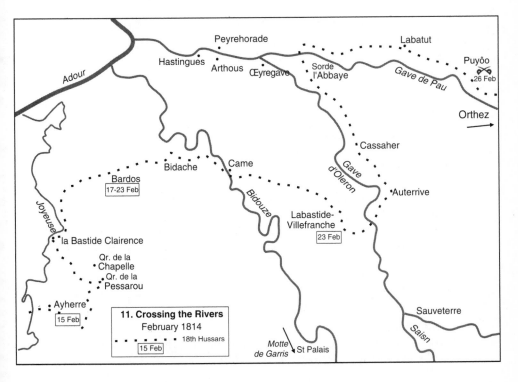

11. Crossing the Rivers
February 1814

18th Hussars

near this. His son the Count de Gramont who is here a Captain in the 10th is gone to see his paternal residence but nothing remains except the wall and the stable . . . During the Revolution it fell into the hands of some Bayonne grocer.

The inhabitants of the village where they were quartered made 'big complaints' against Woodberry's Troop who had stolen some fat, 'but I do not know what to do; our usual fat has been so bad for some time that I am not surprised to see these poor fellows getting their victuals as best they can'.

Pause on the Gave d'Oloron

'Wellington . . . having succeeded in his initial manoeuvre, the drawing off of the greater part of his adversary's army far to the east and the inland, was now about to direct in person the second act – the investment of Bayonne by the crossing of the Adour at its mouth, for which he had left the corps of Hope behind him.'[3]

Russell gained his captaincy and, on 19 February, Woodberry and Pulsford drank to his success. On the 21st Hughes 'found great malpractice in the foraging of the Regiment, ordered arrangements on that head'.

23 February

[GW] I was with the Troop foraging on the banks of the Adour and the enemy fired on us. . . . The infantry have started a move on Bidache. We shall follow tomorrow morning. Hurrah!

[JH] Marched from Bardos, crossed the Bidouze at Bidache, arrived at Labastide-Villefranche . . . the infantry were attacking the French at Hastingues where they had a *tête du pont*, they were driven over the river & out of the town, arrived on a fine plain which however the enemy had abandon'd.

[GW] The Brigade had orders to leave at 10am for Bidache. Waldie and I were sent to find quarters for the Regiment there: we found the town full of infantrymen. At present the enemy occupies the village of Arthous, which our troops attacked immediately. The enemy withdrew to Œyregave and crossed the Gave d'Oloron in boats. Our infantry

182

arrived just when the last boat was leaving and fired a volley, which killed or wounded almost all the occupants. The Brigade was deployed on the plain, ready for action, but with the enemy slipping away, we took up our quarters around Came.

From where Kennedy wrote to his mother:

crossed the Bidouze river to this village . . . The French occupied the town of Hastingues near this in some force but after a little skirmishing took to their heels this evening and fled to the Gave which, under cover of some cannon they had on the opposite bank, they succeeded in passing. I suppose they will be off tonight to Dax on their way to the river Garonne which it is supposed they will now make for, so that I conclude we shall drink a little genuine claret at Bordeaux in a week or so. We shall have fine work hunting them over the level country after we have passed the Adour . . .

The weather continues fine as possible and the French fly on all sides pursued by our troops and by the curses of their countrymen whom they have plundered by all accounts most unmercifully. In fact one can hardly blame them for they have received no pay for twenty months. They take everything they want without payment and carry off what money they can get so that the inhabitants all say they will starve next year and blame Bonaparte as the cause of all their misfortunes. It is impossible to avoid pitying the miserable inhabitants unless one reflects it is a judgement on them for having dethroned and murdered their king.

I met our cousin Sir Lowry yesterday; he enquired after you and desired I would give you his love.[4] You should be highly flattered in being remembered by so great a warrior. *Entre nous* I think him as great a humbug as I ever saw! He is I hear hated most cordially by the army in general. However all this to yourself. . . . I rather think from what Sir Stapleton told me to-day we shall advance to-morrow across the Gave d'Oloron. The country improves in the way of forage as we advance and we now have abundance of both hay and clover to the no small gratification of our hungry quadrupeds who were very nearly famished during our stay at Hasparren.

Fords of the Gave d'Oloron

Vivian's Hussars demonstrated against many fords in the neighbourhood of Taupin's position . . . In one or two places, Vivian's reconnoitring parties got across the river – not without having men drowned, for the water was high.[5]

On 24 February the 18[6] marched at daybreak to Bastide de Béarn[6] and on to the Gave d'Oloron to threaten the fords. 'The infantry cross'd the bridge at Peyrehorade & were repulsed, the enemy's picquets kept a lively fire on us, remained the greater part of the day on the ground, return'd at night to Bastide de Béarn.' Hughes put up at 'a large, cold house where Marshal Soult had slept' and Dolbell went in disguise to reconnoitre one of the fords. Woodberry was agreeably surprised 'to find all sorts of similarities with an English town; cafes and shops of every kind'.

Before marching next day there was a 'severe punishment & drumhead court martial'. Hughes 'address'd the Regiment & was follow'd by Vivian in the same strain, the Regiment growing bad'. They then crossed the Gave d'Oloron, where two men fell and were saved with difficulty, 'particularly the horses'.

Woodberry, ordered to reconnoitre the fords, was up before daybreak. Getting as close to the river as possible, he thought there were enemy sentries at each ford, but, when one of his best shots fired at one of them, 'there was no move and no response'. After a peasant told him that the 'sentries were only uniforms stuffed with straw', he crossed – with difficulty – 'as the current was very strong and the water deep'. Later he was sent back to Auterrive to show the Brigade commander the fords. 'During this crossing I nearly lost my life in going to the aid of a drowning cavalryman. I feel rather sick, having swallowed a good gallon of river water.'

It was night when they arrived at Sorde, where Hughes was 'tolerably well put up' with a 'most killingly civil landlady; my bed broke'. Kennedy encountered some real sentries:

25th Feb. . . . two squadrons were ordered to proceed to reconnoitre the fords over the Gave d'Oloron which with the Gave de Pau form the two great branches into which the Adour here divides. The French picquets were posted all along the opposite bank and on going down near the ford I was received with a very brisk fire of musketry without any possibility of getting across to retaliate. We succeeded however in our reconnaissance without any loss on our part and I was for the first time struck by a musket ball under the short rib, but, it having luckily struck a tree or some other thing before it reached me, it was very harmless not having even cut the cloth of my pelisse. . . . I was the only one touched in my squadron although exposed to a very sharp fire for many minutes. About a league higher up, at Sauveterre, Sir Thos. Picton was attempting at the same time to cross the bridge there and after some heavy cannonading for several hours the enemy blew up the bridge – reckoned to be one of the first in the country. The troops attempted to ford the river afterwards but were repulsed and so in consequence we are halted here today, I suppose till the arrival of the great Lord who is manoeuvring on the Adour near Bayonne whilst we keep the enemy amused in this direction.

The country improves very much as we advance; quite like England . . . The Gascons and the Bearnais whom we are now among are the most amusing ridiculous people you can conceive and civil beyond any conception. What a pity that such a beautiful country should be the seat of war. You can't imagine how annoyed the people were yesterday on hearing of the destruction of their fine bridge over the Gave. It had cost the country 200,000 francs but a few years ago.

The people here almost all speak French which was not the case with the Basques we lately left and I consequently begin to make rapid improvement in the language which is certainly the most useful one of the present time and I now feel the advantage of Diorand's instructions.

. . . I stop the Press to announce the passage of the Gave d'Oloron, which took place today in four different places. We forded across at Auterrive and my Hd. Qrs. are in a small village the name of which is such a jaw-breaker I forget it! but I occupy a magnificent château. We expect to follow up our game tomorrow morning. They are flying like so many hares at the present and we don't expect to see much of them this side the Garonne. Tomorrow we shall most likely wade through the Gave de Pau in pursuit . . . Horses getting into fine condition, roads excellent, weather divine, and as fine as June with you! In short the Wellington Pack are 'in high spirits and in full cry!' – The scent lies well, as the French have had but a short start! I hope we shall be in at the death at Paris before long!

Encounters with the French Rearguard

[AK] the enemy . . . blew up the bridge and retired in the night of the 24th and on the 25th we crossed the Gave d'Oloron and next morning the Gave de Pau, all by fords – very deep! On the opposite bank of the river we again overtook the French rear guard consisting of the 15thRegiment of Chasseurs. The 18th happened to be in front and instantly charged them pursuing them for half a league over the finest road you can imagine. In consequence of which we soon overtook them and such a beating as they had I believe they had not often been accustomed to. The poor wretches we took were cut and sliced in a most merciless manner and Marshal Beresford whose Corps we were immediately attached to was highly pleased with the conduct of our men.

On the 26th Beresford sent Hughes with two squadrons of the Regiment to find a ford and cross the Gave de Pau. They found and crossed 'a baddish ford' and marched on the road to Orthez as far as the road to Dax to which Hughes sent a troop to patrol. He then heard of three squadrons of the enemy at Puyôo, where a deputation came to him from the commune 'begging protection'.

> Came up with the enemy's cavalry . . . charg'd them & took some prisoners, but we pursued so long & so rapidly that we got dispersed & broken, the French charged our broken files who gallop'd back on their support. However we advanced again & they retir'd having narrowly escaped being cut off by the divisions who began to cross.

> [GW] We hit upon the main Orthez road near the village of Labatut. One squadron of the Regiment was sent to the left to reconnoitre and take possession of some villages; the remainder went about one league on the road towards Orthez, and at that moment found the French advance guards near the village of Puyôo. The leading squadron, Burke's, Vivian at its head, chased the French picquet across the streets of Puyôo and Ramous in the most brilliant fashion, capturing several men and horses. . . . Captain Sewell, aide de camp to Marshal Beresford, charged at the head of the Regiment. Having lost his sabre, he seized a broomstick and threw himself at the enemy, landing blows all round.

After 'much delay, many counter-orders & much difficulty' the 18th went into quarters at Puyôo, where Woodberry found the wine at the inn excellent. Hughes dined with Beresford at a dinner given by the Mayor and on his return 'found the Germans foraging in my house, one of them very impudent & I struck him'.

Battle of Orthez

Hughes's diary entry was terse:

> Turn'd out at daybreak; emptied the guardroom & made a severe example; at last order'd to march & on the road heard unexpectedly

186

that the French waited for us at Orthez, march'd at once into position & attack'd them. The French were about 30,000 strong & made a strenuous resistance on the high road to Pau where their grand force appear'd to be collected.

But Kennedy described the day for his mother:

Pursued so closely Marshal Soult was now forced to draw up his army on the following day and give battle to his pursuers. . . . The glorious morning of the 27th had scarcely dawned when I extricated myself from my blankets and mounted my squadron and prepared for the combat . . . The roads in this part of the country are much wider than any you have ever seen and so straight and level that one can see for leagues. Imagine then such a road, covered with troops as far as the eye could reach, all moving forward in the highest spirits confident of victory – a most delightful morning and as warm as June in England rendered the sight truly magnificent.

On arriving near Orthez . . . we found our infantry already sharply engaged and the French drawn up in heavy columns in a most excellent position with two hills in their rear which they afterwards found of great use in their retreat.

The Battle began about midday and for two or three hours they fought more desperately than we have ever yet seen the French fight. A village near the centre was taken and retaken several times by Sir Lowry's division, which at last succeeded in keeping it. Sir Rowland Hill now got round this left flank and, their right being also seriously attacked, about 3 o'clock they gave way in all directions while our guns played among their retreating columns with very great effect and the field was literally strewed with their dead and dying. From one hill to another they retreated and it was a considerable time before any opportunity was offered for the cavalry to take part in this scene of blood and slaughter. At length however the 7th Hussars, who were in front of the line of cavalry, charged and prisoners, guns and tumbrels in numbers fell into our hands whilst those who were fortunate enough to escape scrambled off through woods and an intersected country in every direction. Night put an end to the pursuit, which lasted from near 4 o'clock till eight in the evening.

We bivouacked in a wood and at daybreak next morning continued the pursuit and a great many prisoners were made on the roads; the houses along their route were crammed full of their wounded, which they say amounted to 8,000. We have heard of 2 generals wounded, Clausel and Foy, the former is said to be dead. Our loss has been severe also, we hear about 3,000 *hors de combat*.

187

[GW] The morning started with the flogging of seven men near Ramous . . . Then we joined up with the rest of the English and Allied army and waited for orders. No one could have believed that we were only separated from the enemy by an insignificant hillock.

About nine o'clock, the battle started and our Brigade left the main road to occupy a hill on the left. . . . We then entered the village of Baigts, which had been taken and retaken several times. We could then see the French army in its positions. At this moment, Marshal Soult and his staff officer rode across the length of the battlefront. I could see very well with my spyglass the Marshal exhorting his soldiers . . . We soon came under enemy fire, Vivian wanting to form up the Regiment to the nearest point, in case it became necessary to charge. But the French were playing on us with their guns so two squadrons of the Regiment were sent to the rear guard, and the right squadron sheltered with their horses in a muddy ditch. . . . Marshal Beresford and his staff stayed near us, very exposed, because we were in the centre of the line of battle, waiting for a division to reinforce us. When it arrived, we left the ditch and advanced together. At this moment the enemy withdrew on all sides; General Hill who, having passed the Gave at Orthez, had turned the left flank of the enemy after little fighting.

The pursuit of the infantry continued until nightfall, without opportunity for a charge for our Brigade; the 7th Hussars were luckier and took seventy prisoners.

The road was strewn with corpses, more, I believe, than at Vitoria; and for the time the battle lasted, it was one of the biggest slaughters of the campaign.

The enemy is in full retreat to St Sever. . . . Their cavalry had several hours start on the infantry and were beyond our reach. They occupied the main road, centre of the position; we saw them clearly and were anticipating a hard fight with them. . . .

Lord Wellington was hit by a spent ball, but only slightly wounded . . .

The day ended for the 18th in bivouac 3 miles from St Cricq. Woodberry was delighted to find that, by chance, his baggage and servants had ended up nearby. 'I was able to have my tent pitched and all the officers came to shelter there. I gave them a good supper and most slept under cover.'

CHAPTER 18

PURSUIT FROM ORTHEZ

The Campaign Nears its Climax

Advance to Mont-de-Marsan

While Soult withdrew eastward towards Toulouse, Wellington had good reasons for reaching Bordeaux as soon as possible. Not only were messages reaching him of a planned Bourbon coup in the city, but its capture would be a serious blow to the Bonaparte regime throughout southern France. Beresford therefore advanced on Mont-de-Marsan while Hill followed up Soult and defeated an attempted stand at Aire on the Adour.

Vivian's Brigade resumed the pursuit on 28 February. The 18th, welcomed enthusiastically by inhabitants of the villages, reached Montaut half an hour after the enemy had left. Men and horses were exhausted after a march of nearly 40 miles and Woodberry sought quarters in St Aubin. Several women and children threw themselves on their knees and pleaded with him not to kill them, such was the picture of Allied soldiers painted by the retreating enemy.

At an hotel in Mont-de-Marsan Hughes and the officers had 'a very good dinner, price 10s each'. Next day, less Kennedy's squadron, they left for the Adour, but were not needed, 'Sir R. Hill having beaten the enemy on our right'. Returning to 'a place call'd Artassenx', Hughes took a guide who, mistaking his meaning, brought the Regiment to a house 'inhabit'd by a mechanic or artisan'.

'Several gentlemen have arrived today from Bordeaux to ask the English army to enter their town. Presumably they intend to declare for Louis XVIII.'[1] Mrs Morris also 'showed herself today in the town, on a pretty grey pony, with a fine saddle and a brand new bridle. She had at last persuaded her husband to buy her the lot.' Woodberry thought that a regiment had never been 'more compromised by the wife of an officer than the 18th, by the get-up of Mrs M—'.

Hughes next lodged in a château in Perquie, 'nobody there but a poor woman who was frighten'd, at length a person appear'd who unlock'd the old château which prov'd good quarters'. Woodberry thought the other officers badly housed, 'There is a large château, but our Major, Hughes, occupies it and he likes to be alone, especially when he shares this solitude with a beautiful woman.'

Woodberry took twenty men to clear the main Bordeaux road as far as Roquefort, where the mayor gave him details of all French troops who had passed through (with a list of the provisions they abandoned) and an estimate of their forces in Bordeaux, Langon, and elsewhere. He heard that a French officer, 'by name Florian, with twenty or thirty partisans, was scouting around Roquefort'.[2] On the way back he therefore kept half his detachment on watch while the others fed their horses. Sent next morning to the outposts at Aire, he installed himself comfortably with 'a very obliging old lady'.

Kennedy wrote to his mother from the *Préfecture de Landes* at Mont-de-Marsan:

> I am at present left here with my squadron to keep up the communication with the rest of the army. . . . I am quartered in no less a house than that of the Prefect of the Department who thought proper to take himself off on our approach . . . He was the greatest man in this part of the country and you can't conceive any thing more elegant than his mansion. I do him the honour to drink his fine claret which is really delicious and I am obliged to make use of his letter paper as you may see. . . .[3]

On the 28th we arrived at Montaut near the banks of the Adour which we crossed next morning at a ford and arrived here the same day where we were received by the inhabitants with open arms. You can't imagine the delight of the people to see us and '*Vivent les anglais*' resounded through the villages as we passed. . . . The weather, which had hitherto favoured us so much, changed on the 1st and we came into this town like so many drowned rats; such torrents of rain as we had for two or three days you can't think. It is however now fine . . .

At present I am no small personage being commander of the cavalry here whilst my brother in arms Marshal Beresford commands the infantry . . . We have only one division of infantry here, which is a pleasant circumstance. The people are civil beyond expression and everything is to be bought very cheap. I have got an assortment of necklaces, brooches etc. for you, if I had any mode of conveying them without the risk of seizure in England. Tell Grace I have got her gold chain which she wished for. The beautiful library of the Prefect is a great amusement to me. I mean to give an entertainment here to my subs and I only wish you saw me living in state . . .

I went to pay a visit to the Guillotine here. . . . The executioner exhibited it to us and a more horrid looking instrument I have seldom seen . . .

In the Prefect's library I discovered a curious correspondence between Soult and the Prefect in which Soult says how to raise the *levée en masse* as his army would not be able to oppose us without their assistance. I gave it to Colonel Vivian to send to Lord Wellington.

I am just going to dine with Marshal Beresford and I am sorry to say I am likely to be turned out of my Palace by Lord Wellington who is expected here today with the Duc d'Angoulême. An attempt made here to hoist the White Cockade but the people as yet seem afraid to take any decided part in the business until we arrive at Bordeaux . . . The people here all seem anxious for the fall of Bonaparte although not particularly anxious for the restoration of the old Family. I believe if Lord Wellington declared himself king he would be as well received . . .

7 March

[JH] Rode to Villeneuve for sale of French horses, made some female acquaintances.

[GW] My patrols only returned this morning; the enemy is in force at Nogaro and Manciet, nine leagues from here. His patrols left Montguilhem as mine entered. I dine with my hostess; she told me a lot about her family, which is Irish and lives in Dublin. She has three sons serving in the French armies.

Towards Bordeaux

On 8 March the rest of the Regiment joined up with Kennedy's squadron at Roquefort and Woodberry saw 'two men of Florian's partisans hanging in the market place, by order of Marshal Beresford'. Turning out before daylight, but 'late & disorderly', they had a 'long but pleasant march through a huge pine forest'. Leaving a squadron at Captieux, Hughes marched on to a small village where he lodged at the house of the *Adjoint*, whose family from fear of the English had fled into the woods. There the weather had 'half kill'd the poor woman & her child, but being better informed of the English character were now in their houses'. Hughes called Chambers to the child and the doctor 'prescribed'.

On the 10th Hughes again rose before daylight, 'with a bad headache, miserably cold', but this time the Regiment turned out well and in good time. They marched via Bazas to Langon on the Garonne. At Bazas, 'which we entered with trumpets sounding' Woodberry thought the inhabitants 'overjoyed at seeing us' and the Regiment formed up in the square for about half an hour 'to give them time to admire the English Hussars'. At Langon:

> [JH] A company of the enemy with the *douaniers* employ'd in towing up the boats & sinking them on the other side, fired a few *coups de cannon*, which they return'd with musketry, a party of *Gens des Armes* fell in with our picquet on the Bordeaux road, one wounded & taken, one of the hussars was also wounded, dined with Marshal Beresford, found to my annoyance that the Regiment was to remain & not march in the morn'g.

This time the officers had 'excellent quarters' and dined together at *l'Hotel de l'Empereur*.

Writing to Grace, Kennedy reverts to the vexed question of Vitoria and its aftermath:

> the fine weather and the glorious victory of the 27th at Orthez have at length conducted the British Hussars to the banks of the Garonne where we exhibited our grim visages at noon today. I believe the natives were treated for the first time in their lives with the sight of English troops and it would have amused you to have seen the crowd that collected round me at the door of my hotel here on alighting from my horse and as I am now a tolerable good Frenchman harangued the *bourgeois* on the great advantages they would soon derive from the arrival of the English at Bordeaux of which they all seemed fully sensible and they are really delighted at the probability of their being so soon relieved from the slavery they have been labouring under. . . .
>
> I must not here say too much of the beautiful country we are in lest it might tempt you to leave your own habitation but I really think if I am destined to settle anywhere France will be the place . . . The whole country appears one extensive vineyard. We have the finest Barsac for

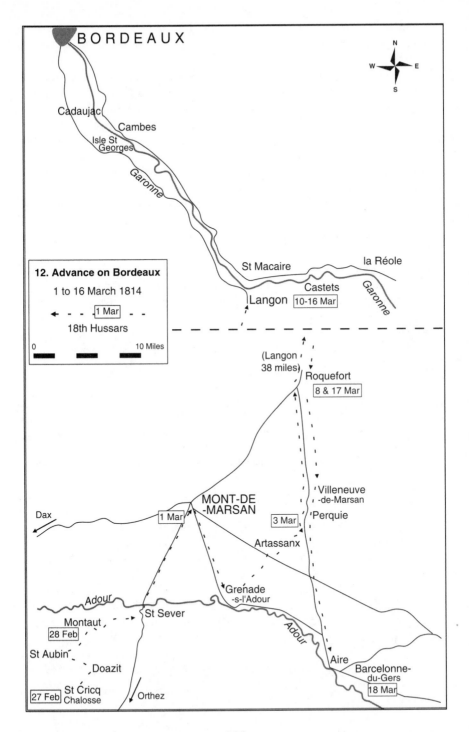

12. Advance on Bordeaux

1 to 16 March 1814

18th Hussars

0   10 Miles

BORDEAUX

Cadaujac

Cambes

Isle St Georges

Garonne

St Macaire

la Réole

Castets 10-16 Mar

Langon

(Langon 38 miles)

Roquefort 8 & 17 Mar

Villeneuve -de-Marsan

MONT-DE -MARSAN

1 Mar

3 Mar

Perquie

Dax

Artassanx

Grenade -s-l'Adour

Adour

St Sever

Montaut 28 Feb

St Aubin

Doazit

Aire

Barcelonne- du-Gers 18 Mar

St Cricq 27 Feb Chalosse

Orthez

Adour

a shilling a bottle which is reckoned dear. The best claret twenty pence and everything else in proportion cheap. We pass through Barsac tomorrow . . .

The few French troops that were in this town crossed the Garonne yesterday on hearing of our arrival. They took off all the boats to the other side of the river, which is here as broad as the Thames at London without any bridge. They carried off all the flour and corn they could and to-day we saw them at the opposite side endeavouring to drag up a boat with flour upon which Marshal Beresford ordered one of our 6-pounders to be brought down and we commenced a fire across the river at them which soon made them take to their heels and set off.

. . . We expect to be received in the handsomest manner in Bordeaux. I hear the warmest invitation has been sent to Lord W. urging his advance there and saying that 1,200 men are in readiness to join us . . .

March 11th. I wrote so far last night. We have an order to-day to halt; the Marshal and our Brigade (Vivian's) are gone to Bordeaux; I suppose to arrange matters for our entry. In the meantime the army is closing up to the Garonne; the infantry are coming in here to-day. The small French picquet still remains on the opposite bank of the river. I amused myself yesterday firing a carbine at them, which they occasionally returned without any casualty on either side. They have got all the boats over so that they can stay there unmolested.

The poor boatmen are going about here out of employment in consequence; they are very numerous and I think will become rioters soon if their boats are not restored. Some of the inhabitants are in rather an awkward predicament. The husbands, who were in the pay of Bonaparte, went off on our approach and the wives stayed behind so now there is no communication between the two banks. The ladies begin to be very clamorous calling across the river to their *cara sposas*. My hotel is close to the water so that I have the advantage of hearing the noisy wretches shouting in all directions. Your sex are in general pretty clamorous and I assure you those in this country are particularly so on the present occasion. . .

Sir Lowry is just arrived with his division, the 7th. I dine with him to-day.

I command the Regiment at present, the Major having set off to Bordeaux to see the town. . . . We have crossed the Garonne last night and driven the French picquet away from the other side. We took the baggage of the Commissaire with about 50,000 francs in money. I am ordered by Sir Lowry to push forward a patrol to the banks of the Dordogne and reconnoitre Libourne. I hope we shall catch the American ships in the river. They amount to thirty or forty, richly laden.

. . . I am sorry to find the rows between the great Lord and the 18th has caused such a number of misrepresentations to go abroad relative to the business and has consequently given you so much uneasiness. . . The story is a long one but the whole sum and substance is that the Regiment was halted in Vitoria by the Commanding Officer to prevent the Spaniards carrying off the treasure, which was lying about in all directions. The men naturally enough helped themselves and some who found means to get drunk were overtaken by Lord W. who was coming on with his staff. For this reason the promotion was stopped; for nothing else, and out of this has arisen perhaps more lies than ever yet were invented. The fact was that he was happy to have an excuse for providing for his friends and he took the opportunity of two captains being killed to provide for his friend Ld. Edwd. Somerset and another to whom he had promised the first vacant troops.

You may suppose what sort of a man this same Lord is when he gave away a troop lately (or rather made an excuse for giving it to Shakespear, Sir Stapleton Cotton's aide-de-camp), because he saw a private of the Regiment chasing a sheep as he supposed with the intention of stealing it. On Shakespear's name being sent to the D. of York H.R.H. wrote to the Lord to say he was sorry he had not recommended Lieutenant Hesse, the senior lieutenant of the Regiment for it, as he the Duke was interested in his promotion. Upon receiving this letter Lord W. wrote to Hesse by his Secretary to say that His Lordship had received the Duke's letter and to express his Lordship's regret he had not known sooner that Hesse was senior lieutenant or he should have recommended him for the troop.

Altogether there never was a Regiment so shamefully used as ours has been for no reason and when the tide of calumny has subsided truth will at last find its level. But in fact you have all made much more of the matter at home than we have here; the subalterns of the Regiment have suffered and many have resigned in consequence. . . . So much for the lies of the British newspapers, the editors of which ought to be ashamed of daily filling their columns with such gross falsehoods against those who are exposing their lives in their defence. For my own part I am quite easy on the subject and I am fully confident the business will stand the test of inquiry, which by the bye the Lord refused to grant. . . . The circumstance stated of the promotion being stopped for three years is contradicted by the appointment of Lieutenant Russell to a troop last Gazette. The charge we made against the French rear guards on the 26th, the day before the Battle of Orthez, under the eye of Marshal Beresford will convince the Lord that although our men will occasionally drink or take King Joseph's cash when it lies in their way yet that they are as good at fighting as any other regiment.

. . . I forgot to tell you the narrow escape I had at the close of the
battle at Orthez, whilst following up the fugitives, almost the last
cannon shot they fired struck a ditch within ten yards of me and
covered me not with glory but with mould, a much more agreeable sort
of wound than if the metal had come into contact with your humble
servant. I thought at first it was a shell that burst but it turned out to
be a ball which threw the earth about in all directions. . .

Pray present my very best regards to Lady Londonderry and return
her a thousand thanks for interesting herself in my promotion. Assure
her I shall never forget it and offer my humble congratulations on the
late happy connubial occurrence. I am afraid you will leave none for
us when we return. All will be disposed of!

I have got you some gold chains; would you wish for some claret?

Woodberry Arrested

Instead of visiting Bordeaux, the 18th watched crossings of the
Garonne against a possible attack on the right flank and on 11 March
Woodberry was sent to Castets. His orders from General Lord
Dalhousie[4] were to prepare 'the equipment to ferry infantry to the
other side . . . to seize the town of Macaire by surprise, at dawn'.

He had put this in hand and gone off to eat, when he heard that
one of his vedettes was being attacked. Galloping to their position he
was greeted opposite la Reole with a volley of musketry, one ball
striking the holster of his gun. Dismounting and crawling to the edge
of the river, he saw the opposite bank 'crowded with people, French
officers and soldiers'. After he had ordered his men to dismount and
open fire with their carbines 'the French soldiers took cover and the
locals fled; my sentries could retake their posts with no further disturbance'.

Hurrying back to Castets he got the waiting company of the 68th
across the river for a successful operation in which the town was taken
without a shot being fired.

Next day Dolbell relieved Woodberry at Castets and later had an
accident, 'showing off in front of the mistress of the house, he put his
horse at a gate; the animal fell and broke its neck, and Mr Dolbell got
a nasty blow on his side'. Woodberry rejoined the Regiment at
Langon to find his writing desk and some of his baggage lost to 'that
scoundrel Florian' who had seized them near Rions. 'Sparem Joe', his

Portuguese servant, was blamed having 'stayed to drink with the rear-guard'.

As he and Russell sat down to dinner an 'exhausted' Woodberry received orders to leave immediately to reconnoitre some 25 miles of the left bank of the Garonne, from Cadaujac to Castets. He was to lay hands on boats of every kind and have them taken across to the left bank. At Cambes, where a number of barges were on the opposite bank, he crossed over to talk to the *maire*, who invited him to land, telling him there was no enemy and that he would fetch the boatmen. However:

> When I followed him to his house, he told me I was a prisoner. The room was full of strong, well-armed men: I sat in front of the fire with his wife; I was allowed to keep my sword. Before long all the men left on various pretexts: I suspected they were looking for the *Gens des Armes* to arrest me. The woman offered me refreshments, which I accepted. After three hours, the *maire* came and told me that a boat was waiting to take me back across to the other side. It was about nine in the evening, raining heavily, and extremely dark. The boatman disembarked me and, without saying a word in response to my questions, pushed his boat into the current. I found myself in a wood; after several abortive attempts to find my way, and several falls into muddy ditches, I lay down under a tree and waited for dawn. Then I saw I was quite near l'Ile-Saint-Georges where I found my servant and my batman with my horses. I have caught a most frightful cold and feel very ill.

In Bordeaux the Mayor had proclaimed Louis XVIII 'in form & thrown off the yoke of Napoleon'. Hughes thought it a magnificent city, with fine promenades and buildings', but the women 'not handsome, their dress horrid'. The reception of the Duc d'Angoulême at the Opera was a ' brilliant affair'.

At Langon, Woodberry 'arranged for some music and we danced. The *maire* of the village came with his two charming daughters and I waltzed with them.'

Kennedy reopened his letter of 6 March to his mother, 'Sir Lowry here with me. I dine with him. He seems to have a strong *penchant* for you I think.'

Soult's Demonstration

Soult advanced on Aire in a 'showy demonstration'[5] against Hill's divisions on 13 March. Wellington rapidly reinforced Hill with three divisions and a substantial force, including Vivian's brigade, assembled under Beresford in order to turn the French right flank. In forced marches, 'both Cole and Vivian found very bad weather and very bad roads; the stages Bazas–Roquefort and Roquefort–Barcelonne were specially remembered as terrible marches of eight and seven leagues respectively, which knocked up all the baggage-horses and mules – mud was up to the horses' fetlocks and the men's ankles'. On the 19th, soon after dawn, the French flank-guard was driven out of Rabasten and towards Vic-Bigorre, through which Soult had been intending to retreat upon Tarbes. After a sharp rearguard action at Tarbes Soult slipped away under cover of darkness to Toulouse.

15 March

[JH] Found that an order had arrived for the Regt. to march tomorrow . . .[6]

[GW] This country is beautiful: I could live here and perhaps even forget England. We danced again this evening, the *maire* and his wife, tired of staying up, entrusted their daughters to me. They were delighted to stay. They sat on my knees, and I have given my heart to the older one, who is delicious; but we leave tomorrow, and probably, like all the other loves of my life, this one will have no future. The mistress of the house sent her husband to Bordeaux and has set her cap at me; but after the delightful daughters of the *maire*, she tempted little and I left her to old Russell – going to bed myself.

On 16 March Woodberry was snatched from his agreeable billet for the forced march. Next day was Saint Patrick's Day and he recalled the year before, at Luz, when the Regiment was drunk to a man. 'This year is very different, everyone stays sober.' It was very hot when they returned through Roquefort, and the march so long that 'we are exhausted and half dead from hunger'. On the 19th they reached Aire and were quartered in 'huts' on the right bank of the Adour. En route they heard that an extra squadron, commanded by Grant and recently arrived from England, was one day's march ahead.[7] At Rabastens on the 20th, 'all evening we heard the sound of cannon in the direction of Tarbes; the armies are engaged a league from here. There is talk of a battle tomorrow morning.'

But Soult made little resistance and retired towards Toulouse. At Cabanac the 18th heard that 'the enemy rearguard of two cavalry regiments is about two leagues away . . . we may engage them tomorrow'. But they had no action and another long march, lasting over nine hours, to Boulogne-sur-Gesse where the Regiment was lodged in farms around the village occupied by Wellington and his staff. 'I am in a miserable hole and have encountered something new – a disagreeable host and hostess.'

By now they had met the new squadron; Woodberry, who thought Captain Grant 'looks a bit mad', was introduced to his two subalterns, 'the Hon. Mr Dawson and Mr Coote'. They heard that Colonel Murray was at Bordeaux 'and will rejoin the Regiment, to the great displeasure of Hughes and the others'. The newly-arrived

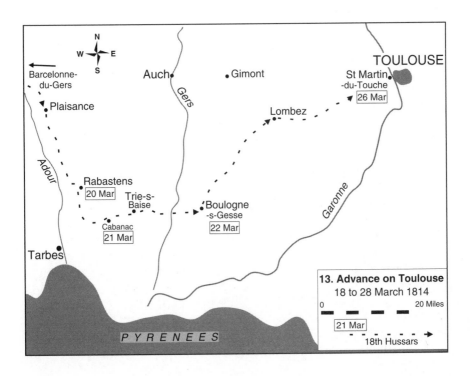

Grant soon 'worked himself into a fury and made a well-earned complaint to Hughes' when 'our Major, in one of his flights of ignorance, today led the Regiment for several miles off our route; he was looking for a house to set himself up'.

Kennedy, wrote again to Grace, from Trie-sur-Baise:

I dare say before this reaches you that the Gazette will inform you of the retrograde movement we have made owing to the troublesome fellow Soult having thought proper to move from Toulouse (where I hoped he had been run to earth) towards Tarbes, evidently with the prospect of drawing us away from Bordeaux which he thought able to effect by menacing our rear.

He has however gone back faster than he came without accomplishing his purpose although he has annoyed our Brigade and the 4th Division of Infantry by giving us a long and rapid march from the Garonne and you may guess how provoking it was to be obliged to come back here without my seeing Bordeaux.

. . . We just arrived in time on Sunday last to witness the enemy's retreat. There had been some skirmishing for two days before but (on hearing of the near approach of the 18th I suppose) the Noble Duke of Dalmatia once more made use of his heels and we are now in full pursuit of his Grace to Toulouse where we shall probably be in 3 or 4 days . . .

I never waged war more agreeably. I am my own commandant having marched with my squadron all the way quite independent. To-day I am appointed to escort the pontoons of the army and am attached to the 4th Division so that I see quite a lot of Sir Lowry who commands it.

. . . On arriving at a village near this yesterday two of the inhabitants (the Mayor and another) actually disputed who should have the honour of entertaining the *Chef d'Escadron*. I was (to use a genteel expression) like a cat in a tripe shop not knowing which way to turn when I decided in favour of the Mayor, from the circumstance of his sister, a very pretty girl, having begged me to stop there, notwithstanding the château of the other was more magnificent. Thereby attending to the advice of the proverb 'Better is a dinner of herbs where Love abideth than a stalled ox when it is absent'. Although not a stalled ox I had a most excellent turkey and a hearty welcome which you would imagine rather a novel circumstance in an enemy's country and Monsieur 'le Chef' (as they call me) was made as much of almost as if Napoleon himself had paid them a visit . . . You can't imagine the various methods the Prefects have taken to rouse the people against us, but without the smallest effect. On the contrary everyone laughs at

200

their proclamations and all those who have been forced to take arms are deserting daily as we advance.

. . . I long much to see Toulouse, which I hear is a fine town. I hope we shall arrive there in time to prevent the fine bridge there over the Garonne from being destroyed; the people here say it is a superb structure.

CHAPTER 19

FINAL DEFEAT OF SOULT

'Gallant and Soldierly conduct'

Wellington now prepared to strike at Toulouse. 'A most careful and elaborate cavalry screen [was] established all round the infantry columns – Bülow's dragoons kept south of the road . . . Somerset's and Vivian's Hussars, on the other flank, sent out squadrons all over the country as far as Auch and Gimont, while Manners's dragoons kept ahead of the main body.'[1]

On 23 March the 18th covered 'seven leagues on the worst roads' Woodberry had ever seen, but he ended the day with a charming family. 'If I ever have the good fortune to have a wife and children, I hope heaven will allow me to enjoy life like the people here.' Next day he was having difficulty in keeping going, 'these forced marches do not agree with me' and his quarters were in 'a dirty and miserable village on top of a hill'. Before marching on the 25th Vivian made 'an admirable short speech' to the Regiment; enjoining the men to be 'brave in action, and keep good order and good relations with the inhabitants'.

As they neared Toulouse Woodberry wanted action straight away, 'I cannot survive more than a day or two and I shudder at the thought of staying in the rearguard'. But on the 28th, 'the doctors have forced me to go to the rearguard, just at the time of the capture of Toulouse . . . They say my illness is the result of exhaustion and cold and that only rest will restore me to health.'

St Martin-du-Touche

As the French withdrew the 18th followed up closely.

28 March

[JH] the enemy withdrew their vedettes & picquets from the front of St Martin-du-Touche . . . found the village barrier'd but abandon'd, advanced thro' it when a few of us in front were saluted by a volley of musketry, & we retired, found it came from a windmill behind the River Touche & from a barrier &c on the bridge, from whence they afterwards kept up a sharp firing, after a long reconnaissance dismounted some riflemen [led by Dawson] . . . received a message to force the barrier, which we did with our dismounted men, charged the French cavalry and pursued them under the walls of Toulouse; we lost two horses by the firing of their rear guard & one by the cannonade which they afterwards open'd upon us.

He wrote to his brother, 'We gained by this action two leagues of ground, and secured what might have cost the infantry a great many men and much time.'

[AK] After about half an hour's fighting we succeeded in gaining the bridge, which we instantly charged, the enemy retreated and instantly galloped off like lightning pursued closely to the very gates of Toulouse when their batteries now opened and checked our further pursuit. It was the most miraculous thing we were not totally destroyed; they allowed us to come close to their guns before they opened on us and the moment Colonel Vivian began to retire showered grape, round shot and shells as must have destroyed our column had the guns been properly directed, so completely did they enfilade us in a broad straight road as level as a floor. We were most fortunate in accomplishing our purpose with the trifling loss of two horses killed and two wounded and only one man wounded. All of my squadron, which was the leading one, of course, caught anything that was going.
   . . . Marshal Beresford and Lord Wellington came up with the infantry and our artillery and the enemy were seen moving out of Toulouse to take up a position on the other side of the Garonne.

Woodberry moaned, 'What a miserable life is mine! To be shut in a bedroom, too weak to ride a horse, and my Regiment perhaps at grips with the enemy.' But on 2 April he heard that he might soon be able to resume active service. His recovery was helped by a quart a day of 'delicious Bordeaux' from the cellar of his billet.

The best crossing point of the Garonne was found to be near Grenade, north of Toulouse; the west bank commanded the opposite side, and woods would screen troops assembling. After dark on 3 April the pontoon train moved forward followed by 4th Division and Vivian's Brigade. By dusk on the 4th, 'the three leading infantry divisions with Vivian's, Manners's and Somerset's cavalry, and divisional field batteries were across the water. They took up a semi-circular position, covering the bridge . . . the hussars pushed forward both across the Ers and up the bank of the Garonne, and established a cavalry screen well in front of the main position.'[2]

It was a 'dark, dismal & rainy morning' when the 18th moved forward to the pontoon bridge. 'Pakenham came up & was very civil'[3] to Hughes whose patrols met no opposition, but 'seized a great quantity of supplies, bullocks &c.' as well as intercepting a courier with 'interesting dispatches to Soult'. He spent the night 'rather on the alert, strong picquets, patrols &c'.

Kennedy told his mother:

> Being senior captain with the Regiment and consequently having the Right Squadron and our Brigade the first to cross the river I was of course the first across and as such packed off to clear away the French picquets who all retired without opposition to Toulouse. On the way we continued to help them to some of their eatables which they could not get away fast enough and no less than ninety or a hundred fine bullocks fell into the hands of Drogheda's Cossacks. A quantity of shirts, cloth etc for their troops also fell into our claws, the former not at all out of the way to some of our *sans chemise* gentry who were considerably put to their shifts in that useful article.

Heavy rain had swelled the Garonne and the bridge swayed so ominously that those crossing later had to lead horses across in single file. During the night the moorings broke and one pontoon was lost.

That day Woodberry felt well enough 'to share the dangers of my comrades'. However, after crossing the pontoon bridge, he had to turn back and stay the night at Beauzelle. Hughes heard that the current was so strong that the bridge would be destroyed and had an 'uneasy night' expecting an attack. Although all was quiet next morning the 18th were ordered back to Castelnau, 'our post being supposed dangerous'. It was four days before the bridge could be relaid, during which Wellington kept in touch with Beresford by rowing boat.

On 4 April Napoleon abdicated, but the news did not reach the south for another eight days.

Success at Croix d'Orade

The water subsided on the night of the 7th and the bridge was replaced, while the next day was spent in moving forward toward the outer defences of Toulouse. 'Soult's *chasseurs à cheval* kept falling back before Wellington's advance on both side of the Ers, breaking each bridge as they passed by southwards . . . no bridge was saved till that of Croix d'Orade, which was captured by a bold stroke of Vivian and the 18th Hussars.' The 5th and 22nd Chasseurs had prepared the bridge for demolition and were 'retiring at leisure' when the 18th came up, flanking the left brigade of 4th Division.

Hughes wrote to his brother:

> the Regiment's patrols attacked the cavalry picquets of three regiments of the enemy's cavalry that were in the villages of St Loup and St Geniès. From these picquets the Regiment killed and took some prisoners. Two of these regiments retired, and formed on the high ground below the heights from St Geniès to Toulouse, and the other retired on the great road to d'Albi, keeping on our flank. . . we charged, drove them from the road; our flank now being much harassed by the fire of a detachment from the 5th Hussars. I halted and detached Captain Luard's troop, with Lieutenant Dunkin, to attack them, and they drove them from the village on our flank, and it was here that poor Vivian's arm was broken by a carbine shot. I then attacked the two regiments who opposed us on the bridge over the Ers, and charged into them, taking 200 prisoners, chiefly wounded, and an officer. My horse 'Percy' was shot.[5] Our loss was only four killed, and one officer, Captain Croker, a gallant fellow, wounded. It was reckoned the best cavalry affair that had occurred, and all the praises which we have acquired have met my most sanguine expectations, and Lord Wellington has been most kind to me.

Kennedy told his mother:

> the 18th has been most fortunate in having had one of the finest opportunities you ever heard of for regaining the favour of the Great Lord

and that, go home when they will, we have completely done away by gallantry in the field any unfavourable impression his Lordship may before have had.

. . . It was about 5 in the evening when we came up with the 15th Regiment of Chasseurs à Cheval within 2 leagues of the town. Lord Wellington was on a height reconnoitring close by and Soult on the opposite side at the distance of about ½ a league from one another. In the plain between the heights we encountered the enemy, charged them through a village where they in vain made an attempt to defend and pursued them at full gallop nearly a league in the very highest style almost to the gates of Toulouse, having killed or wounded or taken almost all opposed to us. Lord W. in the greatest delight all the time exclaimed 'Well done 18th. By God well done.' . . . It is so fortunate that no other Regiment was engaged at the time and it is quite the conversation of the whole army.

And in a later letter:

Never was an exhibition at Astley's more clearly seen than the whole affair by all parties. The French cavalry were pursued for nearly a league as fast as they could go, after suffering severely at length formed near a bridge across the great road in column. It was their great object to defend it long enough to give time for its explosion but all in vain; never was cavalry more desperately attacked nor more completely overthrown and one division was driven back upon another in such rapid succession that they had not time to form and the whole 15th Regiment of Chasseurs was nearly cut to pieces in less than ten minutes. Some Polish lancers who came to their assistance got also pretty roughly handled and horses, prisoners, pikes and standards became our prey – not to mention numbers of killed and wounded which were strewed over the road. But for the barriers they had thrown across the road and the number of infantry they brought down to prevent our further progress, ten minutes more would have brought us to the gates of the town. On a heavy fire of musketry being opened on us, which by the bye it is only surprising did not kill half the Regiment, Sir Stapleton Cotton sent down to order us to retire. He then came himself and expressed his and Lord Wellington's highest approbation of what they had witnessed.

. . . it is thought Major Hughes who commanded will get a lieutenant colonelcy. If so I think I might have some claim (from being senior captain so long) to a brevet majority which is the only promotion I can look for at present and which might be had easily should some kind friend whisper softly in the ear of the Royal Frederick. A majority in

207

the Regiment I have at present no chance of as there are two captains who will purchase above me, therefore the brevet is the only possible step I could procure and could not only be easily had by interest, but may be of the most essential service afterwards towards my getting the rank of lieutenant colonel at some future period. Numerous however and powerful as my friends and relations are both civil and military I have certainly gained but little rank as yet by favour and I much fear am likely to gain as little as the termination of the war will make promotion very slow indeed.

By now Woodberry had rejoined:

The French dragoon who had wounded Croker was cut down immediately afterwards by Sergeant Major Black; almost all the men went at it tooth and nail after this poor devil: in a few seconds his face was completely unrecognisable.

British delight at the capture of the bridge was matched by French fury, 'Soult had to lay the blame for this check on his own brother, Pierre, who was present with Vial's brigade at the moment, and narrowly escaped being captured. He had been offered two companies of infantry to support him and had not accepted them, and he had distinctly been surprised.'

On the 9th Hughes found Vivian doing well and 'most happy in having received a flattering testimonial from the officers'. He also encountered Beresford, Lowry Cole and 'a great variety of generals' all of whom congratulated him 'on our fortunate affair with the enemy'.

Official congratulations followed:

Brigade Orders

It is with the most heartfelt satisfaction that Colonel Vivian congratulates Major Hughes the officers non commissioned officers and men of the 18th Hussars on the conspicuous gallantry and extreme steadiness of that Regiment in the action with the enemy yesterday under the immediate notice of His Excellency the Commander of the Forces and the Colonel feels most happy to learn that he expressed himself in the highest terms of approbation. Colonel Vivian laments most truly that his wound will prevent him for some time partaking of the honours and dangers of his Brigade and he trusts he shall hear by the pursuance of the same system of steadiness of movements and gallantry of execution of their having reaped fresh laurels and nothing will give him greater pleasure than finding himself once more at the their head.

Cavalry Orders

Lt. General Stapleton Cotton witnessed with the greatest satisfaction the gallant and soldierly conduct of the 18th Hussars when engaged yesterday with a superior force of the enemy near Toulouse. The Lt. General's thanks are due to Col. Vivian who with so much judgement and gallantry commanded his Brigade and who was unfortunately wounded at the commencement of the charge. The Lt. General begs Major Hughes, the officers, non commissioned officers and men of that Regiment will accept his thanks for the steadiness, good conduct and courage they displayed on the occasion.

Battle of Toulouse, 10 April

Kennedy described the battle for his mother:

all remained tranquil next day which was passed by the Field Marshal in reconnoitring the strong position of the enemy which consisted in a chain of heights in front of Toulouse (from whence they were distant about 300 yards) strong by nature and rendered as strong as it was possible for the art of engineers to make them, aided by the labour of thousands of peasants . . . forced much against their inclination to work gratis for several months before. . . In front of this fortified chain of heights and along the bottom ran a small river which completely defended the approach to them in front; and in rear of them was the famous canal of Languedoc – the finest probably in the world. The French had of course everything prepared for a most desperate defence. Their position was excellent and in case of defeat they were certain of a retreat into the town, which they well knew Lord W. would not bombard or destroy.

. . . long before daybreak on the morning of the 10th in expectation of the attack we heard all their drums beat to arms, our army was under arms at 5 o'clock at which time the curtain rose and discovered the formidable chain of redoubts filled with troops, probably from 30 to 40,000. Their cavalry was formed on the right which was the weakest point and where our Brigade was ordered to proceed so as to take the first opportunity of attacking the cavalry placed there and thereby endeavour to turn that flank which it afterwards appeared was in a great measure decisive in the fortune of the day. By the time we gained the right flank our infantry were beginning to ascend the heights in all directions under the most tremendous cannonade and musketry imaginable whilst they were unable to fire a shot until they had gained the summit of the heights, even then our artillery could not get into play for a length of time so that the French had every advantage possible without being able to profit by it for nothing appeared to have any effect on our men who steadily pursued their course until they carried their point. I never witnessed anything finer than their ascending those heights.

Their cavalry, which appeared on the right, was charged by our Brigade and we found ourselves opposed to the 22nd Chasseurs and 2nd Schonbroun Regiment of Hussars, reckoned one of the most famous in their service. We soon sent them to the right about taking, killing and wounding a great many and pursuing the rest almost to the gates of Toulouse, by which means we found ourselves completely in rear of the French position.

Towards midday almost all the principal redoubts had surrendered

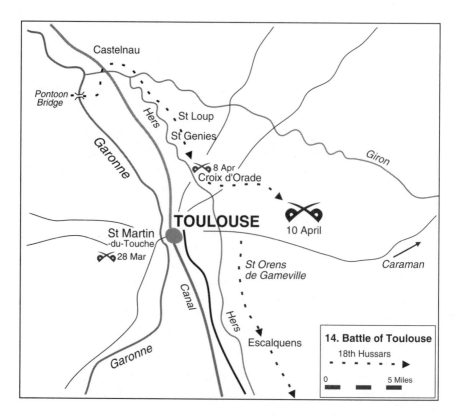

in rapid succession, the enemy retiring into the town. One strong one only held out which would have been taken much sooner, but for the bad conduct of the Spaniards who were employed in attacking it and who, according to ancient custom ran away most valiantly and left the poor 42nd Regiment of Highlanders to be almost annihilated by the superior force of the enemy. They were most desperately cut up in consequence having left upwards of 400 on the field out of 500 and odd that attacked. General Pack who commanded them had three horses shot and was himself wounded. The Fort was at length carried but not till sunset and after a most dreadful slaughter on both sides. Lord W. was most annoyed at the Spaniards and ordered a brigade of our heavy cavalry to form in rear of them to cut down any that might again attempt to run. He was himself at the head of them and was I hear much exposed.

About 2 o'clock it was evident the day was ours, the heights had been carried except this one and the enemy's coaches caravans wagons etc. were all soon flying out of the town in full retreat. . . . I was sent down with a squadron towards the road by which they were retreating to try what we could cut off. The canal however prevented us from getting at them but I had the good fortune to take six boats laden with arms ammunition and provisions and about a hundred prisoners who were endeavouring to get off up the canal, several of them severely wounded. The cavalry had now done all they had allotted for them, we were accordingly halted within gun shot of the town into which the enemy had retreated, and I took the opportunity of visiting the whole field of battle which was one of the most horrid I have seen.

Our loss was very great, but wonderful to say, it is thought that of the French has been greater. 7,000 men and five generals, two killed and three wounded. Passing over the field I saw some men of the 10th Hussars digging a grave and to my astonishment and grief heard it was destined to contain my poor friend Captain Gordon, a most uncommon fine handsome young man. A cannon shot had passed thro' both thighs and he lived half an hour after. FitzClarence was also wounded but is doing well. Seeing our Brigade pursuing the French cavalry they mistook us for French and were coming to attack us when passing by one of the Redoubts they were considerably exposed to fire and suffered much in consequence.

Thus with the close of the day ended the great and sanguinary battle of Toulouse, a day which will cut a conspicuous figure among the many that have been gained by Lord Wellington or what they call him here, the English Turenne. What a glorious termination for the war and what an opinion the people of Toulouse must have of British valour and discipline, for certainly no other troops on earth could have taken those fortified heights defended as they were, and never were troops exposed to a more tremendous cannonade.

Hughes ended the day in posting picquets and lodged for the night in a large château. Next morning Somerset's and Arentschildt's brigades[6] were sent along both sides of the Ers, to reconnoitre along Soult's likely withdrawal routes. The 18th cantoned around St Orens de Gameville and Hughes, having 'unfortunately surprised & frighten'd' him', lodged with the Mayor, where he found 'various pretty & agreeable females' and dined well.

Wellington enters Toulouse

The Prefect and Mayor of Toulouse fled with Soult, but 'the Deputy Mayor, accompanied by practically the whole of the municipal council was awaiting Wellington at the gates, with a band, the city keys on a velvet cushion . . . Unfortunately Wellington, unaware of these arrangements, entered by another gate – whereupon there was a general rush to the square in front of the Capitol, where the ceremony took place.'[7]

Most of the Regiment was otherwise occupied, but Kennedy was there:

> Such a scene as I witnessed yesterday morning I never shall forget. No less than the triumphant entry of Lord Wellington into this town, after the battle Soult driven from all his positions retreated into the town, which was also fortified and after remaining a day to rest evacuated it by capitulation at midnight on condition that our light troops should not pursue till 9 next morning. At that hour Lord W. entered at the head of the cavalry, all the National guards who had been the day before arrayed against us now lined the streets with the Mayor etc. etc. received us with open arms all wearing the white cockade. Whilst the inhabitants in thousands rent the air with cries of Long live the English, the King, and down with Bonaparte. . . . The windows crowded with women clapping and shouting, waving handkerchiefs etc. etc. and absolutely shedding tears of joy.

On 12 April, after confirming there were no French in Labastide, Hughes was told 'to take the Regiment to feel Bazière' and, before

212

being relieved, the 18th 'got several prisoners, posted picquets, had a man wounded', Hughes lodged with the Marquis St Felix at Mauremon, 'he & his family excellent people, arranged my picquets, an excellent supper'.

Woodberry went to Toulouse to find provisions, '*Vivent les Bourbons* echoes on all sides and all are wearing the white cockade.' Women were 'bustling around, cleaning their windows and arranging candles for lighting this evening'. All the windows were filled with pretty women wearing white ribbons waiting for Wellington's entry.

Napoleon's Abdication

On the 13th a letter arrived at Mauremon announcing Napoleon's abdication. Hughes took the letter to show Beresford, 'of course he did not believe it, but he was yet reading it when the fullest confirmation arrived!! Went back to the château & in the presence of a large party announced Peace & the dethronement of the despot, their transports, embraces & the whole scene that follow'd was most extraordinary & striking, a large party dined together.'

On Woodberry's twenty-second birthday, 'What pleasure, what joy to be able to write about the news just arrived from Paris! Bonaparte has abdicated from the throne of France and a new government has been formed! It is peace!'

In Toulouse next day Hughes received 'a thousand congratulations on my success with the 18th' and, after dining with Beresford, 'went to the play and afterwards to Ld. Wellington's Ball, very much crowded, Ld. Wellington accosted me in a frank & pleasant manner'. Woodberry was also in Toulouse with Luard, Hesse and Dunkin:

Each of us bought a white cockade and we dined at an hotel in the square . . . Then we went to the theatre. . . . Lord Wellington honoured the play with his presence and the place was full of English officers. During the play there was a loyal song in honour of the Bourbons at which the whole audience responded with '*Vive le Roi*'. Women of a certain kind thronged all the streets leading to the theatre: their conduct would make their equals in England blush. All the military speak of nothing but the brilliant conduct of the 18th. Our men really fought like lions.

15 April

[JH] dined with a large party at the *Hôtel des Princes*, went to the play, *une demoiselle bien instruit.*

[GW] the shopkeepers, knowing the depth of the pockets of John Bull, have doubled all their prices since our arrival.

16 April

[JH] Called on Sir R. Kennedy, Vivian, Croker &c, rambling, dined at a *Table d'Hôte*, Murray arrived, rode back to Mauremon.

[GW] An old admiral, who is a jolly chap, owns the chateau of this pretty little village (Escalquens). He has paraded all round the hamlet in his uniform with a white cockade in his hat.

On the 17th Hughes 'took leave of the St. Felix's & march'd against Soult, who is not disposed to give in'. Woodberry 'learnt that the enemy was at Castelnaudary and followed the high road from Revel to Castelnaudary, until about half a league from the latter, and confirmed that the enemy had a strong picquet hidden behind a fold in the ground. I went forward to investigate and was hard pressed to escape from three enemy dragoons. After placing an outpost, I returned and reported to Colonel Arentschildt.'

Meanwhile Hughes had 'abdicated to Murray who join'd here & march'd to Mourvilles with half the Regt. Sergeant Jeffs[8] got into a scrape with the enemy in consequence of disobeying my order.'

16 April

[GW] Everyone believes there will be another battle tomorrow, as Lord Wellington will no longer be a party to parley with Soult: he wants an immediate declaration in favour of the new constitution and of the new government. We think several regiments will desert this evening: orders have been given to receive them in our lines.

17 April

This morning Soult agreed an armistice with Lord Wellington and we have been in the French lines to talk to the officers. We evacuate the village and surrounding area tomorrow; the French troops will occupy it. We will withdraw to the banks of the Garonne and stay there until peace is signed.

18 April

[JH] thus I have brought my adventures & the discriminations of my reign as Commanding Officer of the 18th Hussars.

From 'A Château, 6 leagues from Toulouse on the Carcassonne road', Kennedy wrote to his mother:

part of my squadron that was in advance attempted to enter a village and was already engaged with the enemy's *chasseurs*, when the French General Berton, who commands the cavalry, rode up to me waving a white handkerchief as a flag of truce and informed me of General Gazan having just set off to propose terms of some sort either for an armistice or surrender, and at the same time to say he had received orders not to commit further hostilities requesting also that I would order the same; for, (as he observed) the war was now likely to be over in a day or two there was no use in cutting each others' throats unnecessarily . . . I was graciously pleased to withdraw my army the more especially as I was considerably fagged after a long day's march. I accordingly took possession of my present mansion which is so close to that occupied by the foe that previous to parting from the General I felt it necessary to extort a promise from him, that should any orders for the re-commencement of hostilities arrive during the night, he should give me an hour's notice to prepare my legions, this was agreed to mutually and after shaking hands as cordially as if we had been the best of friends I relied on French honour and committed myself to the blankets and although within a gun shot of their vedettes I don't remember having experienced more felicity in the society of the somniferous Divinity.

I forwarded a letter from him to Lowry Cole (whose division we are attached to), informing him also of the *négociation* for the armistice having commenced, and accordingly we have received orders to suspend hostilities also and the army is halted to-day in consequence. . . . The delight of the people at their emancipation from tyranny is really inconceivable; men, women and children almost all shed tears with joy. . .

what a proud attitude England must now assume . . . Wonderful times we live in certainly, posterity will stare a little when they read the history of the present year . . . Six months ago I bet 10 guineas we should have peace (and not with Bonaparte) before the 1st May. This I think I shall win, for by all accounts it must have been proclaimed at

Paris last Sunday when the grand review took place by the Emperor of Russia and the King of Prussia. It is a pity that Lord Wellington could not have been there for certainly no small part of the merit of having overthrown Bonaparte belongs to him.

. . . Even successful as we have been I can't wish to see any more bloodshed. Nine pitched battles and numberless petty affairs have been quite sufficient to satiate my appetite in the slaughtering line, and I don't care if I never see a sword drawn again during my abode on terra firma. The only thing I wish now to hear of would be one or two divisions of this army being sent to America to finally settle with Jonathan, who I suppose will be well inclined now to come unto terms. I must say I should rejoice to see those gentry beyond the Atlantic get a good thrashing and then let the war cease in all quarters.

. . . when you write to Lady Londonderry pray remember me in the kindest manner and return her in my name a thousand thanks for her introduction to Sir Stapleton Cotton . . .should I be fortunate enough to obtain the brevet I might then retire on half pay with the rank of major and receive a large difference; after peace is concluded troops of light cavalry will fetch any price you choose to ask and there will be so many reduced to half pay they will give anything to be restored to full pay again. We have now 12 troops which will be most likely reduced to 8.

Croker rejoined, bearing the scar of his sabre wound, and Woodberry was treated well in a house whose owners' son was a prisoner in England, 'I have promised that their letters will reach him.'

On the 20th they set off back to Toulouse where they found Sir Charles Stewart, 'in the greatest delight & animation of spirits about the conduct & honour acquired by the 18th. He had arrived from Paris with despatches for Wellington'[9] and inspected the Regiment while they crossed the bridge, expressing great satisfaction at their conduct at the battle. 'He told us of the flattering terms in which Lord Wellington spoke of us.'

Hughes 'stay'd in Toulouse, took a bath, where I conversed with two ladies also in the Bath, went home with one; dined with Grant, follow'd the Regt. after dinner, got late to my château'. Kennedy and Woodberry went to the ball given by Wellington, 'There was such a crowd that we had great difficulty in entering the ballroom. Among the strangers, I saw Suchet: he was wearing hussar uniform, with a huge moustache, and a lock of hair hanging down to each shoulder. The Great Lord was covered in stars and orders.'

CHAPTER 20

A NEW WORLD OF PEACE?

April to July 1814

After a sortie 'as wanton as it was useless', the Governor of Bayonne did 'like the rest of the world' and made peace.

> Thereafter the British army took its ease. The Cavalry . . . rode home across France to Boulogne and Calais, feasting off champagne at a shilling a bottle and delighting in a countryside unravaged by war. The infantry marched to Bordeaux to await transportation to England or America, where war with America was still continuing. As the troops tramped the sunny roads of southern France . . . a new world of peace seemed to be opening before them and mankind.[1]

A Month of 'friendship and hospitality'

Woodberry lodged for the next month at Lisse, near Mézin, with a marquis 'of the old nobility' and became fast friends of the family.

Hughes made the final entry in his diary on 1 May, and the 'society' of Mézin entertained the officers of the Brigade to a ball. Woodberry and his host's son, the count, went beforehand to the theatre where, 'until the curtain was raised, Grant and Hesse amused us, as well as the whole audience, by various buffooneries and songs, etc.' Woodberry thought French women 'admirably light on their feet; they have pretty feet and fine limbs' and the men also danced well, 'Some of them too well: you could take them for dancing masters.' Next day he was 'overwhelmed with questions by the ladies; I had to tell them all the details of the fête yesterday, tell them the names of my partners, etc.'

'What a difference with life in England! Here, a man of good family can run an establishment for two or three hundred pounds, which would cost 1,500 in England.' He visited a small property which his 'friends from Lisse would like me to buy'; it was 'quite a nice house, good for a family of eight to ten people, with sixty acres of ground around, price: 1,000 napoleons'.

The Brigade returned local hospitality with a ball, in rooms decorated with laurels, roses and coloured lanterns and a 'transparency' represented an Hussar bending his knee before a French lady. The Band of the 18th was a great success and Woodberry danced the cotillion, with 'several elegant women', but made himself so dizzy trying to waltz that he fell, 'to great amusement'. He hunted several times and one day, 'we put up a wolf, running it to ground with great difficulty. It held its own with the hounds, but the youngest son of the marquis shot it dead.' Next day, during which they found a number of hares, hounds 'wanted to return . . . paid no attention to horns, shouts, or whipping, and just went where they wanted. Dawson and I, the only English there, were very amused.'

Orders arrived for the cavalry and horse artillery to prepare to march to the Channel. Woodberry could not take his 'faithful Sparem Joe to England, which he wants so much' as officers' Portuguese servants had to be repatriated.

On 29 May, Woodberry's Troop, parading with oak leaves in their hats,[2] were delighted to hear that they were to set off home at last. Woodberry and the count exchanged mementos, 'a little bowl in coconut, prettily carved by him' and from Woodberry, a small powder flask. He had no need of tokens 'in order never to forget the young ladies and their mother: their generosity will never be erased from my memory'. Just before they left 'Vitoria' gave birth, so 'I have a small family to move' in a pannier on his mule.

From the Garonne to the Charente

Kennedy left Mézin on 30 May, 'amidst the regret of all the inhabitants, whose friendship and hospitality we had experienced more than a month'. Crowds followed them for some distance 'repeatedly cheering us in the most enthusiastic manner, which was returned by our men. Ladies in tears were to be seen in many directions and some of the men detained by soft persuasion even remained behind with inamoratas and have not since been heard of.'

At Casteljaloux, Woodberry stayed with 'an old officer, who was in the service of the rebels in America and taken prisoner'. His wife, deranged by the loss of a son in the wars, took Woodberry for him and came into his room, 'taking me in her arms and hugging me passionately. I locked my door.'

They marched 'through a rich and well-cultivated country . . . crowded with Spaniards and monks returning home from confinement'. At Langoiran, Kennedy had excellent quarters and a 'very civil landlady'. At Bonnetan, however, 'with no small difficulty, I procured quarters for my troop from a most stupid mayor who had been since 4 o'clock in the morning puzzling his brains to accommodate the Regiment, notwithstanding he had the assistance of his wife and four or five pretty daughters, who all seemed to know more of his business than the mayor himself'.

At Aubie he was 'most hospitably received by a M. Choumeil who, with his wife and daughter (a very pretty girl) were most expeditious in producing all manner of things for supper and most vociferous in abusing the *ci devant* Emperor, hailing us as their liberators'. He wrote to his mother:

> Anything more delightful than the country we are now in and have passed thro' already, it is impossible to imagine; one extensive garden and vineyard. . . . The roads excellent and the weather as fine as possible, rather too hot in the middle of the day.
>
> [Bordeaux] is one of the finest cities I ever saw.
>
> . . . I see by a French paper to say Sir J. Warren has arrived and of course the Governor with him. If in London tell his Excellency he had better come and meet us on the road between Calais and Mantes.

Woodberry had been with the adjutant to Bordeaux, where Duperier was born. 'He knocked on the door of a handsome house where he had lived previously and asked the people who were living there how long they had occupied it. "Nineteen years," was the reply. – "Who lived here before you?" – "A young madman called Duperier who died in England."'

On 5 June the march proper began. Eighteen regiments and horse artillery were in two columns; Arentschildt's Brigade was in the left column, commanded by Vandeleur. With new instruments from Bordeaux, the 18th Hussars' Band could play on the march for the first time since Portugal.

219

Kennedy's squadron reached Châteauneuf-s-Charente, 'The river winds here most beautifully through a very rich cultivated vale. We are two leagues from Cognac, famous for the best brandy in France, and about the same distance from the beautiful château of Charnac, formerly belonging to Chabot's father,[3] and now sold to some brandy merchant.'

Charente to Loire

Marching through Angoulême the Band attracted a large crowd 'who followed us some distance', but, because of the unfavourable picture painted by French officers, 'almost all the best families have left their houses until the departure of our army'. After crossing the Charente at Mansle 'over a handsome bridge' to Ruffec and then Couhé, Woodberry thought most officers were tired of the march across France. 'I am myself bad tempered, as the inhabitants are far less friendly than around Bordeaux. . . It is not unusual here to see the tricolour again.'

After a long dusty march in intensely hot weather they entered Poitiers, a ' handsome town . . . famous for the great battle and victory gained by the British about 400 years ago'; the inhabitants could recount the details 'as if it had taken place in the last campaign'. The public walk was the finest Kennedy had so far seen in France, after Toulouse, but it was so hot that he and Woodberry had to shelter in a café until mid-afternoon. 'The women of Poitiers are extremely pretty, dress demurely and also quite expensively.'

In a remarkable encounter, they came on 'the horse of poor Carew;[4] a French soldier was riding him to his regiment quartered at Rochelle'.

After another 'most hot and dusty march' to Châtellereault, Kennedy was 'happy to immerse my corporeal faculties in the bosom of the river Vienne . . . This place is the Sheffield of France and after dinner we are beset with the clamorous natives particularly women with all sorts of hardware for sale which, although far inferior to the English, they insist on being better and we have no small difficulty in getting rid of the noisy wretches.'

Woodberry thought Châtellereault, 'not only large, but also pretty'. After dinner, 'our musicians played and we danced with some young women from the town', but, 'after the champagne and this impromptu ball, we were very tired. The weather is exceedingly hot and we march at 4 am every day.'

Overtaken by a storm on the road to Tours, they were 'completely drenched to the skin, . . . not disagreeable after the excessive heat and dust we had lately encountered'. 'A few minutes before it broke, the heat was so oppressive that we could scarce stay in the saddle: we could only breathe with difficulty. The thunder rolled around our heads, the lightning flashing all round the column and frightened everyone. At last the rain fell in torrents; the horses could scarcely walk on' (GW).

Woodberry heard Bonaparte was dead, 'I hope not, as I dream of new picquets and patrols: this life of inaction wearies me.'

At Tours, throngs of people crowded the streets and they were 'received in the Rue Royale by the French garrison. . . . Our musicians were a great success.'

[AK] we arrived yesterday on the banks of the Loire, one of the finest rivers in France . . . The country around is called the garden of France and is rich beyond any description. Indeed the whole country from Bordeaux is one extensive garden.

Kennedy thought they were the first British troops to have entered Poitiers 'since the famous victory gained by the Black Prince about 400 years ago'.

The roads are covered with French soldiers and conscripts now returning home; an immense number of prisoners who have just landed from England where they have been confined many years, many of whom (whether well founded or not) complain much of their treatment there. Among the soldiers we saw several very well inclined to cry *Vive Napoleon* and some of them, indeed almost all of them, seem fond of the rascal and go so far as to say they think he will come back among them. I think if great care is not taken of him there will be a disturbance in this country before long. . . . The soldiers seem in general by no means to relish our march through their towns with green boughs in our caps and the bands playing on horseback. The small garrison guard here turned out yesterday on our arrival and affected to salute us with carried arms and drums beating although I have no doubt they wished us far enough at the same time.

. . . I am sorry it should have cost you anything to insert the orders in N. Papers respecting the 18th. Do you think Lady Londonderry has applied about the Brevet for me? One word from Lord C. or Sir Chas. would get it. I suppose you know the latter remains at Paris doing Lord Wellington's duty until he arrives. . . . If the Governor is with you tell him I wrote to Farran to desire him to come and meet us near Rouen . . . remember me to Conolly if in Dublin, and congratulate John on the birth of my niece . . . I hope he and Dix have taken some steps with Curtis respecting the money which is now due as I find neither interest nor principal have been paid although he has joined the 10th and I suppose is dashing away at Brighton as usual.

The neighbourhood appealed to Woodberry; 'if I ever left the land of my birth, it is Tours or the Lisse area that I would choose to live'.

Wellington, passing through Tours on his way to Paris, was 'particularly satisfied with this column, whose conduct has given no cause for any complaint' and told Vandeleur to allow officers to go to Paris. (The right column, by comparison, had 'quarrelled and fought with the locals. Several men have been killed. The most culpable are the Life Guards.')

Excursion to Paris

Across the Loire, Murray authorized Woodberry to go to Paris with Kennedy. Halfway to Cloyes they

> found Hughes, Clements and Luard on the post coach. Knowing that it would be impossible to travel together, as there were neither enough coaches nor horses, we led them to believe that we would stay the night at Cloyes. But, as soon as they had left, we took a carriage and followed them as far as Bonneval, where they were in the middle of dinner. We heard them laughing and making a lot of noise, little realising that we were going to trump them. In fact, thinking that we were behind them, they failed to keep the post chaise: we took it and we arrived in Chartres at 2 am. We went to bed, having ordered a coach and horses to be ready at six.

They passed Rambouillet 'the favourite hunting lodge or rather palace of Bonaparte and Maria Louisa' and the 'Military school of St. Cyr', from which the 800 pupils were ordered by Bonaparte to assist in defending Paris; '600 are said to have fallen on the heights of

Montmartre.' Versailles gave Kennedy 'an idea of princely magnificence' beyond anything he had seen; whereas 'The small palace of Henry 4th . . . and the house of his Minister Sully, one would never suppose had been the abode of such great men.' Their postilion observed, 'they were not very proud in those days'. After Sèvres and St Cloud, they crossed the Seine and could see the Dome of the Pantheon.

'At 7 in the evening we entered Paris . . . The first striking object on the right is the great dome of the Invalides, which has been lately gilt by Bonaparte . . . Passing the new bridge of Jena . . . we saw the École Militaire a fine building situated on the Champ de Mars.' At an hotel near the Tuileries they took 'two bedrooms and a sitting room for a week, all of this for a mere ten pounds sterling'.

Sightseeing

First call was on a tailor who took their measurements for civilian clothes – 'promised for tomorrow morning'. They then sauntered in the Palais-Royale, 'looking at the women and the shops. . . The fashion shops, jewellers, tailors, bookshops, porcelain shops, cafes, public baths, money changers, gaming houses – all come together in friendly rivalry to part a fool from his money without realising it.'

Setting out 'to explore the curiosities of the capital', they climbed 'the immense column of brass' in the Place Vendôme made of the cannon taken from the Austrians, '. . . and from the summit we had a complete view of Paris and the country for many leagues around. . . . The most prominent character here and on every other public work that has been erected by him in Paris is the image of Bonaparte himself . . . it will be impossible to get rid of him without spoiling the appearance of the building.'

They saw the 'beautiful triumphal arch . . . surmounted by a car of Victory the horses etc. all gilt and as large as life . . . brought from Venice by Bonaparte or rather stolen from thence,' and, at the Louvre, 'the finest collection of sculpture and painting in the universe . . . The Apollo Belvedere, the Venus de Medici and thousands of the finest sculptures taken from the Vatican at Rome and all parts of Italy'.

At dinner with officers of the 1st Hussars some Russian officers joined them, 'to the great confusion of the French who were there, in a toast to the health of Lord Wellington and the army which had fought on the same day in the previous year at Vitoria'. The Opera they thought 'inferior to that in London in every respect except the dancing, which is excellent'.

Notre Dame was, for Kennedy, 'an immense pile but containing nothing worth notice' while Woodberry thought it inferior to Westminster Abbey. At the Pantheon they were 'conducted by candles underground to visit the tombs of Voltaire, Rousseau' and went on to the Jardin des Plantes, with its 'flowers and shrubs of every species' and 'thousands of curiosities brought from all parts of the world'. Birds, beasts and 'fish of every sort' were to be seen stuffed in the Museum, while in dens round the garden were many wild beasts including an 'elephant of great size'.

At the Palace of the Luxembourg the 'apartments are elegantly furnished and in the body of the House are deposited all the colours taken from the conquered nations, mostly Austrian and Prussian. The Senators' chairs beautifully ornamented and painted in velvet and the *tout ensemble* forms a striking contrast with the shabby appearance of our English House of Commons.'

In evening visits, Woodberry greatly enjoyed the songs at the Opera-Comique, while Kennedy thought the Theatre Français 'not so large or as handsome as either Drury Lane or Covent Garden in London'.

Full dress was donned for a Royal levée at the Tuileries. 'H.M. was dressed in plain blue coat with epaulettes and broad sky blue sash, he appeared very gouty.' After Mass they viewed the portraits in the hall of the Marshals while waiting to be presented. 'His Majesty spoke to us first in French, and then in English, which he speaks remarkably well.'

At the Invalides, where there were 3,800 wounded soldiers 'besides many officers', they saw the tombs of Turenne and Vauban in the chapel. 'The former is remarkable for its simplicity having no inscription but merely "Turenne", which is a volume in itself.' From the *Champ de Mars,* where Napoleon 'would review 30 or 40,000 men' they walked to the *Place de la Revolution,* 'where the unfortunate king and queen of France were guillotined' and the Tuileries garden.

Time had come to rejoin the Regiment and Kennedy summed up, 'Upon the whole Paris altho' very inferior to London in many respects is certainly very superior in almost all its public buildings which have been much embellished by Bonaparte.'

They briefly visited Saint-Cloud and Versailles on their way back – and were 'amazed' by the chateau of Trianons. 'The elegant pavilion . . . rises like a fairy palace in the middle of the rustic scene of the Trianon.'

Paris to Calais

On 25 June the 18th reached Normandy where Woodberry heard that, a few days after the battle of Paris, a considerable number of corpses were floating in the Seine. They were all French, 'as the Russians and the Prussians buried all their dead and threw those of the enemy to the fishes'.

Kennedy sent Grace his diary of the journey:

> As I find you have some intention of paying France a visit next summer (which I think will most likely terminate as the generality of your projected excursions generally do) in the second week of January or in more plain English in sitting quietly over the fire at Cultra, I think I cannot employ a halt day better than giving your Majesty an extract of my journal since our march commenced . . . relying on your Royal generosity in excusing (from the cursory manner in which it is written) the usual consequence, blunders which are as natural to the Hibernian as the potato which he eats.

Woodberry went ahead to find quarters. At Gournay-en-Bray, they were busy 'scraping the eagles and the imperial arms from the public monuments and replacing them by the coat of arms of the Bourbons', but he feared that 'there will be another change around in a few months, such is the fickleness of the French people'. He dined with the *sous-préfet* at Neufchâtel-en-Bray, who held himself out to be a good royalist, 'he spoke a lot of good king Louis XVIII' and of 'that rascal Bonaparte', but also met 'a lovely young girl' who told him that almost the whole town was devoted to Bonaparte. (When Kennedy reached Neufchâtel he, 'for the first time met with a very uncivil disobliging landlord and consequently not sorry to depart'.)

Woodberry had trouble with the mayor of Blangy-s-Breste, 'a great idiot', and found quarters for the Regiment only after much difficulty. At Abbeville, his host told him that the friendly *sous-préfet* of Neufchatel, 'who I took for a true Royalist, made himself famous during the Revolution by choosing the victims for the guillotine'. He had, nevertheless contrived to be chosen to take a loyal address to Louis XVIII. 'The poor King will do well to mistrust him.'

Next day the Regiment arrived and the officers dined at the Hotel d'Europe, which Kennedy thought the best he had seen in France outside Paris.

They crossed the Somme into Picardy, passing 'the great forest and famous fields of Crécy and Agincourt' and that evening Woodberry enjoyed a coal fire for the first time since leaving England. He and Kennedy then had 'a most hospitable and elegant reception' at the château of the Comte de Mountbrun, where Ney lodged during the preparations to invade England.

They had expected to embark at Boulogne:

[AK] but find we must wait some days for a spring tide as the transports are so large they can't go out of the harbour loaded, although they can come in empty. In the meantime we shall have time to explore . . . this far famed place from which Bonaparte so long threatened John Bull with invasion. On the road . . . we passed the Château de Briquer where he used to reside when here and saw the beautiful column of marble erected by the army to Bonaparte – and having written so far, the route has arrived for us to go to Calais . . . where we go into quarters and are likely to remain several days as the harbour is just as bad as that of Boulogne and we can't move till the spring tides think proper to come and export us to the shores of old England.

From Boulogne Woodberry could see 'the chalk cliffs of Albion, on which I gaze entranced. More than once I had given up hope of ever seeing my country again; but thank God! I rejoice at my good fortune.' After dinner on the 7th the officers went to the theatre, but, 'The production was miserable: I could have had the principal actress for one napoleon.'

At Calais, a parade was held to select 150 horses of the best horses from the two columns as a gift for the King of France of which only three came from the 18th. The officers also set about selling mules acquired in Lisbon; Woodberry's, 'though in much better trim now than then', fetched only fifteen dollars.

He was staying in the mayor's house in a small village, 'there was a meal for twelve, including myself. It was more of a banquet than a dinner. My servant Ipper did the cooking. Immediately afterwards, the violins and the clarinets entered playing and the dances started: they lasted until eleven at night.'

Embarkation began next day and by 18 July the whole Regiment had been shipped across the Channel in sixteen small transports. Woodberry was the last officer to leave:

12 July

it was night before we got every body on board. I put my troop and my horses on transport V, but I fear it is too big to get out of port for several days.

13 July

waiting for the wind and the tide; we have little chance of leaving Calais for a week. Murray, Hughes and the adjutant left last night by the packet. . . . The only distraction we have is to walk in the town: we look at the shops and the pretty English serving women. Almost every business in Calais has an English girl as shop assistant.

14 July

Dr Chambers left yesterday and today I received a letter from him posted from Dover. He tells me that the Regiment will go to Lewes and that Mr D . . . is married. Ah! poor woman, whoever she is, I pity her.

16 July

The wind has changed and most of the ships have left. I am now the only officer in the Regiment in Calais. There has been a disturbance in the arsenal between some men of the 18th and people in the port. I was dining with the Commissary and was not told of it until it was all over. For all that, I have received a severe letter on the matter, from General Vandeleur.

17 July

This morning, early, I found General Vandeleur and explained to him I was not to blame, as the disorders took place on board boat No 611 and I had no command there. But he said I was responsible for everything my men did and gave me a good dressing down.

. . . towards midday we left port and put to sea in a fresh breeze: but, at about four, in the middle of the crossing, the wind dropped, and we remained stationary for several hours. Half of my troop are sick, the other half laugh at their expense. About ten in the evening, the breeze picked up and we reached the approaches to Dover.

But their ship failed to make Dover, and they were taken to Ramsgate, entering the harbour at noon on the 18th, from where they marched to Canterbury.

Phoney Peace

Peace celebrations had been going on throughout Britain for the past two months, but the homecoming for many men had little of cheer about it. As Arthur Bryant described it in *The Age of Elegance*, 'They were recruited from the gutter, and to the gutter they returned. They had done what the nation need and were wanted no more. They were given their arrears of pay – without interest – and disbanded so that the taxes could be reduced. At Chelsea thousands of idle soldiers, awaiting demobilisation, lined streets and lounged before the doors of public houses.'

'There,' wrote Rifleman Harris, discharged after seven years' campaigning with a wound pension of 6d a day, 'hobbled the maimed light-infantryman, the heavy dragoon, the hussar, the artilleryman, the fusilier . . . the Irishman shouting and brandishing his crutch, the Englishman reeling with drink, and the Scot with grave melancholy visage sitting on the step of the public-house amongst the crowds.'

Light cavalry regiments were reduced to eight troops; each had to discharge some 350 men and cast a similar number of horses. But, as Kennedy and Woodberry had forecast, there was soon a reaction in France against the Bourbon restoration. 'The Emperor, brave men whispered hoarsely, would return in the spring with the violets . . . an English traveller was informed that Leghorn Jews were shipping eagled buttons to Elba. The British Commissioner in the island sent a warning to London that something was afoot, the French Government pleaded nervously for the Emperor's removal to St Helena.' On 26 February a small flotilla slipped away from Elba. The Hundred Days were about to begin.

PART V

THE GREAT WAR
FINALLY ENDS

CHAPTER 21

RENDEZVOUS IN FLANDERS

March to June 1815

'Bonaparte in Paris'

On 7 March the officers of the 18th were at a ball in Canterbury when orders arrived for two squadrons to march immediately to London, where the proposed Corn Law had led to serious rioting. After a march of 69 miles – and being 'booed by the riff raff' – they reached London by the end of the 8th. Their principal task was patrolling the streets and Woodberry spent a number of days on picquet in the West End, but with no incidents. On the 20th he wrote in his diary: 'BONAPARTE IN PARIS'. The Regiment heard they were to be sent to Belgium, to 'reinforce the army of Lord Wellington' and on 19 April they set off. Their establishment had been restored to ten troops, but only six were available to march for Dover and Ramsgate.

They sailed for Ostend and Woodberry passed the night on the bridge, with Monins and Luard, wrapped in his greatcoat. Monins was miserable, having left a wife and child at Ramsgate. They marched through Bruges and Woodberry lodged at Oedelem with a widow 'left with two pretty daughters and two sons. . . . She gave me a good dinner, and in return, I offered her two bottles of English beer and a loaf, left over from my rations at sea.' At Eeklo, Woodberry 'could have believed I was in England, visiting one of my best friends, from the cordial reception my host gave me when I produced my billeting order. "Sir," he said, "I am happy to meet you. My house is yours for as long as you remain in this town. I invite you to take coffee with me. Our dinner is ordered for three o'clock; is that convenient for you?"'

Woodberry thought Ghent cathedral superb, 'I had time only to dismount and put my head round the door, but I was astounded by the magnificence of the interior.' Marching past the Grand Palais they saluted the 'unfortunate King Louis XVIII, who stood at the window between the Dukes of Feltre and Marmont, two great blackguards.'

Next stage was to Oudenaarde and Woodberry was finding Flemish 'diabolical'. 'If we ask a local a question, their response is: Yo! Yo!'

'Lord Uxbridge has arrived to command the cavalry: we are all delighted.'[1] The 18th, with the 10th Hussars and 1st Hussars KGL, were again under Vivian; Colquhoun Grant commanded the other hussar brigade, consisting of the 7th and 15th and the 3rd Hussars KGL.

Avelgem and Area

They stayed a week in Avelgem and other villages on the Escaut. 'The champagne is good and at a good price: five francs a bottle. Bread is three times as dear as in England.' Woodberry was messing at Anzegem with Luard and Monins when a Lieutenant Prior arrived. Kennedy's officers wanted nothing to do with him; he had apparently been 'placed under arrest by the Commander in Chief when he rejoined the Regiment at Ostend'. Woodberry and his friends were in a quandary: 'We have asked him to dine today, but we do not intend to make him a member of the mess.' Next morning Prior went out with him, making route maps for Murray, and Woodberry hoped that 'in the future, he will change his ways of doing things'.[2]

Racing began, but just before the start of a race on 1 May, between the 18th and the 10th and 7th Hussars, orders arrived for the Brigade to go immediately to the banks of the Dendre. Bonaparte was reported to be at Valenciennes.

Kennedy wrote to Grace:

I recommend you as soon as you become a reduced gentlewoman on a moderate fortune to come out and live here. We have a splendid dinner of 2 courses for about 18 pence a day. . . . It is certainly a famous country for making war in, some difference between it and Spain.
. . . I should think we shall move forward soon. . . . The Prussians

have already been skirmishing with the French near Givet 16 leagues from hence; and about 5 leagues from this is their outpost, a league from Tournai . . .

I never saw our Regiment in finer order than at present which is a favourable circumstance and I hope under our old friend Vivian we shall do well. There are no troops out here in better order. . . . When you write to the Governor tell him he will be perfectly safe if he comes out here as an Amateur and that I strongly recommend him to do so, if not better employed . . .

2nd May. We go to Ninove to-day . . . where we go from thence we know not but suppose the frontiers. 60,000 Prussians are come up to join us besides the Hanoverians and Brunswick army. Today a heavy firing is heard in direction of Valenciennes supposed to be for Bonaparte's arrival there. . . .

Iddergem

Next day was terribly hot and the Regiment did not reach Iddergem until eight in the evening. ' men and horses were exhausted'. A gloomy silence hung over the crowd of peasants who came to watch them pass. 'The population is really French at heart, and the lower classes, I am convinced, prefer Napoleon to their present king.' Woodberry was comfortably installed with the priest, 'a large, old, good-natured, happy man, previously the confessor of a convent nearby'.

He went to Brussels with Chambers:

we had great difficulty in finding a place for ourselves and our horses at the *Hotel de l'Imperatrice*. After refreshing ourselves, we went to the promenade in the Park, where thousands of people of quality gathered; among them were many foreigners of distinction. I met several of my old friends from England, Lord Arthur Hill, who is the Duke of Wellington's aide de camp, and Lord Greenock, who brought me a letter from Canterbury.

After dinner, they rode to 'the fashionable promenade', where there were 'more than a 1,000 people and at least 500 carriages of various kinds. In the throng I noted some of the royal family, and the Dukes of Wellington and Richmond. The King of Belgium and his chief of staff were riding and greeting all who passed by.' At the Opera,

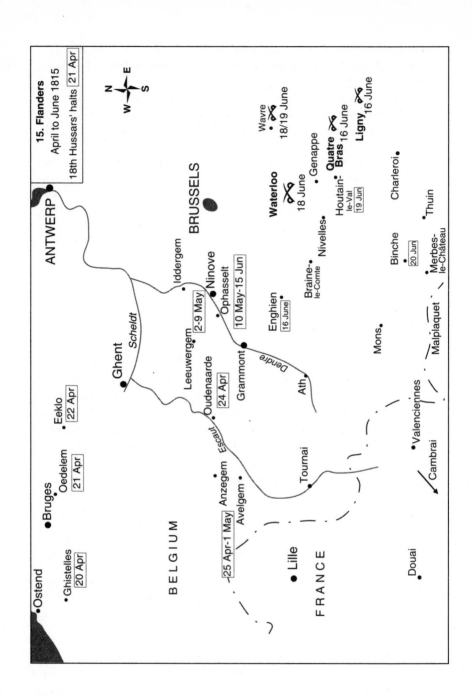

15. Flanders
April to June 1815
18th Hussars' halts 21 Apr

packed because of the presence of the King, he was received by the audience with cries of *Vive le Roi!*

A soldier had free entry everywhere, 'other than the theatre, and even there he pays only half price'. At the Dyle museum they 'saw beautiful pictures by Van Dyck, Rubens, and many other well-known masters'.

> The magnificent Belgian *carabinier* regiment, formerly in the service of France under Napoleon, is in barracks here . . . They are said to be particularly devoted to Bonaparte, and I imagine will cross to his side at the first opportunity . . . their commander Nevers, one of Napoleon's favourite cavalry generals, appears to enjoy the favour of the King. . . . Personally, I would not trust him, and I would not want either him or his regiment in the capital.'

Ophasselt

Next move was to Ophasselt, a village near Iddergem, with 'six to eight decent houses and some mud shanties: nothing in Ireland can give you an idea of this misery'. A division of the Belgian Army passed through, who 'looked to be good troops . . . (but) they are being moved because Bonaparte is concentrating at Lille, and these fellows cannot be trusted in the front line'.

Officers in Brussels were now ordered to rejoin their regiments and no officer was to visit there without his general's authority.

Woodberry relates a story, which could have come straight from *Vanity Fair*. B— of the 10th, had won several races at Ninove:

> This young gallant has carried off a woman who was living with Captain S— of the 16th Light Dragoons. This woman, a widow, had been kept for several years by Captain S— and B—, having seen her recently, offered her 200 pounds a year if she would come and live with him and leave her lover, which she accepted. Captain S—sent his thanks to Mr B— for having taken the woman off his hands, adding that he had done so, moreover, more honourably than could a man of breeding. Some say that Mr S— should call Mr B— out. For my part, I think he acted quite correctly.

A few days later, while schooling his chestnut 'Varment', Woodberry encountered B— on the racecourse and 'his woman, who was watching him exercise his horses; she was wearing pantaloons in the Cossack style'.

Vivian soon had his Brigade out on manoeuvres and on 18 May led them to Grammont, for inspection by Hill: 'all those who saw the Hussar Brigade said it was the best brigade in Europe'.

Kennedy arrested for spying

One day Woodberry rode to see Deane and met the Brigade Major:

> and several others who were dining with him . . . During the meal, a peasant brought a letter to the Adjutant who opened it and, to his great surprise and ours, saw that it came from Captain Kennedy who was being held as a spy by the mayor of Leeuwergem. He asked him to write or come to release him. Kennedy likes to reconnoitre the country and question the locals as to their attitude to the government. Apparently he went into the cantonments of the Belgian troops and was asking the men about their strength and their loyalty to their country's cause: it was then that he was arrested and imprisoned as a spy.

All the cavalry officers gathered on 23 May to watch the Hussar Brigade races. Afterwards: 'we withdrew to a small grove of trees in whose shade the officers of the 10th Hussars provided refreshments at the expense of the Brigade, with a great abundance of champagne and hock. Next day Woodberry watched a review of the two brigades of heavy cavalry by the Prince of Orange. Blücher had been invited to watch, but replied that he was an old hussar and would not go out of his way to see English troops, other than the hussars, 'whom he held to be the best soldiers in Europe'.

Woodberry was scandalized by 'The women in this country' who he thought 'the most shameless creatures; . . . I have seen such scenes in public, on the street, that I am rendered completely stupefied by them. How the women of my country would blush to see them behave.'

Dunkin was sick in Brussels and Moller in his quarters. 'Ellis, just as unwell, will not be capable of active service for some days. Even I had some aches and pains in my limbs and back, but tobacco and toddy have put me right without the help of the doctor.'

Inspection by Wellington and Blücher

29 May

[GW] At eight o'clock this morning all the cavalry paraded together on the plain by the Dendre . . . At midday the Duke of Wellington arrived with the Prince and was received by Lord Uxbridge. A twenty-one gun salute was fired and the three lines saluted. His Grace took nearly three hours to ride through the lines, each one of them being nearly three quarters of a mile long. There was then a march past by half squadrons. It was a beautiful day and there were innumerable spectators. . . . the Duke had Lord Uxbridge on his right and Prince Blücher on his left. I wanted very much to see this brave old soldier: he saluted all the hussar officers. Behind them came the Prince of Orange, the Duke of Brunswick, the Duke of Berry, the Duke of Feltre, the Duke of Richmond, all our general officers and a large number of Russian generals, Prussians and Saxons. I have never seen such a display. Some of them were so covered in stars, orders, gold braid and magnificent plumes that I almost wished to be at war with them in the hope of ransoming even one of the least important.

On the 30th there were more races. Wellington and Prince Blücher were expected, 'but the rain prevented them from coming. . . . There were several matches, but scarce half could take place. . . . At one time there were nearly two thousand riders, nearly all officers.' Afterwards Woodberry dined with Luard, Quincey, and Gordon, 'they made me so fuddled that I fell off my horse several times going home. This is the first and last time that I will get myself in such a state while in this country.'

A familiar complaint went off to Grace:

[AK] Mail after mail comes in without a line from anyone. . . . I saw Lady Emily who looks very well and I think will very soon increase the illustrious house of Stewart, she mentioned having had a letter from you.

 . . . we had a most superb review of all the British Cavalry at present in Flanders. Old Blücher came over from Liege to see such a sight as I believe neither he nor anyone else has ever witnessed. 46 of the finest squadrons of cavalry ever seen were drawn up in a place in their lines, with 6 troops of Horse artillery and a Brigade of Rockets, in all about 6,500 men. The day was remarkably favourable for all the *haut ton* of Brussels to come and see the review, the crowd in consequence was as great as if it had been at Hounslow Heath. Blücher and all the foreign princes were highly delighted and the most handsome orders were issued by the D. of W. expressing his high approbation of the excellent appearance of both men and horses, which certainly exceeded anything I ever saw.

. . . Lady Londonderry has very kindly volunteered to be my post-mistress so you have only to send your communications to her in future . . .

Tell Hugh he ought to visit the Pays to see fine crops; I never saw such corn 9 or 10 feet high in some fields and such quantities of it. I only wonder how half of it is ever consumed. Where is the Governor? He never writes.

The Brigade went out frequently and one day, 'General Vivian showed the picquets the way of working on the ground.' Woodberry was nominated to command the skirmishers and Waldie the reserve ones. 'These are posts of honour and I am confident I will do my duty, when I have to, in a way that will merit the praises of my superiors.'

6 June

[GW] To see the roads leading to the racecourse today, one could imagine that the whole population of the department is there. All the carriages have been requisitioned and one party of the *'beau monde'* from Brussels has honoured us with its presence. . . . It started towards midday with a race for half-breeds, then another for thoroughbreds, both very interesting. Eleven horses ran in the first one, and thirteen in the second. There were also several matches between ponies and mules, which amused us a lot.

In the middle of the fete, there was a violent rainstorm . . . We took refuge in an old house, where refreshments had been prepared. We sat down, about seventy of us, to an excellent cold dinner, washed down by a lot of champagne. It had all been done under the direction of the mayor of Ninove. . . . In two hours, the whole lot had time to eat and get drunk together: I seem to remember that a bad character from the 10th Hussars, standing on one of the tables, set out to break, with a large stick, all the plates and dishes, all the bottles and all the glasses; that the remainder of the company took part in this fatuous entertainment, and that, throwing themselves on to their horses, went back to the racecourse, half of them falling off on the way, and many of the horses galloping to the stables without their riders. The maddest rushed headlong into a race to the bell tower, across the fields, at night, and gave the peasants some idea of the independence of the English Hussars by shouting in the village streets 'Long live Napoleon!' In the last place . . . it either happened or I dreamt it – they upturned two carriages and terrified, in a way giving them hysterics, the women who were inside, in charging their husbands or protectors in a truly cossack manner.

I injured my horse Dick, as well, through steeplechasing; but though I left the saddle three times, I was not the slightest the worse for it.

Not surprisingly, 'there have been numerous complaints to the General; I suppose we will also have to pay for all the damage caused in the area. The mayor of Ninove has declared he never again wants to have anything to do with such a gang of ENGLISH COSSACKS.'

On 8 June Ellis seems to have had a stroke – 'an attack of apoplexy' – and was in bed, unconscious; 'the whole of his left side is twisted horribly'. Soon afterwards he was sent home. Fortunately Hesse arrived, 'in good health and in good humour', to take command of his troop. 'When he left England, Captain B – [Burke?] was serving at the regimental depot, and I strongly suspect this gallant of trying to stay there. The officers have written to Major Hughes, asking him to advise Captain B – that if he does not change posts immediately, his behaviour will be reported to the Duke of York.'[3]

Deserters were arriving from Cambrai and Valenciennes and one day Woodberry saw two cavalry officers from Cambrai. 'On leaving there were three of them, but some leagues from the frontier, they were discovered by a patrol of French lancers: one of them was taken and killed, the other two escaped by the speed of their horses.' In the opposite direction, 'The Belgian troops are deserting in large numbers to the enemy. They are dissatisfied with the reunion of their country with Holland; I fear that the rest will follow their example at the first opportunity.'

A letter arrived from the War Ministry:

To Lieutenant George Woodberry, 18th Hussars, in Flanders.

Sir,

I am charged by the Secretary of State in the War Department, to tell you that a mandate has been sent to the treasury of the army to deliver to you the sum of 164 sterling pounds and 5 shillings, that is to say one year's pay of a lieutenant of cavalry, which His Royal Highness has pleasure in according you, in the name of, and to the charge of His

Majesty, because of the gravity of the wound which you received at Mendionde and for the necessary expenses incurred in your recovery.

I am, Sir, your very obedient and honoured servant.

W. Merry

It was 13 June before there were reports of Napoleon concentrating on the frontier. Outposts reported that the 'whole French Army it appears is concentrated at & near Maubeuge', but during that night, Hill heard that the French had fallen back from there and were concentrating behind Charleroi.

Woodberry came across a proclamation from Soult to the French Army, finishing:

> Aux armes! Le signal va être donné. Que tout homme soit à son poste. L'ennemi est nombreux, mais nos phalanges victorieuses n'en auront que plus de gloire. Soldats! Napoléon guide nos pas; nous combattons pour l'indépendence de notre belle patrie; nous sommes invincibles!

On 14 June Fraser of the 7th Hussars won a gold cup, presented by Uxbridge and 'worth fifty guineas' in a race for the chargers of officers ridden by their owners. 'Each officer will have his sabre drawn and if he touches the reins with his right hand during the race, he will be disqualified.' Next day there were reports that 'the enemy, with Bonaparte at its head, has advanced towards Charleroi'.

'Lord Wellington gives a grand ball in Brussels this evening'[4] to which Lord Arthur Hill had invited Woodberry, 'but it is too far away'.

As people dressed for the Duchess of Richmond's Ball, news reached Brussels that Prussian outposts at Thuin had been driven in that morning. Wellington having ordered the Army to be ready to move, heard later that the French were at Quatre Bras, within 17 miles of Brussels. The cavalry, who had been ordered to collect that night at Ninove, were ordered forward to Enghien.

CHAPTER 22

THREE DAYS IN JUNE 1815

Quatre Bras to Waterloo

'The Cavalry will march immediately from the Left to Enghien'

Uxbridge returned from the Ball and issued 'General Cavalry Orders':

June 15th, 1815 – ¾ past 11pm

The Cavalry will march immediately from the Left to Enghien.

Whatever Brigade arrives first within a mile of Enghien, will choose a convenient spot near the road, to form in column of half squadrons at quarter distance.

The Brigades as they arrive in succession will form in rear of that first form'd.

The Baggage will march in the rear of each Brigade under a sufficient guard.

The Royal Horse Artillery of the Cavalry will also march by Troops independently to near Enghien. Lt Col Webber Smith's Troop is attached to Maj. Genl Sir C. Grant's Brigade. Lt Col Sir Robt. Gardiner's is attach'd to M. Genl. Sir H. Vivian's Brigade.

An officer of each Brigade, and an officer per Troop from the Rl. H. Artillery will meet Lt. Genl. The Earl of Uxbridge at the Hotel Royal at Enghien.

Uxbridge, Lt. Gl.

Such sick as are unable to march, will be sent to Brussels. Horses unable to march with the Brigades will be sent to Ninove.

Quatre Bras, 16-17 June

Vandeleur's brigade arrived before the fighting at Quatre Bras ended, late on the 16th. With them, Uxbridge 'shewed a front and kept the enemy's cavalry in check'. The infantry were replaced next morning with cavalry and horse artillery, hussars in the first line, light dragoons in the second and 'heavies' some way behind. As the last of the infantry withdrew, an enormous mass of French cavalry formed some 2 miles away, but did not advance until 2 p.m. Each line gave place in succession until the two heavy brigades faced the French. Uxbridge wrote later:

> the moment the squadrons of the Rear Guard halted and fronted, those of the enemy invariably avoided a collision, and the retreat was covered at a walk. The artillery however on both sides were occasionally at work, and our Congreves rockets were pitched into them with good effect . . . Thus ended the prettiest Field Day of Cavalry and Horse Artillery that I ever witnessed.

When his Brigade reached Enghien Vivian sent Woodberry to Tournai with orders for the 1st Hussars to rejoin at Nivelles. He covered the 35 miles to Tournai by two o'clock. Exhausted, but not wishing to miss the action, he returned as quickly as he could via Braine-le-Comte, where, 'A party of Belgian infantry arrived in this town . . . the men's only idea was to pillage and the officers watched them doing it . . . I have never seen such a shameful display.' When he reached Nivelles and found the 18th, the town was 'full of wounded English'. By now Kennedy was *hors de combat*, as he explained to his stepfather:

> My dear Sir,
>
> . . . You are indebted for this early communication of our movement very much to my horse who unintentionally so much injured me yesterday as to oblige me to lay up here to-day . . . We had halted between Gramont and Enghien and to avoid the heat of the sun I jumped over a ditch behind a hedge, and whilst sitting in the shade holding the bridle of my horse . . . he thought he might as well be in the shade as well as his master and accordingly sprang over the hedge ditch and all on me, most fortunately his feet came so lightly on my legs only as to bruise them severely and cause them a good deal of pain and consequent lameness which I hope I shall soon get rid of. Had his

forefeet come on my stomach or breast laying as I was, the consequence must have been much worse . . . I am resolved at all events on pushing on to-morrow in a carriage or cart as I should not like to be absent should a general battle take place.

I can give you no certain information of the business at Charleroi having heard nothing to be depended on as yet but the noise of the cannon which we could hear distinctly yesterday evening it being only 11 or 12 leagues off.

James Hughes's father had died on 1 June. Duperier wrote to him on the 19th:

Dear Major,
I have no word to express my sorrow at your late misfortune; philosophy, that of which you possess so great a share of, is in this case wanted, and I have no doubt but you submit quietly to that great 'power providence', who rules majestically every event of this world.

Although, dear Major, that I begin in a way as if I intended to make a long letter of this, if I intend to finish it, it must be a short one, for I am in a great pain, caused by a ball which I received in my head, charging a French battalion with about forty of our men. It would have killed an Englishman, having passed through my scull, opened the scull and out the other side. When I say it would have killed an Englishman it is because he has brains, but you know that I have none. On the 16th inst. we marched from our respective quarters, and made with all speed for Enghien and Charleroi, but the French was too quick for us, and before we arrived, had driven the Belgian troops as far as Abbeville; we had a little skirmishing with their cavalry, but nought came on, and we was forced to remain on the spot until 2 o'clock on the 17th, when they began like fury at us, being determined to pass between us and the Prussians.

We fought bravely; all the cavalry that we could muster was flying about deploying here, forming column there, but all in vain for Lord Wellington received information from General Blücher that Boney with 10,000 of his best cavalry had forced his centre, and consequently forced him after a loss of 14,000 to retreat precipitately a great way.

. . . the aides de camp &c flew in all directions, and by degrees nothing did remain but the cavalry, who being of course obliged to cover the retreat. Indeed Major, I wished you there, it was done in that majestic way which indeed do great honour to the commander; it was like playing at shake here and there, a battalion gone at last nothing before us.

For about three hours the French apparently made no movements, but they being covered by a thick wood we could not see over. In an instant the cavalry fell on us in all sides besides artillery, the rascals began to shout at a fine rate, and fell on us at all corners. It began at the same moment that we went threes about, a most tremendous shower of rain, the hardest that I ever experienced, with loud claps of thunder accompanied with the French artillery, who began sending the shells very heavily among at that moment; we lost only one man. We covered the retreat during a shower, which endured almost half an hour. Then the 10th took over, we was cut off from the main road, and map in hand, we run round by roads at full trot, took up guides behind a hussar . . .

At last we overtook the infantry who had taken position and the French popped at them. But they had gone as far as intended, and stood their ground. We bivouacked in a small wood, and had such a night as we had on entering France, nothing to eat, nor drink, nothing so much as water.

Battle of Waterloo

On 18 June the two armies faced each other across a shallow valley. Between ten and eleven o'clock the cavalry brigades moved out to their positions; Vivian's brigade was on the extreme left of the Allied line, with detachments to the east charged with giving early notice of the arrival of the Prussians. After the battle had raged for some six hours most of the Allied cavalry had taken heavy punishment and Uxbridge had little left but Vandeleur's and Vivian's brigades. At last the Prussian cavalry were sighted and Vivian could move his brigade, followed by Vandeleur's, to counter Napoleon's last advance.

> The arrival of Vivian and Vandeleur at this most desperate moment for the Allies, when, for the third time during the day, it seemed that all was lost, greatly revived the spirits of the harassed infantry. Then, suddenly, and to the surprise of nearly everyone present except the Duke, the end was at hand.

Wellington gave the order for the whole line to advance and 'the sun had just set when Vivian's hussars. . . charged down upon the enemy taking two squares of infantry and a column of infantry in their way'.

Duperier's letter continued:

We remained very quiet on the morning of the 18th, till half past eleven, when it was reported that the Prussians had received a reinforcement of 30,000 men, and was advancing, would be with us by two o'clock. We then began to show fight, and pushed forward in all directions. We manoeuvred a good deal before the enemy, and the guns on both sides was tremendous, a little rain now and then, but nothing to hurt. At three an express came from the Prussians to say that they would be up in an hour, but the roads were so bad that it was past the time they took a position very quick, and began opening a good fire of artillery, but the French stood them well, did not appear the least checked by it, and in a moment opened a good fire on that column and continued so till a second column of Prussians made its appearance between us, and their first, they was forced to give way a little on which the whole army gave three cheers.

Now for the best. Very few of us being in the affairs of Cabinet, all the light cavalry and hussars were withdrawn and put for very few minutes under a hill considerable on our right and entirely under the position of our army, leaving, as we wise creatures usually do, our left flank open. Don't be alarmed, dear Major, it was to make place for 5,000 of Prussian cavalry, who was coming for one thing, and the next, as I conjectured, and I find I was right, to come on step by step on the fleeing infantry, that is the Belgian troops, which I saw of my own eyes, officers behind them lathering away (as the drover did the cattle in Spain) to make them smell the gunpowder. We then took more ground to the right in a column of half squadrons and brought up a movement of echelon our right shoulder and formed close to our infantry close to their heels, and them almost nose to nose with the French. It might be about eight, with the smoke and the view we could not see one another. . . . to pass the time I done like the Belgian officers, every one that faced about I laid my sword across his shoulders, and told him that if he did not go back I would run him through, and that had the desired effect for they all stood it. I must at this critical period inform you that Lord Uxbridge got a ball in his leg which fractured the bone so much that he was forced to leave us, but he done it so well that nobody saw it. I suspected it by his slow pace and his shaking hands with Gen. Vivian.

. . . when Bonaparte found that he was so close pushed, he feebly returned the shots of the Prussians and put all his force on us with himself at the head of his men, promising the whole town of Brussels to plunder if they stood. After a long contest . . . of perhaps half an hour altogether, but at entire close quarters about ten minutes, Lord Wellington brought some little red-coated fellows from where I do not know, I could just see them through the cloud of smoke, who charged, we shouted and the whole of the French army give way that very

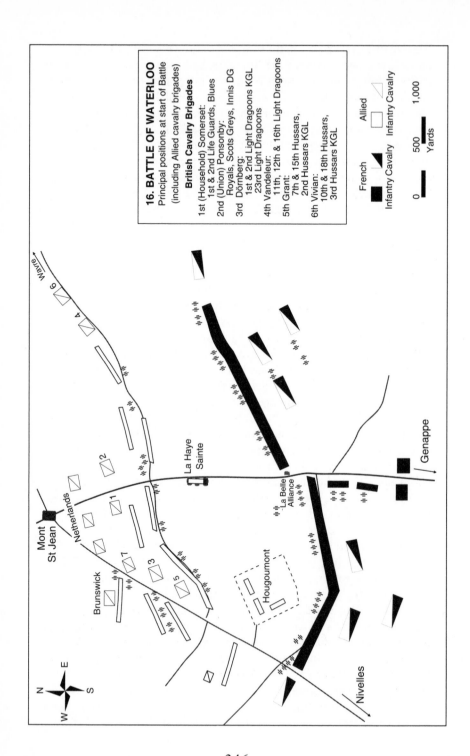

16. BATTLE OF WATERLOO

Principal positions at start of Battle
(including Allied cavalry brigades)

British Cavalry Brigades

1st (Household) Somerset:
    1st & 2nd Life Guards, Blues
2nd (Union) Ponsonby:
    Royals, Scots Greys, Innis DG
3rd Dörnberg:
    1st & 2nd Light Dragoons KGL
    23rd Light Dragoons
4th Vandeleur:
    11th, 12th & 16th Light Dragoons
5th Grant:
    7th & 15th Hussars,
    2nd Hussars KGL
6th Vivian:
    10th & 18th Hussars,
    3rd Hussars KGL

French   Allied

Infantry Cavalry   Infantry Cavalry

0   500   1,000

Yards

Wavre

Mont
St Jean

Netherlands

Brunswick

La Haye
Sainte

La Belle
Alliance

Hougoumont

Genappe

Nivelles

N
W   E
S

instant, the very finest I ever beheld. We charged, and of course overtook them, in an instant we fell on the cavalry who resisted but feebly; and in running, tumbled over their own infantry. From that we came on the artillery, who was not better treated by the Irish lads in their attentions. There was perhaps three 18th Hussars on a regiment of the French, nothing but 'Vive le Roi', but it was too late, beside our men do not understand French, so they cut a way all through till we came to the body of reserve, when we was saluted with a volley at the length of two swords. We tacked about and had the same fun in coming back, but unfortunately the Prussians not coming as soon as it was expected, owing to the badness of the road, too late by about ten minutes we found in coming back some ones that had rallied and to us grate[?] . . . me for one, who got a ball and poor Hesse a broken arm, Machell's horse killed, under him, Rowll's likewise; . . . My grey mare was shot in the first beginning of the action.

You will excuse the irregularity of this, the stooping is too much. I must close. I will write when I get better.

I remain, dear Major, your most humble servant,

H Duperier

Woodberry headed a lengthy account of what he had gleaned of the events of the day: BATTLE OF MONT-SAINT-JEAN OR WATERLOO. So far as his own observations were concerned:

remained in our bivouac till ten o'clock; we left it on the sound of the trumpet. We thought the allied army was going to advance in concert with Blücher's Prussians, but when we arrived at our position (on the extreme left), we saw several strong enemy columns marching to the attack and found our pickets attacked by the French cavalry and pushed back by them quite a distance.

The skirmish lasted until about eleven, the moment when the battle commenced, and which continued until eight in the middle of the most horrible carnage.

. . . At half past ten there was considerable movement in the enemy lines and a coming and going of many officers around one particular place where there was a large body of infantry, which we learnt later, was the Imperial Guard. Bonaparte was there in person, and it was from this point that all the orders were issued.

During all this time the enemy masses were forming up and it was said battle would commence at half past eleven. The enemy attacked the country house on our right with one of his corps shouting their usual cries. The Nassau troops soon gave ground, but the enemy

247

experienced such resistance on the part of the Guards holding the house that they were forced to call off their enterprise, leaving a great number of dead and wounded on the ground. Wellington sent fresh troops who retook the wood and the garden, and the battle ceased on this side for the moment.

We then saw enemy columns advancing towards the centre of our line. There was a silence of the grave: we did not hear a single explosion for nearly an hour. We anxiously watched the enemy movements. The French cavalry, formed in a square alongside the infantry, marched on our centre. At the same time, about two o'clock, a Prussian aide de camp of Blucher arrived from the left flank. . . . He told us 30,000 Prussians were marching to our aid, and shortly afterwards we could see them clearly, but at a great distance.

Nothing can equal the spectacular sight, which the attack on our centre offered. Over two hundred cannon opened a terrible fire upon us. Under the cover of their smoke, Bonaparte made a general attack with the cavalry and the infantry . . . General Picton, who was on the road from Brussels to Charleroi, marched with fixed bayonets to receive the enemy, but he was unfortunately killed at the very moment when the French, terrified by the sight of the division, . . . took flight. Thus departed one of the very best men of the British army. . .

. . . Vivian's brigade had passed the whole day on the extreme left flank of the army; it had not been engaged before half past seven when the Prussians arrived. We then had to cross over to the right and charged the Imperial Guard, the cuirassiers, the lancers and the artillery, blazing a trail through the middle of the whole of this mass until we came up to the farm of la Belle-Alliance, where we were ordered to halt, and where we gave three cheers at the fleeing enemy.

Vivian had placed himself in front of the centre, beside Colonel Murray, in order to put the Regiment in the required direction. He then said, '18th, you will follow me' on which the Sergeant-Major, Jeffs,[1] said, 'By Jasus, General, anywhere – to hell – if you will lead us.' He then ordered the Charge, 'when the Regiment dashed forward with the greatest impetuosity, and at the same time with as much steadiness and regularity as if they had been at field day exercise on Hounslow Heath'.

After they went into bivouac Woodberry 'had a good supper with Luard and I slept deeply after the exhaustions of the day'.

The Day After

At first light the 18th were under arms and at about ten o'clock Woodberry was sent to the battlefield to collect wounded and bury the dead. He found a large number of men of his own troop, 'several of whom had been wounded and spent the night without help, while we were taking care of ourselves in camp. I am appalled that I could have forgotten, even without orders, these poor lads and neglected the performance of this duty.' He loaded them into two carts and sent them to the hospital in Brussels, having given them his purse. He buried twenty-seven bodies.

On his return from the battlefield, the Regiment had left for Nivelles. The efficient Ipper arrived with his baggage, but 'he has lost my bitch Vitoria'.

Thirteen of the Regiment's rank and file had been killed. As well as Duperier, Hesse had been wounded, together with seventy-two other ranks; seventeen were missing.

Kennedy finished his letter to his stepfather:

18th My bruises are better today, excuse scrawl & hurry. French in complete rout. I hobble after them.
20th Glorious and decisive victory.

and wrote to his mother:

. . . I am in such a hurry at present getting on after the remains of the regiment which is to-day beyond Mons in full pursuit, that I have scarcely a moment to write, . . . It almost exceeds credibility that so immense a carnage should have been made in so few hours and it is quite impossible that my description can give you an idea of the field of battle I have passed over. . . . we have begun and terminated (I think) the war completely and Mr Nap. may go back if he can and improve his island of Elba for the game on the continent is up with him. The flower of his army, almost all his Guards, his cavalry in particular (the finest men without exception I ever saw) are strewed in thousands over the field at Genappe. His cuirassiers (certainly the most beautiful regiments in the world) are literally cut to pieces by our cavalry and the road strewed with their armour and coats of mail. . . . Such a scene as the road exhibited by which he fled (for a retreat it cannot be called) I had no idea of. It equalled Vitoria in every thing but riches, but the French officers who have been at Leipzig and Austerlitz say that the battles there were but skirmishes compared to this and the retreat from Moscow nothing in comparison. Our regiment behaved most gallantly and indeed all the cavalry have immortalised themselves . . . We had not more than 7,000 British cavalry, which with Belgians and Dutch might amount to 10,000 against 22,000 of the elite French dragoons . . . The French army estimated at 85,000 in all against our British, Belgian and Dutch only 55,000 strong. It was a fair trial of strength. The two first Captains in the world against each other on an open plain where neither party had any advantage of position and our communication with Blücher's army cut off previously by the French at Fleurus left Lord Wellington to his own resources. What a wonderful man this has proved him to be . . .

I should not be surprised if my next is from Paris.

. . . You may communicate this to your tea table friends etc. I am getting much better and shall endeavour to catch the Regiment at Mons today if possible.

Advance on Paris

On the 20th they went via Nivelles to Binche on the main road, crowded with English, Belgian, Prussian, and Hanoverian troops. 'It was a terribly long march; and there was absolutely nothing to distract our attention, the countryside was absolutely flat with many ditches and not a hedge in sight.' Woodberry 'slept half the way, and was nearly suffocated by the dust and the heat'.

The victors marched into France from Belgium along two main routes. Blücher moved via Charleroi and Avesnes to Guise while the main Prussian columns hurried on to St Quentin. Bent on avenging French excesses in Prussia, they left a trail of devastation behind them. Grouchy, after fighting several minor actions against them, reached Paris with some 50,000 men on 29 June.

More considerate than the Prussians and determined to keep his forces under control, Wellington marched more slowly through Nivelles and Maubeuge. The fortresses of Cambrai and Péronne had to be assaulted, but surrendered without offering too much resistance. Wellington had issued a proclamation to the French nation on the 21st saying that he was entering France with a victorious army, not as an enemy, but to help the French to shake off the yoke of iron that crushed them. The possessions of those who followed Napoleon would be sequestered.

Vivian, who had been wounded in the ankle, was following his Brigade in a closed wagon into France. The 18th camped near Malplaquet, where a large farm had been reserved for the officers and Woodberry confessed:

> We romp'd it completely . . . one of these individuals had the audacity to tell us that he had expected to be protected by the English army and that he found us, on the contrary, to be worse than the Cossacks . . . after we had crossed the frontier, my heart bled for these unfortunate peasants: their harvest, which offered such good promise, has been wilfully destroyed by the Prussians, the Hanoverians, the Belgians, and I am ashamed to say, by the English. We received complaints, but replied that they had to thank their Emperor for all their misfortunes. They say . . . it is the fault of the army; that Napoleon would never have left Elba if the army had not insisted on having him back. . . . We had some good lambs at this farm and paid the farmer one franc apiece, when he was asking twelve. We gave nothing for chickens and pigeons, and nothing for the beer, which we had for the whole Regiment. The men had marched a long way; they were tired and thirsty and got through three tuns.

On the 22nd they marched for le Cateau-Cambrénsis, 'having said farewell to the poor people of this farm, who whole heartedly called down curses on us'. Woodberry, on picquet duty, was out at daybreak on the 23rd to patrol to Brancourt, where the French were thought to have a picquet only to find that they had left. The day before there had been 450 cuirassiers, whose general dined with the mayor before leaving. 'I followed his example.' The British army halted for a day's rest and the 18th could hear cannon fire, probably from Cambrai, which was taken on the 25th. Woodberry wrote to Duperier 'who is in bed in Brussels, seriously wounded; I included a bill for ten pounds sterling. The brave fellow is thought to be dangerously wounded. . . my friend Hesse is getting better.' Recalled to the Brigade, he went through several villages razed to the ground; 'I cannot recall such miserable hovels in any of my travels.'

Second Abdication

News came of Napoleon's abdication. 'Never, since the famous day at Poitiers, has the pride of France been so completely humiliated by

251

English arms. If only this last victory could serve to assure the peace of the world for centuries to come.'

On 2 July Kennedy wrote to his mother:

I thought myself almost awake from a dream when at sun rise yesterday I saw the dome of the Invalides and Mont Pantheon of Paris, Montmartre distant only 3 miles. I could scarcely help exclaiming 'How are the mighty fallen' when I found it was not a dream but that the man who this day fortnight advanced with so much confidence at the head of 150,000 of the finest looking troops in the world, apparently certain of entering Brussels triumphant, should on this day be himself hunted to his usurped capital and like a fox after a hard day's chase completely run to earth, from which I trust we shall dig him out before many days elapse . . . I think it most likely before to-morrow we shall enter the city. The heights on this hill are strongly fortified with upwards of 300 pieces of cannon and Montmartre appears quite a second Gibraltar. Old Blücher however has crossed the Seine in two places with his Prussians who have been heavily cannonading all yesterday evening in the direction of Versailles. The British army are closing fast round this side of Paris and by to-morrow we expect 40,000 Bavarians up from the Rhine so that the 80,000 gentlemen who are said to be enclosed in the walls of Paris must shortly surrender or be destroyed with their capital, which the Prussians have resolved on pillaging should they attempt to hold out. Lord Wellington's head quarters are about four miles from this at Genappe and flags of truce are continually passing through here from the enemy with proposals but I believe none will be accepted but the unconditional surrender of Bonaparte's person; should he escape with his life . . .

It is impossible to give you an idea of that part of our march which the Prussians have already passed through; the inhabitants almost everywhere fled and their houses and villages converted into complete deserts. If all the other allied troops follow the same system there must be a famine here next year, thousands of people along our line of march must be completely ruined and one would be inclined to pity them did we not reflect that the French army have done the same thing wherever they have yet been. In short Bonaparte after having scourged the rest of the world has been reserved to be the scourge of the French nation.

. . . I am happy to say the 18th behaved most admirably. Sir H. Vivian after the battle told the Regiment they had even exceeded his expectations and he issued the most flattering orders in consequence. Several regiments have been nearly destroyed. Our loss is about 100 killed and wounded, two officers only wounded.

For some days after the Battle the rain continued. We were obliged to halt a day at Cateau until Valenciennes, Cambray and Mauberge were invested and on the 25th we reached St. Quentin, the 27th Compiegne, the 29th Senlis where we overtook old Blücher's army. He pushed on by St. Denis and crossed the Seine near Versailles where he now is so that we have Paris now nearly invested. I hear the Prussians have totally destroyed the finest Porcelain manufactory in the world at Sevres near Versailles. This will be good news for the English manufacturers; in short they have spared nothing wherever they have been. The crops of corn, all nearly ripe, have of course suffered in no small degree and in short France is ruined and not impossible but the Coup de Grâce will be the burning of Paris.

July 1st. I had got so far when the news of an armistice arrived, the abdication of Bonaparte you of course know of . . .

I am to-day at the outposts with my squadron close under the heights of Montmartre and Belleville near the forest of Bondey . . . where the enemy's advanced picquets are also placed. . . . I am on Picquet in a most splendid château, *sans* windows doors or furniture like the rest of the châteaux of this devastated country, literally *sans* everything that could be carried away or destroyed; for what the Prussians left undone the Belgians have finished. . .

5th July. The business is nearly over, a capitulation has been signed and we expect orders every hour to enter Paris. The troops have orders to make clean for the occasion and to put green boughs in our caps; we are to pass the Duke in review, I believe, on the famous Champ de Mars so that we shall have a Champ de July instead of de Mai! The town of St. Denis is given up to our troops and by the day after to-morrow all the scattered remnants of their army will be on the Loire where I dare say they will be ordered to ground their arms. . .

You cannot think how high the English rank among the few inhabitants we have yet met. On entering the town of Senlis, where the Prussians had been the day before, their shops and houses close shut but on finding we were English, instantly the town crier went about desiring everyone to open their houses to receive the English, the white flag was displayed and numbers of well dressed ladies distributed fleurs de lys to all the troops hailing us as their liberators.

CHAPTER 23

PARIS

July 1815

Lodging with a Princess

July 8th Château de Sausne near St. Cloud.

[AK] We have just arrived here, a most delightful village on the Seine close to St. Cloud and a league from Paris. I am in hopes we shall remain some time, as I was never put up more to my satisfaction. I occupy the country house of the Princess Montmorency Vaudimet, a most excellent establishment of servants and famous feeds, the finest view of Paris St. Cloud and all the course of the Seine for many miles, you can imagine. My Hostess lives in Paris at present, I hear entertains Lord Castlereagh and Talleyrand to-day, whilst she entertains in the country the next greatest personage! Lord Castlereagh passed through Bouget yesterday and he and the Duke entered Paris to-day.

9th Louis entered yesterday amidst cries of *Vive le Roi*, the tri-coloured cockade was universally worn in Paris at 11 o'clock, at 3 the white had universally replaced it, what an extraordinary weathercock nation.

He wrote to Grace on the 12th:

Lord Castlereagh arrived in good time just as we were taking posses-sion of Paris . . . I have called and left my name at his hotel, but he is so busy as you may suppose there is no seeing him. The Emperors of Russia and Austria and the King of Prussia are also come . . . They have all got hotels close to Wellington who seems to be the Polar star among them. We expect a grand review of our cavalry in a day or two by these aforesaid big wigs, who testified a wish to that effect I hear. Well they may wish to look at the British troops for they have saved them many broken heads and have accomplished in our day what they have been all trying to do this 20 years. Never was a nation so completely humbled as this. . . . You can't think how their tone is altered and how completely abased the rascals all appear whilst on the other hand the high admiration they hold the English in is not to be told. The Prussians they hold in abhorrence and I think they will have some reason for doing so before all is over with them.

I am most comfortably fixed at a beautiful village near St. Cloud in the country château of the Princesse Vaudimet. She has a house in Paris also, and servants and establishments at each. She is too happy to have me there to prevent the Prussians pillaging her house and I live in the most splendid style you can possibly imagine. Two courses every day and nothing but the finest Madeira and Claret, so that I don't care if the war lasts a little longer at this rate. She and her friend the Countess of Jarnac (Chabot's mother dines with me there to-day and I have some idea, as she is a widow, of proposing for Her Highness! I don't know how it is I am always stumbling over a Princess somehow.) It would really make you faint to see the style I keep up. As a particular mark of my esteem I have [made] room in my stable to-day for her coach horses. This was being more civil than the Prussians who carried off her cows the day before we came and about 300 bottles of her wine.

To-morrow we march into the Tuileries to do duty for the day, we take it by regiments turn about. . . . I saw Blücher a few days ago. Old Louis arrived on Saturday and on Sunday I saw him go in state from the Tuileries to Notre Dame to say his prayers.

I am anxious to hear some further intelligence of poor unfortunate Tom.[1] What an extraordinary unaccountable proceeding. . . .I saw Lowry Cole yesterday who was speaking to me about it, but knew nothing more certain than he was supposed to be going to America with some woman that he was ashamed of. It was really a melancholy business and shews in the strongest light the dreadful effects of a young man getting into low and bad company without anyone to direct him. I trust it may not turn out worse than it at present appears.

Excuse hurry as I am just going to dine with my hostess. Don't be surprised if I become a Prince ere long, more unlikely things have happened I can tell you.

Forage was increasingly scarce and the Allied garrison of Paris was reduced. 'The Guards only are to occupy Paris in conjunction with the Guards of Prussia, Austria and Russia.' The 18th moved into Picardy and Kennedy told his mother, 'It was quite a tender separation between the Princess and her guest, I assure you, and I have promised to correspond with her.'

256

Dining with the 'Greatest Men in Europe'

[AK] The day before we marched she had Prince Metternich the Austrian ambassador, the Duke d'Alberg the French minister, Prince Louis of Austria and the last not least in roguery the famous or rather infamous minister of Police Fouché, Duke of Otranto, to dine with me! The latter is again very high in favour at Court having been the President of the Provisional Government and the principal person in making Bonaparte abdicate; in short they attribute the salvation of Paris to him and he is now as great a man with Louis as he was formerly with Bonaparte. My curiosity to see a man who has acted so conspicuous a part in the great drama of the revolution was as you may suppose rather great and it was highly gratifying to meet two such opposite characters as Fouché and Metternich. The latter is a very gentlemanlike man not unlike Lord Castlereagh whereas the former is the most villainous looking fellow you ever saw but at the same time contains something in his ugly visage denoting great talent. You of course know his character; he is the most complete spy in France and as such may, if he is faithful, be of great use to the King. I had a good deal of conversation with Metternich and after dinner by way of amusement he got a pen & ink & was quizzing Fouché about Bonaparte. He drew up a sort of ridiculous form of abdication for the ex-Emperor which he made Fouché sign and as a witness I put my name to it which I daresay he will shew Lord Castlereagh the first time they meet. I think they will be rather surprised to find my name to a paper under those of the two greatest men in Europe. It amused the Princess extremely.

I suppose you have seen the account of our famous review. . . . We were drawn up on the road from Paris to Neuilly and passed by the sovereigns by half squadrons in the Place Louis Quinze, on the spot where Louis 16 was guillotined! It was one of the finest sights ever beheld at Paris I believe and you have no idea of the crowd that came over to see it. . . The Emperors all wore the Order of the Garter on the occasion. But by far the most splendid as you may suppose amongst the rich dresses was his Lordship of Stewart, absolutely one sheet of stars and lace. The Prince of Orange came up from Brussels for it. He marched past and saluted with his arm in a sling, as he has not yet recovered his wound.

Still No Promotion

His letter continued with further agonizing over his lack of promotion. His accident meant that, although the senior captain, he was not eligible for one of the traditional promotions after a major victory. A brevet majority went to one captain in each regiment, usually the most senior present, but in the 18th Wellington gave it to the second senior, Grant:

> passing over Croker who was the eldest so that I suppose had I been there I should have gained nothing by it. Grant had been in India with him, which I believe was his reason for recommending him.

Both Croker and Kennedy sent 'memorials' to Wellington, in Kennedy's case pointing out the accident which prevented his being on the field, but, 'He is such a positive man in everything he does that I fear neither of us have any chance of success.' He was therefore relying on private approaches to the Duke of York through Castlereagh or Stewart:

> [AK] You need not say anything of this to anyone, I mean of my having memorialised, till you hear further from me on the subject. Col. Murray and General Vivian have backed my memorial the latter in very handsome terms but I know it will have no effect on the Duke of Wellington whatever it may have on the Duke of York if Castlereagh presents the memorial.

Prize Money

Vivian's Brigade had captured some sixty French horses at Waterloo. Some of the proceeds were used to buy the trumpet-major in each regiment a silver trumpet. On that of the 18th is inscribed 'Purchased by desire of the soldiers of the Eighteenth Hussars, with part of the prize money arising from the enemy's horses captured by their brigade, under the command of Major-General Sir Hussey Vivian, KCB, etc, at the battle of Waterloo, 18th June, 1815.'[2]

Napoleon had been exiled to St Helena on 7 August, but it was 20 November before the second Treaty of Paris was signed. A month earlier Wellington had been appointed Commander-in-Chief of the Allied Army of Occupation.

POSTSCRIPT

Honours and Awards

In 1815 the campaign honour 'Peninsula' was granted to eighty-six regiments including the 18th, for service between 1809 (after Wellington returned) and 1814. The battle honour 'Vittoria' was awarded to forty-seven regiments between 1816 and 1832, and two more in 1890. Not surprisingly, perhaps, the 18th were not amongst them. However, neither they nor the 10th were recognized for their presence at any of the other battles of the campaign. 'Orthes' and 'Toulouse' were awarded to some cavalry regiments, but not the 18th. Individuals fared better when a General Service Medal was introduced in 1848 and bars or clasps were awarded retrospectively for 'Sahagun and Benavente' (79), 'Nivelle' (28), 'Nive' (5), 'Orthes' (69) and 'Toulouse' (124). Waterloo was a different matter. As well as the award of the Battle Honour to the Regiment, all 'Waterloo Men' received a medal and subaltern officers and men were credited with two years' service.

'Whatever happened to—?'

James Hughes

Awarded a CB in 1815, Hughes was a Lieutenant Colonel by army rank from 1817 and a Colonel in 1837. He also received the gold medal with gold clasps for Orthez, Toulouse and Vitoria. In 1841 he married Fanny Anna Jane, daughter of the Hon. Francis Stanhope. There were no children and he died in Florence in November 1845.

Arthur Kennedy

In December 1815 Kennedy was still writing to his mother, from France, about promotion. After reminding her of various relations and contacts she could pursue he asked her to tell his sisters that he would reply to their letter 'when we get settled and that I can bring my thoughts to any other subject than this cursed promotion which at present engrosses my attention'. Through his own or his mother's efforts he received a Brevet majority dated from 4 December 1815. He became a lieutenant colonel in the Rifle Brigade and in 1837 married a widow, Mabella Hamilton-Jones, daughter of Major Charles Hill of Bellaghy Castle. They had three daughters, one of whom, Elizabeth, married Sir Anthony Weldon, the fifth baronet. Kennedy died in 1855 at Hollybrook, Randalstown.

George Woodberry

Efforts to find any trace of Woodberry's family, or of his life after leaving the 18th, have so far drawn a blank. Army Records show his having haled from Worcester (to which his diaries refer several times), but there were no Woodberrys recorded in the 1851 Census for Worcestershire. His name was no longer on the Army List in 1819.

Some of the others

Castlereagh succeeded as Marquis of Londonderry in 1822 and, on his death, his half-brother, *Charles Stewart* became the third Marquis. He became a general in the Army and held numerous public appointments before dying in 1854.

Loftus Otway CB, was knighted by the Spanish and became a lieutenant general in the British Army; he also died in 1854.

Henry Murray, awarded a CB after Waterloo, was promoted General in 1855.

Charles Hesse was claimed as one of his most intimate friends by Gronow in his *Reminiscences,* and said to be a son of the Duke of York 'by a German lady of rank', but Malet refers to his father as a Prussian banker. After being badly wounded at Waterloo he left the Regiment the following year. Amongst ladies with whom he was said to have attachments were Princess Charlotte and the Queen of

Naples. He died from wounds in 1832 after a duel with Count St Leon, a natural son of Napoleon.

Disbandment

The 18th Hussars remained with the Army of Occupation until November 1818, but survived only three more years before being disbanded in a general reduction of the Army. 'On the 22nd of December, 1821, heart-broken it seems, at the loss of his Regiment, died Field Marshal Charles, Marquess of Drogheda, KP, the Colonel of the Regiment.' At the time of disbandment Murray, Hughes, Luard, Clements, Kennedy, Duperier, Chambers, Deane, Quincey and Pilcher were still shown in the Army List as officers of the Regiment.

When Napier published his *History of the War in the Peninsula*[1] Sir Hussey Vivian, by then Master-General of the Ordnance, wrote to him about the actions at St Martin-du-Touche and Croix d'Orade. He finishes:

> I cannot conclude this letter without embracing the opportunity (and I rejoice in being afforded it) of speaking of my gallant friends, the late Eighteenth Regiment of Hussars, as in my estimation they justly merit being spoken of. For many years this Corps had been well-known to me, having myself commanded a regiment in the same Brigade with them under Lord Paget at Ipswich. At the conclusion of the Peninsular War I was appointed to the command of a Brigade of which they formed a part. Prior to the Battle of Waterloo they were again placed under my orders, and continued so during the whole time the army of occupation remained in France. I can truly say a more cheerful, willing, and braver body of men it never was the good fortune of any officer to command. Collectively I valued and admired them as soldiers; separated, I esteem them as men and friends, and I trust and hope that should this letter ever meet the eyes of any of them, they will do me the justice to believe that the feelings I have now expressed will cease only with my existence.

Resurrection

In 1858 Lieutenant Colonel Knox (from the 15th Hussars) was ordered to re-raise and command the Eighteenth Hussars. Ten years later Captain Harold Malet prepared *Records of the 18th* Hussars, regretting that he was 'unable to produce more perfect annals', but in 1907 he produced *Memoirs of the Eighteenth Princess of Wales' Own Hussars*. A 'fortunate chance', had enabled him to use 'unpublished diaries and letters, penned by officers of the Regiment during the wars in the Peninsula and Netherlands. They comprise a diary (partly in cipher and partly in French and English), as well as letters, all written by the officer in command, also a diary and letters written by one of the senior captains and by a subaltern during the same eventful period. Not much use had evidently been made of these, as for the most part the sand of the Peninsula was still adhering to them.' The subaltern was Woodberry and the only one of his original diaries now known to exist is the first – that turned up in a 'junk shop' in the 1950s.

The 'Waterloo Trumpet', which had been presented to Vivian at disbandment, returned to the Regiment in 1880:

> On the 10th September, 1821, the day on which the Eighteenth Hussars were disbanded, this trumpet was presented to Major-Gen. Sir Hussey Vivian, KCB. Having commanded them upon many glorious occasions, they offer to him this memorial of the last victory it was their fortune to be led by him, as an assurance that while he gained their admiration as a soldier, he secured their lasting and unfeigned esteem as a friend, and in the hope of living in his recollection and estimation, when they have ceased to exist as a corps. On the 10th September, 1880, the fifty-ninth anniversary of the disbandment of the old Regiment, this trumpet was very generously entrusted by Charles Crespigny, second Baron Vivian, to the care of the Eighteenth Hussars, believing that in this record of glorious deeds the memory of his father, who led the Regiment to victory on many occasions, will ever be cherished in the corps whose admiration he secured.

After service in the South African War the 18th were in France and Flanders throughout the First World War and then another Army of Occupation, before returning to India. When the 'Geddes Axe' fell across the services they were summoned home for amalgamation with the 13th Hussars. Yet another economy drive finally saw '18th' disappear from the Army List in 1992, when the 13th/18th Hussars amalgamated with the 15th/19th Hussars to form The Light Dragoons. That Regiment, however, looks back proudly to the history, traditions and honours of each of its forebears – and long may it continue to do so.

NOTES

Introduction

[1] They were raised from Drogheda's home at Moore Abbey, Co. Kildare.

[2] The official title remained 'Light Dragoons (Hussars)' for many years.

[3] Known as a 'busby' from about 1850, after a cap-maker of that name.

[4] Wellesley had exchanged into the 18th from the 41st Foot in 1791, as a lieutenant, but did not serve with the Regiment before he obtained a captaincy in the 33rd Foot three years later.

[5] Castlereagh was then Minister of War.

[6] 400 strong, of whom only 180 had horses; it had been thought that horses could be obtained locally, but that was soon found to be impracticable.

Chapter 1

[1] Each was paid an allowance to carry them and their children home – for most that meant Ireland.

[2] He was 'without equipment of any kind, either for the carriage of the light baggage of regiments, artillery stores, commissariat stores or any other appendage of an army'. Moore to Castlereagh from Lisbon, 9 Oct 1808.

[3] The three other regiments of hussars: 7th, 10th and 15th.

[4] Villa Viçosa had at one time been the seat of the Dukes of Bragança.

[5] All Saints' Day.

[6] At Espinosa de los Monteros.

[7] 15 November. Maurice J.F. (ed.) (1904), *Diary of Sir John Moore*.

[8] Moore to Frere from Salamanca, 27 Nov 1808.

[9] Malet, *Memoirs of the XVIIth Hussars*, p. 25. (The original is not with the Kennedy letters held by Sir Anthony Weldon).

Chapter 2

[1] Carola Oman (1953), *Sir John Moore*, p. 559.

[2] Letter to Baird, 6 Dec 1808 (James Moore, *A Narrative of the Campaign of the British Army in Spain 1809*, p. 149).

[3] Making use of the carbines with which light dragoon and hussar regiments were equipped.

[4] Diary of Captain Edward Hodge (7th Hussars) during the Corunna Campaign, October 1808–March 1809.

[5] The dispatch also gave the full disposition and immediate plans of the Army of Spain.

[6] Gordon A (1990), *A Cavalry Officer in the Corunna Campaign 1808–1809, The Journal of Captain Gordon of the 15th Hussars*, Worley, p. 86.

[7] Oman, *A History of the Peninsular War*, Vol I, p. 532.

[8] Lord Paget's brother, Edward, commanded the Reserve Division.

[9] Wylly, H.C., *XVth (The King's) Hussars 1759 to 1913*, Caxton, p. 155.

Chapter 3

[1] Fortescue, Sir John, *History of the British Army, 1899–1930*.

[2] Manuscript Journal of Sir John Slade, (Wylly).

[3] PRO WO12 Muster Roll for 1808.

[4] Oman Vol I, p. 547.

[5] Napoleon was in the area that night. See David Chandler's Appendix to *Dictionary of the Napoleonic Wars*: 'Napoleon's Military Movements'.

[6] Oman Vol I, p. 548.

[7] Gordon, *A Cavalry Officer in the Corunna Campaign*, p. 137.

[8] Charles Stewart quoted by Malet, *Memoirs of the XVIIth Hussars*, p. 28.

[9] Gordon, pp. 148–9.

[10] Oman, Vol I, p. 570.

[11] Gordon, pp. 180–4.

[12] To an unknown correspondent.

[13] Gordon, p. 200.

Chapter 4

[1] Gordon, p. 207.

[2] Not a little effort had to be made to obtain the reward money; amounts due from a seizure in 1801–2, of 325 gallons of 'Geneva', were still being argued about in 1811.

[3] Malet, p. 32.

[4] Following King George III's permanent incapacity from porphyria, the Regency Bill had been passed in February.

[5] The Dukes of York, Kent, Cumberland and Cambridge.

[6] An elaborate centre piece in silver-gilt of which the base panels included two relief presentations of hussars in action: 'presented to Lieutenant-General Lord Paget by the Prince Regent, by H.R.H. The Duke of Cumberland, and

the inscribed officers of the Hussar Brigade who served under his Lordship's command in token of their admiration of his high military acquirements and of the Courage and Talent constantly displayed by him in leading the Hussars to Victory during the Campaign on the Peninsula in 1808'.

[7] Murray and James Hughes had served together as cornets in the 16th Light Dragoons, Hughes then being the senior by a month. However, Murray obtained his majority in 1807, probably by purchase; Hughes had to wait until 1812, after Oliver Jones's promotion to major general and Murray's to lieutenant colonel.

[8] In the absence of a constabulary, cavalry regiments were often needed to deal with civil disorder.

[9] Stewart had been appointed Wellington's Adjutant General in 1809.

[10] Stewart was a younger brother of Castlereagh, and would eventually succeed him as the Marquis of Londonderry. The Kennedys were related; Arthur's great-great-aunt was a Stewart, her nephew became the first Earl of Londonderry in 1796.

[11] Caleb Underwood had been with the Regiment in the Peninsula.

[12] Kennedy's correspondence makes frequent reference to his concern for promotion and his hopes that he can obtain it through patronage. However, since the scandals of the previous century, this was far harder to achieve.

[13] MPs could frank letters without charge.

[14] Sarah Siddons already had a great reputation in the provinces when she became the 'unquestioned queen of the stage' after playing at Drury Lane in 1782. She retired in 1812 aged 57 and died in 1831.

Chapter 5

[1] 'I have always been of the opinion that Portugal might be defended, whatever might be the result of the contest in Spain, and that in the meantime measures adopted for the defence of Portugal would be highly useful to the Spaniards in their contest with the French. My notion was that the Portuguese military establishment ought to be revived, and that in addition to those troops His Majesty ought to employ about 20,000 British troops, including about 4,000 cavalry. My opinion was that, even if Spain should have been conquered, the French would not be able to overrun Portugal with a smaller force than 100,000 men. As long as the contest may continue in Spain, this force [the 20,000 British troops] if it could be placed in a state of activity, would be highly useful to the Spaniards and might eventually decide the contest.' Memorandum to Castlereagh, 7 March 1809.

Chapter 7

[1] General Leith, who had been wounded commanding the 5th Division at Salamanca in July 1812, was now a lieutenant general. The Marquess of

Worcester, son of the Duke of Beaufort, was a Lieutenant in the 10th Hussars who was serving as extra ADC to Wellington. His family had got him out of England in order to extricate him from a protracted involvement with Harriet Wilson, the notorious courtesan.

2 [Peacock] Commander of the Lisbon Garrison.

3 As the 18th hoped they would come under Charles Stewart's command again, the appearance of his horses and hounds in Lisbon seemed promising. Stewart had asked to command a cavalry division, but Wellington thought he should remain Adjutant General: 'although it may be more agreeable to you to take a gallop with the Hussars, I think you had better return to your office'.

4 Lord Paget had succeeded his father in 1812. The rumour was false; not only had Paget antagonised the Wellesleys by eloping with Wellington's sister-in-law, but Wellington wanted Stapleton Cotton as his cavalry commander.

5 Hamilton commanded a Portuguese division; nothing more is heard of Woodberry joining his 'family'.

6 This report, like many that reached the Peninsula Army about what was going on elsewhere in Europe, was inaccurate. There had been no major action between the Russians and French since the latter managed to force the crossings of the River Beresina in late November 1912, but the Russians were now advancing into Westphalia. The French had captured Danzig in 1807 and their garrison was besieged by the Prusso-Russians from January to November 1813.

7 Regimental Courts Martial could award up to 300 lashes; a General or Field Court Martial up to 1,200 (a very rare award).

8 Each of the three regiments of Household Cavalry had found two strong squadrons for Peninsula service. When they disembarked in late November 1812 Beresford had inspected themn and 'pronounced The Blues to be in excellent order, men and horses, with an efficient commanding officer, but would not say as much for the two regiments of Life Guards. Their colonel, terrified at the weight of responsibility which had, as he imagined, fallen upon him, lost his head completely. Both regiments had thrown away their curry combs and brushes, under the impression that those implements were useless on active service; such were the defects bred by sixty years at home, unvaried by active service.' Fortescue.

9 'none under one hundred & eighty dollars. When the Regiment was in Portugal and Spain four years back, mules sold for twenty-five dollars'.

10 See Annex B.

11 Bât = baggage and Bât Forage was for feeding baggage animals; hence Bât-man.

12 See Annex B.

Chapter 8

[1] *quinta* = country estate.
[2] Schaumann was then with the 3rd Hussars, King German's Legion.
[3] According to his own memoirs he passed through Badajoz six months later.
[4] Frequent use is made of 'rompa'ing', as a general description of looting – and rape? French *rompre* = to break.
[5] Duperier, who had been commissioned from the ranks of the 10th Hussars, was preceded by a considerable reputation.

Chapter 9

[1] *Military Adventures of Johnny Newcome* (pub 1816), p. 152.
[2] *The Letters of Private Wheeler*, Liddell Hart (ed.) p. 112.
[3] Malet, p. 48.
[4] Oman Vol VI, p. 358.
[5] The Prince of Orange was one of Wellington's ADCs; Woodberry who met him a short time before wrote: 'He is a very thin young man, about my height and age and is here universally beloved by all who has the honour of knowing him.'
[6] From the reference to Russell as Adjutant he must have taken over from Foster; the latter's temporary appointment had seemed curious as he was the most junior cornet, whereas Russell was the senior lieutenant.
[7] Battle of Lützen 2 May. Napoleon defeated Russo-Prussian force under Wittgenstein.

Chapter 10

[1] 'Wellington, on reaching Vitoria, set Robert Hill's brigade of Household Cavalry to guard the town from plunder.' Oman, Vol VII, p. 441.
[2] Oman, Vol VI, p. 440.
[3] Oman, Vol VI, p. 441.

Chapter 11

[1] Malet, *Memoirs of the XVIIth Hussars*, p. 60.
[2] Elsewhere in the Hussar Brigade four officers of the 15th, Grant's own regiment, were told that they had 'disgraced themselves by participating in the plunder'.
[3] Oman, Vol VI, p. 523.
[4] The 18th confused Bock with another German, Victor Alten.
[5] The officers met the costs of the Band. Nearly a year later Woodberry refers to their having lost all their instruments in Portugal and the musicians having been 'put in the line'. Presumably they had other instruments for performing at dances.

[6] Malet, p. 60.

[7] The 'piece of embroidered cloth' was probably another product of Vitoria looting. Schaumann attended a 'jumble sale' not long after the battle and was astonished by 'the vast number of military and court uniforms . . . made either of fine cloth or brown, blue and scarlet velvet, and covered with gold lace. We had jackets and forage caps made out of them.'

[8] Griffith's letter was dated 21 July, but it anticipated events by several months.

Chapter 12

[1] Soult had been recalled to France in early 1813, but was charged by Napoleon, after the Vitoria debacle, with sorting out the disorganised remnants of Joseph's army.

[2] One of Picton's brigade commanders.

[3] 'Rifles', presumably rifled carbines.

[4] Vedettes warned outlying picquets according to a series of previously arranged signals: 'When the enemy appeared, the vedette put his cap on his carbine. When he only saw cavalry, he turned his horse round in a circle to the left; when infantry to the right. If the enemy advanced quick, he cantered his horse in a circle, and if not noticed, fired his carbine. He held his post until the enemy came close to his, and in retiring kept firing.'
(*British Light Cavalry* by John Pimlott, Almark Publishing Co. 1977)

[5] 'the Governor' – probably his stepfather. His father had died in 1802.

Chapter 13

[1] Russell received allowances as the acting Quartermaster for the first half of 1813.

[2] 'Miss Murphys'; from a letter reference, there was a Captain Murphy with the Spanish Army, their father?

[3] Wellington's military secretary, the future Lord Raglan.

[4] Two subalterns from other regiments were to have the vacant troops. Luard of the 4th Dragoons and Owen of the 16th Light Dragoons.

[5] Rowlls was to be the subject of an oft-quoted *Reminiscence* of Gronow:
'I knew an officer of the 18th Hussars, young, rich, and a fine-looking fellow, who joined the Army not far from St Sebastian. His stud of horses was remarkable for their blood; his grooms were English, and three in number. He brought with him a light cart to carry forage, and a fourgon for his own baggage. All went well till he came to go on outpost duty; but not finding there any of the comforts to which he had been accustomed, he quietly mounted his charger, told his astonished sergeant that campaigning was not intended for a gentleman, and instantly galloped off to his quarters, ordering

his servants to pack up everything immediately, as he had hired a transport to take him off to England'.

Much of that was nonsense. Rowlls had come out with the Regiment early in 1813 and had served throughout the campaign to date.

[6] Charles Blackett's resignation must have been withdrawn, he continued with the Regiment until 1820, but Hughes told Enos Smith that he was 'free to go to England' a fortnight later. Woodberry included a rough copy of his 'Memorial to Field Marshal The Marquis of Wellington' in the *Idle Companion*:

'Sheweth that his personal affairs in England being much derainged [four lines mostly obliterated] that Memst. had volunteered his service to accompany the Regiment to this Country in preference to remaining in England and should now feel it painful to solicit Your Exy. at the present Crisis for the shortest leave of absence, were it not for the above circumstances, which as nothing but his personal attendance would need to adjust and humbly prays your Excy. for two months Leave of absence. This is submitted. Geo. Woodberry Lieut 18th Hussars Olite 25th. August 1913'

Chapter 14

[1] Duncan was reduced to corporal, but was promoted again to sergeant the following February.

[2] 13th & 14th Light Dragoons.

[3] Brunswick Oels Jägers (The 'Black Brunswickers').

[4] General Carlos Le Cor, a Portuguese general, commanding 7th Division.

Chapter 15

[1] Hughes's original diary has sketches of the barn and the 'contrivance' – see Illustrations.

[2] Major Brotherton and Lieutenant Southwell of the 14th Light Dragoons had been captured in what Oman describes as 'a mad venture to charge across a narrow bridge' at Hasparren. In the mid-nineteenth century there was a deal of controvery about the incident.

[3] Oman, Vol VII, p. 315.

[4] Remainder of letter missing.

Chapter 16

[1] Oman, Vol VII, p. 316.

[2] Morris had taken over Woodberry's detachment when the Regiment was ordered abroad in January 1813.

[3] Mount Stewart, seat of the Stewarts in County Down.

Chapter 17

[1] Oman, Vol VII, p. 320.

[2] Hill's force consisted of 2nd Division, the Portuguese (Le Cor) and Spanish

(Morillo) divisions with 13th and 14th Light Dragoons under Fane. Beresford had 4th and 7th Divisions; the Light and 6th Divisions were following up.

3 Oman, Vol VII, p. 329; bad weather prevented the crossing and after four days Wellington had to leave the operation to Hope while he returned to direct the main operations.

4 Lowry Cole, a relative of Kennedy's mother, had been a suitor of Kitty Pakenham before she married the future Duke of Wellington.

5 Oman, Vol VII, p. 345.

6 Bastide de Béarn – Labastide Villefranche?

Chapter 18
1 On 4 March Wellington was visited at St Sever by the Mayor of Bordeaux's agents.

2 'Florian, a celebrated Franco-Spanish partisan, who had served King Joseph. . . . His men, and those of one or two other bands, according to French sources, were mere highway robbers, and more dangerous to the peasantry than to English stragglers. Complaints as to their doings led Wellington to authorise the local *maires* to form 'urban guards' to defend themselves. . . . the 'partisans' were considered as public enemies in Gascony, and the British as friends!' Oman, p. 440.

3 See Illustrations.

4 Dalhousie was now commanding 7th Division.

5 Oman, Vol VII, p.436.

6 In the flurried activity of the next ten days Hughes perhaps made no more entries in his diary until 25 March. If he did, none has survived.

7 Two more troops had been added to the establishment in November 1813.

Chapter 19
1 Oman, Vol VII, p. 449.

2 Oman, Vol VII, p. 460.

3 Pakenham had taken over from Stewart as Adjutant General.

4 Oman, Vol VII, p. 463.

5 Hughes had ridden 'Percy' throughout the campaign.

6 Arentschildt from the KGL Heavy Brigade had taken over from Vivian.

7 Oman, Vol VII, p. 497.

8 Sergeant Jeffs; there were two Jeffs in the 18th. Thomas, who was referred to by Otway as taking part at Benavente in 1808, was now Regimental Sergeant Major. William was Troop Sergeant Major in Russell's Troop.

9 The despatches included the offer of the Paris embassy, which Wellington accepted.

Chapter 20
1 Arthur Bryant, *The Age of Elegance*, p. 98.

[2] 'Oak-apple Day'; at the Restoration Charles II entered London on 29 May (his birthday). An Act of Parliament commanded it to be a day of thanksgiving.

[3] Viscount W. de R. Chabot served with the 18th from 1794 to 1808.

[4] Mortally wounded at Vitoria.

Chapter 21

[1] Wellington wanted Stapleton Cotton, now Lord Combermere, back in command of his cavalry. However, Horse Guards prevailed on him to accept Uxbridge.

[2] Prior was to figure in an incident in 1816, when 'hostility between French and British officers was an increasing problem. . . . there was an affray at Boulogne caused by a Lieutenant Prior of the 18th Hussars ("a very bad subject") twitting a French actor backstage. After due warning the Frenchman knocked Prior down, Prior's comrades rushed the stage and were in turn attacked by the *gendarmerie*, one of the British officers being seriously wounded. Prior was officially blamed but not without the Duke's insistence. He had the Duke's verdict revised when it enlarged upon French violence.' Elizabeth Longford, *Wellington – Pillar of State*, p. 42.

[3] Burke obtained a majority in the 100th Foot during 1815.

[4] It was, of course, being given by the Duchess of Richmond.

Chapter 22

[1] Jeffs later became Adjutant of the 7th Hussars.

[2] Malet, p. 33.

Chapter 23

[1] Perhaps Thomas Kennedy, a younger brother; *The Landed Gentry of Ireland* 1912 lists him but gives no other information.

[2] See Illustrations.

Postscript

Published between 1828 and 1840.

BIBLIOGRAPHY

Published Works

Anglesey, Marquess (1961), *One-Leg,* Jonathan Cape.

Bryant, Sir Arthur (1944), *Years of Victory,* Collins.

Chandler, David (1999), *Dictionary of the Napoleonic Wars,* 1979, Wordsworth Editions.

Fortescue Sir John (1906–20), *History of the British Army* (Vols IV-X), London.

Glover, Michael (1977), *Wellington's Army in the Peninsula 1808-1814,* David & Charles.

Gronow, Captain (1991), *His Reminiscences of Regency and Victorian Life 1810-60,* C Hibbert (ed.), Kyle Cathie.

Helié G. (1896), (trans.) *Journal du Lieutenant Woodberry* [1813–15], Paris.

Hibbert, Christopher (1961), *Corunna* Batsford.

Liddell Hart, Captain B.H. (1951), *The Letters of Private Wheeler* 1809-1828, London.

Longford, Elizabeth (1969), *The Years of the Sword,* Weidenfeld & Nicholson.

Mollo, John (1997), *The Prince's Dolls; Scandals, Skirmishes and Splendours of the Hussars 1739–1815,* Pen & Sword Books (Leo Cooper).

Napier, Sir William (1842), *History of War in the Peninsula and the South of France 1807–14,* Warne.

Oman, Sir Charles (1903–30), *A History of the Peninsular War* (7 vols). OUP.

Oman, Sir Charles (1913), *Wellington's Army 1809–1814,* London.

Paget, Sir Julian (1990), *Wellington's Peninsular War,* Leo Cooper.

Schaumann, A.L. (1924), *On the Road with Wellington, The Diary of a War Commissary in the Peninsular Campaigns* (tr. & ed. A.M. Ludovici).

Wylly H.C. (ed.) (1913), *A Cavalry Officer in the Corunna Campaign 1808–9, the Journal of Capt Gordon of the XVth Hussars*, John Murray.

Manuscripts

Hodge, Edward, *Correspondence & Diaries (A to D) 1808–09, 1813–14*, Queen's Own Hussars Museum Warwick.

Hughes, James; Diaries & papers 1808, 1813-15: Kinmel 1572 & 1573 Dept of MS, University of North Wales, Bangor

Kennedy, Arthur; Letters in the possession of Sir Arthur Weldon, Bt.

Otway Loftus; Small calf bound notebook – diary during 1808–09 campaign in the Peninsula (NAM 7406-34. 1-20)

Woodberry, George, *The Idle Companion of a Young Hussar during the year 1813* (NAM 1968-07-267)

ANNEX A

OFFICERS OF THE 18TH HUSSARS (1808–15)

(Names are followed by dates of service and campaigns (in *italic*) with the Regiment. Surnames of those referred to in text are in **bold**.)

Allen, Thomas L., 1799 to 1812 *Coruña*
(Captain 1799, Major 1801)

Ball, George, 1806 to 1813
(Cornet 1806, Lieutenant 1808)

Blackett, Charles, 1810 to 1820 *1813–14*
(Lieutenant 1810, Captain 1816)

Blaquiere, G., Hon., 1813 to 1814
(Lieutenant 1813)

Bolton, Robert Dawson, 1802 to 1813 *Coruña, 1813–14*; d. of wounds 19 Dec 1813 (b. 1779, Cornet 1802, Lieutenant 1804, Captain 1807)

Brett, R.R.W., 1814 to 1818
(Lieutenant 1814)

Brooke, Richard, 1805 to 1813 *Coruña, 1813–14*
(Lieutenant 1806)

Burke, Edward, 1804 to 1815 *Coruña, 1813–14*
(Lieutenant 1804, Captain 1812, Major 100ᵗʰ Foot 1815)

Carew, Robert, 1804 to 1813 *Coruña, 1813–14*; d. of wounds 22 June 1813
(Cornet 1804, Lieutenant 1805, Captain 1811)

Clements, John O'Marcus, 1804 to 1822 *Coruña, 1813–14*
(Cornet 1804, Lieutenant 1805, Captain 1806, Brevet Major, Beresford's staff 1813–14, Major 1814, Lieutenant Colonel 1819. Became MP for Co Leitrim)

Conolly, James, 1808 to 1814 *Coruña, 1813–14*
(Cornet 1808, Lieutenant 1809)

Coote, R., 1814 to 1818 *1813–14, Waterloo*
(Lieutenant 1814)

Croker, Richard, 1805 to 1821 *Coruña, 1813–14 & Waterloo*; wounded at Coruña, Mendionde and Toulouse (b. 1786, Cornet 1805, Lieutenant 1806, Captain 1812, MFH to Regimental pack in France; Major 1815)

Curtis, Daniel, J., 1813 to 1814 *1813–14*
(Cornet 1813)

Curtis, Robert J., 1813 to 1814 (older brother of Daniel) *1813–14*
(Cornet 1813)

Davison, H.P., 1809 to 1814 *1813–14*
(Captain 1809)

Dawson, L.C., Hon., 1814 to 1818 *1813–14, Waterloo*; marched with 18th 16 June, baggage guard 17 June
(Lieutenant 1814)

Deane, W., 1797 to 1803
(Cornet 1797, Lieutenant 1800, to Paymaster 1803 – *see below.*)

Dolbell, John, 1813 to 1816 *1813–14*
(Cornet 1813, Lieutenant 1814)

Dunkin, Thomas, 1812 to 1820 *1813–14, Waterloo*; to Ostend with Ellis June 1815 (Cornet 1807, Lieutenant 1808. Served with 13th Light Dragoons, 4th Dragoons and Royals before joining 18th)

Duperier, Henry, 1813 to 1821, Adjutant 1813 to 1821 *1813–14, Waterloo*; wounded at Waterloo (Sergeant Major 10th Hussars, Cornet 1808, Lieutenant 1809)

Ellis, Richard, 1807 to 1817 *Coruña, Waterloo*; fell sick on leave in Flanders before Waterloo (Lieutenant 1807, Captain 1812)

Evans, Thomas, 1805 to 1813
(Cornet 1805, Lieutenant 1805)

Fane, T., 1810 to 1811
(Lieutenant 1810, ADC to Major General Skerrett in Peninsula)

Foster, W.H., 1812 to 1813 *1813–14*; d. of wounds at Vitoria July 1813
(Cornet 1812, acting Adjutant 1813)

French, Martin, 1814 to 1818 *Waterloo*; sick on 18 June
(Lieutenant 1814)

Gibbs, William, 1808 to 1822 *Coruña*
(Cornet 1808, Lieutenant 1811)

Gordon, J.R., 1815 to 1816 *Waterloo*
(Lieutenant 1815)

Grant, James, 1814 to 1820 *1813–14, Waterloo*
(Captain 1814, brevet Major 1815, later promoted Major General)

Greatheed, S., 1811 to 1813?
(Cornet 1811, Lieutenant 1812)

Greville, R., 1809 to 1810
(Cornet 1809)

Harris, Thomas Noel, 1805 to 1813 *Coruña, Waterloo*; ADC to General Stewart, then General Walker; wounded at Badajoz; Brigade Major to Vivian at Waterloo, charged with 18th (Lieutenant 1807, Captain 1808, sold out as Captain 1809, re-entered as Cornet)

Harvey, G.F., 1804 to 1812?
(Cornet 1804, Lieutenant 1806, Captain 1808)

Hay, C. Peter, 1802 to 1811 *Coruña*
(Captain 1802)

Hay, Philip, 1803 to 1822 *Coruña*
(Captain 1803, Major 1812)

Hesse, Charles, 1809 to 1817 *1813–14, Waterloo*; wounded at Waterloo (Cornet 1809, Lieutenant 1810, Captain Staff Corps 1816, half pay 1819, killed in duel 1832)

Hoey, W.R., 1807 to 1811 *Coruña*
(Captain 1807)

Hughes, James, 1803 to 1822 *Coruña, 1813–14*; wounded during Coruña campaign and at Mendionde. CB, Gold Medal with clasps for Vitoria, Orthez, Toulouse (b. 1778, Cornet 1800, 16th Light Dragoons 1800–02, Captain 1802, Hompesch's Mounted Rifles, Major 1812, Lieutenant Colonel 1817, d. 1845)

Johnson, J.A., 1808 to 1812 *Coruña*
(Cornet 1808, Lieutenant 1809)

Jones, Charles, 1799 to 1813 *Coruña*
(Lieutenant 1799, Captain 1803, Major 1812)

Jones, Oliver Thomas, 1801 to 1814 *Coruña*; Gold Medal with clasp for Sahagun & Benavente (Lieutenant Colonel 1801, d. 14 Nov 1815)

Jones, Valentine, 1809 to 1813 *1813–14*
(Lieutenant 1809, to 3rd Dragoon Guards 1814?)

Kennedy, Arthur, 1804 to 1822 *Coruña, 1813–14, Waterloo*; accident with horse prevented his being present at battle (Ensign 1803, 24th Foot 1803–4, Cornet 1804, Lieutenant 1805, Captain 1811, Major 1815, d. 1855)

Lloyd, J.R.L., 1814 to 1819 *Waterloo*
(Captain 1814)

Luard, George, 1814 to 1822 *1813–14, Waterloo*
(Captain 1814, from 4ᵗʰ Dragoons)

Machell, J.T., 1814 to 1822 *Waterloo*
(Lieutenant 1814)

Mansfield, W.H., 1810 to 1813
(Cornet 1810, Lieutenant 1811)

McCartney, 1811 to 1818?
(Cornet 1810, Lieutenant 1811)

McDuffie, Donald, 1814 to 1818 *Waterloo*
(Lieutenant 1814)

Milner, Charles, 1805 to 1820 *Coruña*
(Miller in some Army Lists. Cornet 1805, Lieutenant 1805, Captain 1810, Major 1813)

Moller, C.C., 1814 to 1818 *Waterloo*, but sick for battle
(Cornet 1814, Lieutenant 1816)

Monins, William, 1815 to 1817 *Waterloo*, but sick for battle
(Lieutenant 1815)

Moore, Edwin, 1800 to 1808? *Coruña*
(Cornet 1800, d. 1808?)

Moore, Charles, 1759 to 1821
(6th Earl and 1st Marquis Drogheda; raised 19ᵗʰ Light Dragoons 1759, renumbered 18ᵗʰ 1761, Lieutenant General 1777, General 1793, Field Marshal 1821, d. 1821)

Morris, James, 1813 to 1816 *1813–14*
(Lieutenant 1813)

Murray, Henry, Hon., 1810 to 1822 *1813–14, Waterloo*; invalided home 1813–14 (b. 1784, Cornet 1800, Lieutenant 1801, Captain-Lieutenant 1802, Major 1807, Lieutenant Colonel 1812. CB 1815. Served in 16ᵗʰ Light Dragoons, 20ᵗʰ Light Dragoons, 10ᵗʰ Hussars and 26ᵗʰ Foot from 1800 to 1810, Major General 1838, General 1855)

Otway, Loftus William, 1807 to 1810 *Coruña*; Portuguese Army 1811–14? (b. 1775, Lieutenant 1796, Captain 1798, Major 1803, Lieutenant Colonel 1805. Served in 5ᵗʰ Dragoon Guards, 8ᵗʰ Dragoons, 24ᵗʰ Dragoons 1796–1807. Portuguese and British knighthoods, General 1851, d. 1854)

Owen, H., 1813 to 1817 *1813–14*
(Captain, from 16ᵗʰ Light Dragoons 1813)

Pearson, W., 1808 to 1814
(Lieutenant 1808)

Prior, Thomas, 1814 to 1818 *Waterloo*
(Cornet 1814, Lieutenant 1814)

Raynes, John Thomas, 1808 to 1810 *Coruña*
(Cornet 1797, Lieutenant 1799)

Richards, Thomas W.R., 1806 to 1811 *Coruña*
(Cornet 1806, Lieutenant 1808, changed name to Edwards)

Rowlls, C., 1811 to 1813 *1813–14*; deserted September 1813
(Cornet 1811, Lieutenant 1812)

Rowells, W.H., 1814 to 1816 *Waterloo*
(Cornet 1814, Lieutenant 1816

Russell, Robert, 1806 to 1815 *Coruña, 1813–14*
(Cornet 1806, Lieutenant 1808, Captain 1814)

Seymour, H., 1814 to 1816
(Lieutenant 1814)

Shakespear, 1814 to 18? *1813–14*; ADC to Vivian at Waterloo
(Captain 1814, from ?, to vacancy caused by Bolton's death, but did not appear in Army List)

Sherwood, I., 1809 to 1814 *1813–14, Waterloo*; killed in battle
(Cornet 1809, Lieutenant 1810)

Smith, Enos, 1809 to 1814 *1813–14*
(Cornet 1809, Lieutenant 1810)

Somerset, Henry, 1814 to 1816; ADC to Major General Lord Somerset at Waterloo (Lieutenant 1814)

Stewart, Charles W., Hon., 1798 to 1813 *Coruña*, commanded Hussar Brigade (b. 1778, Ensign 1794, Lieutenant 1794, Captain 1794, Major 1795, Lieutenant Colonel 1799, Colonel 1808, Major General 1810. Served in Macnamara's Regiment, 106th Foot and 5th Dragoons 1794–8. Adjutant General to Wellington 1809–14, diplomatic mission to Berlin April 1813, created Baron June 1814. Marquis Londonderry 1822, d. 1854.)

Turing, William, 1808 to 1814 *Coruña, 1813–14*; killed at Vitoria
(Cornet 1804, Lieutenant 1805, Captain 1807)

Underwood, Caleb, 1804 to 1812 *Coruña*
(Lieutenant 1804, Captain 1809, d. 1812)

Vanneck, T., Hon., 1810 to 1814
(Cornet 1810)

Waldie, James H., 1812 to 1821 *1813–14, Waterloo*
(Cornet 1812, Lieutenant 1814, Adjutant 1812–13)

Webster, G., Sir, Bt., 1810 to 1813

(Lieutenant 1810; 'superceded' after consistent overstaying of leave when Regiment stationed at Kent)

Woodberry, George, 1812 to 1819 *1813–14*, *Waterloo*; wounded Vitoria and Mendionde (b. 1792, Ensign 1812, Cornet 1812, Lieutenant 1814; 10th Foot 1812)

Paymaster

Deane, W., 1803 to 1822 *Coruña*, *1813–14* and *Waterloo*
(From Lieutenant – *see above*)

Surgeons

Chambers, W., 1799 to 1822 *Coruña*, *1813–14* and *Waterloo*
(Asst Surgeon 1799, Surgeon 1804)

Jebb, F., 1805 to 1809
(Asst Surgeon 1805)

Pulsford, Lucas, 1812 to 1820 *1813–14*, *Waterloo*; absent from battle, sent to Ostend with sick officer (Asst surgeon 1812)

Quincey, J., 1813 to 1818 *1813–14*, *Waterloo*
(Asst surgeon 1813)

Veterinary Surgeon

Pilcher, Daniel, 1812 to 1822 *1813–14*, *Waterloo*

Commissary

Schaumann, A.L.F., 1813 to 1814 *1813–14*
(b. 1778, Lieutenant 7th Line KGL 1809–12, Commissary 3rd Hussars KGL 1809–12, 9th Light Dragoons 1812, d. 1840)

Volunteers

For *Waterloo* the 18th were joined by two volunteers:

Grant, Peter
(Captain, 'in the service of the India Company')

Williams, C.
(Captain, 'of the West Middlesex Militia', brother-in-law of R.L. Lloyd)

ANNEX B

GEORGE WOODBERRY'S BAGGAGE AND HOUSEHOLD

May 1813 – Baggage on mule

2 Pelisses

1 Dress Waistcoat

1 Bear Skin Bed

Dressing Case

2 Blue Waistcoats

2 White –Do–

2 Flannel –Do–

3 –Do– Waistcoats

12 Shirts

Dress sabretache

2 Foraging Caps

1 Hussar –Do– & oil skin Cover

1 Cap line

2 Feathers

3 Gloves   1 shoes

1 Dressing Gown

1 Rug

2 Blankets

Writing Case

10 Books

1 pr Hussar Pistols

1 Pocket   –Do–

1 Pouch Belt (plain)

Dress sword

Plain sword

–Do– sabretache

Racing Jacket

1 Pelisse Line

2 Night Caps   2pr Slippers

1 Jacket

4 Regimental Pantaloons

3 White   –Do–

1 Leather   –Do–

Cotton Drawers

1 Powder Flask

12 Hose

1 Pistol Belt & pouch

4 Black Handkfs

6 Pocket –Do–

Sword knot

1 Sash

6pr Boots

Canteen – Breakfast & Dining Service compleat   1 Hussar pipe compleat

Hussar Horse accoutrements compleat   1 Leather Trunk

2 Horse Cloths

Basket with Locks

Great Coat

Flannel Jacket

Leather Bucket

15 Cakes of Soap

Double Saddle Bags

1 Plain Saddle

2 –Do– Bridles

3 Shoe Brushes & Blackg

Oil Skin & Straps (to go over the Baggage)

Boot Jack

2 Horse Blankets

Spy Glass

Pack Saddle, Bridle &c (compleat)

May 1813 – Trunk with Heavy Baggage

4 Leather Pantaloons
1 – Do – Britches
2 Cloth – Do –
3 Cloth Pantaloons

1 Dress White – Do –
1 Dress Blue   – Do –
7 Waistcoats
1 Dress Pelisse
1 – Do – Jacket
1 Blue Overals
5 White neck Handkfs
1 Black Silk Stockgs.
2 White Silk – Do –

4 Pantaloon Hose
1 pr Flannel Drawers
1 Cotton   – Do –
2 Coats

2 Silk Handkfs.
1 Pantaloons
1 Dress Belt
1 Pumps
1 Boots
1 Sett of Horse Cloths
3 Shirts
2 Cotton – Do –
1 Shabraque

1 Great Coat
1 Whip
Account Book, Ledger
2 Books (Syntax &
Sword Exs)
Hat Brush
Pistol Case
2 Pipe tubes &c
3 Sheets
L? Picture
1 Dress Sash
1 – Do – Cap line

September 1813, 'My Horses, Mules – Servants &c &c'

No.1 – Grey Horse — Crafty
    2 – Bay Horse — Worcester (my Battle Horse)
    3 – Black Horse — Andalusian, (late King Joseph's)
    4 – Bay Mare — Morales — for Baggage
    5 – Pye Bald Mare Poney – Belisarda — for The Small Breakfast Canteens
                      2 Years Old, in foal. She is 4 foot high.
    6– a Mule — Doctor— for Baggage
Fly, Swift Two french Grey Hounds
Vitoria – my French Prisoner – a Faithful companion
John Porter – Valet & Cook
John Ipper – Groom
Jossa – a Portuguese Servant – hired him at Sovillida (very faithful)
& Kington – a Mounted Dragoon.

INDEX

287